'Australia's Most Important Writer

'The winner of Australia's richest literary prize did not attend the ceremony. His absence was not by choice. Behrouz Boochani, whose debut book won both the $25,000 non-fiction prize at the Victorian premier's literary awards and the $100,000 Victorian prize for literature, is not allowed into Australia. The Kurdish Iranian writer is an asylum seeker who has been kept in purgatory on Manus Island in Papua New Guinea for almost six years, first behind the wire of the Australian offshore detention centre, and then in alternative accommodation on the island. Now his book *No Friend but the Mountains* – composed one text message at a time from within the detention centre – has been recognized by a government from the same country that denied him access and locked him up.'   *Guardian*

'The systems of containment and control that the rich world applies to many thousands of migrants and refugees work by reducing people to a faceless presence to either be feared or pitied, but never listened to. In the face of this oppression, Behrouz Boochani's lyrical yet unsparing account is a vital act of resistance, and a unique examination of people pushed to life's extremes.'
                    Daniel Trilling, author of *Lights in the Distance*

'A chant, a cry from the heart, a lament, fuelled by a fierce urgency, written with the lyricism of a poet, the literary skills of a novelist, and the profound insights of an astute observer of human behaviour and the ruthless politics of a cruel and unjust imprisonment.'   Arnold Zable, author of *Jewels and Ashes* and *Cafe Scheherazade*

'To understand the true nature of what it is that we have done, every Australian, beginning with the Prime Minister, should read Behrouz Boochani's intense, lyrical, and psychologically perceptive prose-poetry masterpiece, *No Friend but the Mountains* . . . Boochani is a man of delicate sensibility and fine, sometimes severe, moral judgment but also, in his willingness to lay bare his soul before us, of mighty courage.'   *Sydney Morning Herald*

'Boochani has produced a literary, journalistic and philosophical tour de force. It may well stand as one of the most important books published in Australia in two decades'

Saturday Paper

'In the absence of images, turn to this book to fathom what we have done, what we continue to do. It is, put simply, the most extraordinary and important book I have ever read.'

Good Reading Magazine

'Not for the faint-hearted, it's a powerful, devastating insight into a situation that's so often seen through a political – not personal – lens.'   *GQ Australia*

Behrouz Boochani graduated from Tarbiat Moallem University and Tarbiat Modares University, both in Tehran; he holds a Masters degree in political science, political geography and geopolitics. He is a Kurdish-Iranian writer, journalist, scholar, cultural advocate and filmmaker. Boochani was writer for the Kurdish language magazine *Werya*; is Honorary Member of PEN International; winner of an Amnesty International Australia 2017 Media Award, the Diaspora Symposium Social Justice Award, the Liberty Victoria 2018 Empty Chair Award, and the Anna Politkovskaya Award for journalism; and he is non-resident Visiting Scholar at the Sydney Asia Pacific Migration Centre (SAPMiC), University of Sydney. He publishes regularly with *The Guardian*, and his writing also features in *The Saturday Paper*, *Huffington Post*, *New Matilda*, *The Financial Times* and *The Sydney Morning Herald*. Boochani is also co-director (with Arash Kamali Sarvestani) of the 2017 feature-length film *Chauka, Please Tell Us the Time*; collaborator on Nazanin Sahamizadeh's play *Manus*; and author of *No Friend but the Mountains: Writing from Manus Prison* (Picador, 2018).

Translator Omid Tofighian is a lecturer, researcher and community advocate, combining philosophy with interests in citizen media, rhetoric, religion, popular culture, transnationalism, displacement and discrimination. He completed his PhD in philosophy at Leiden University and graduated with a combined Honours degree in philosophy and studies in religion at the University of Sydney. His current roles include Assistant Professor of Philosophy at the American University in Cairo; Honorary Research Associate for the Department of Philosophy, University of Sydney; faculty at Iran Academia; and campaign manager for Why Is My Curriculum White? – Australasia. He has published numerous book chapters and journal articles, is author of *Myth and Philosophy in Platonic Dialogues* (Palgrave Macmillan 2016) and translator of Behrouz Boochani's book *No Friend but the Mountains: Writing From Manus Prison* (Picador, 2018).

NO

FRIEND

The true story of an illegally imprisoned refugee

BUT THE

MOUNTAINS

Behrouz Boochani

Translated by Omid Tofighian

PICADOR

First published in 2018 by Picador Australia
Pan Macmillan Australia
Level 25, 1 Market Street
SYDNEY NSW 2000

First published in the UK 2019 by Picador
an imprint of Pan Macmillan
20 New Wharf Road, London N1 9RR
Associated companies throughout the world
www.panmacmillan.com

ISBN 978-1-5290-2848-5

1 3 5 7 9 8 6 4 2

A CIP catalogue record for this book is available from the British Library.

Printed and bound by CPI Group (UK) Ltd, Croydon, CR0 4YY

Visit **www.picador.com** to read more about all our books
and to buy them. You will also find features, author interviews and
news of any author events, and you can sign up for e-newsletters
so that you're always first to hear about our new releases.

For Janet Galbraith
Who is a bird

Foreword

No Friend but the Mountains is a book that can rightly take its place on the shelf of world prison literature, alongside such diverse works as Oscar Wilde's *De Profundis*, Antonio Gramsci's *Prison Notebooks*, Ray Parkin's *Into The Smother*, Wole Soyinka's *The Man Died*, and Martin Luther King Jr's *Letter from Birmingham Jail*.

Written in Farsi by a young Kurdish poet, Behrouz Boochani, in situations of prolonged duress, torment, and suffering, the very existence of this book is a miracle of courage and creative tenacity. It was written not on paper or a computer, but thumbed on a phone and smuggled out of Manus Island in the form of thousands of text messages.

We should recognise the extent of Behrouz Boochani's achievement by first acknowledging the difficulty of its creation, the near impossibility of its existence. Everything has been done by our government to dehumanise asylum seekers. Their names and their stories are kept from us. On Nauru and Manus Island, they live in a zoo of cruelty. Their lives are stripped of meaning.

These prisoners were all people who had been imprisoned without charge, without conviction, and without sentence. It is a particularly Kafkaesque fate that frequently has the cruellest effect – and one fully intended by their Australian jailers – of destroying hope.

Thus the cry for freedom was transmuted into charring flesh as 23-year-old Omid Masoumali burnt his body in protest. The screams of 21-year-old Hodan Yasin as she too set herself alight.

This is what we, Australia, have become.

The ignored begging of a woman on Nauru being raped.

A girl who sewed her lips together.

A child refugee who stitched a heart into their hand and didn't know why.

Behrouz Boochani's revolt took a different form. For the one thing that his jailers could not destroy in Behrouz Boochani was his belief in words: their beauty, their necessity, their possibility, their liberating power.

And so over the course of his imprisonment Behrouz Boochani began one of the more remarkable careers in Australian journalism: reporting about what was happening on Manus Island in the form of tweets, texts, phone videos, calls, and emails. In so doing he defied the Australian government which went to extreme lengths to prevent refugees' stories being told, constantly seeking to deny journalists access to Manus Island and Nauru; going so far, for a time, as to legislate the draconian section 42 of the *Australian Border Force Act*, which allowed for the jailing for two years of any doctors or social workers who bore public witness to children beaten or sexually abused, to acts of rape or cruelty.

His words came to be read around the world, to be heard across the oceans and over the shrill cries of the legions of paid propagandists. With only the truth on his side and a phone in his hand, one imprisoned refugee alerted the world to Australia's great crime.

Behrouz Boochani has now written a strange and terrible book chronicling his fate as a young man who has spent *five years* on Manus Island as a prisoner of the Australian government's refugee policies – policies in which both our major parties have publicly competed in cruelty.

Reading this book is difficult for any Australian. We pride ourselves on decency, kindness, generosity, and a fair go. None of these qualities are evident in Boochani's account of hunger, squalor, beatings, suicide and murder.

I was painfully reminded in his descriptions of the Australian officials' behaviour on Manus of my father's descriptions of the Japanese commanders' behaviour in the POW camps where he and fellow Australian POWs suffered so much.

What has become of us when it is we who now commit such crimes?

This account demands a reckoning. Someone must answer for these crimes. Because if they don't, the one certainty that history teaches us is that the injustice of Manus Island and Nauru will one day be repeated on a larger, grander, and infinitely more tragic scale in Australia.

Someone is responsible, and it is they, and not the innocent, to whose great suffering this book bears such disturbing witness, who should be in jail.

This book, though, is something greater than just a *J'accuse*. It is a profound victory for a young poet who showed us all how much words can still matter. Australia imprisoned his body, but his soul remained that of a free man. His words have now irrevocably become our words, and our history must henceforth account for his story.

I hope one day to welcome Behrouz Boochani to Australia as what I believe he has shown himself to be in these pages. A writer. A great Australian writer.

Richard Flanagan, 2018

A Disclaimer

This book has been written to give a truthful account of the experience of Australia's Manus Island Regional Offshore Processing Centre, and to convey a truthful first-hand experience of what it has been like to be detained within that system. There are some limits to what can be revealed, particularly about fellow detainees. Changing details such as hair colour, eye colour, age, nationality, name . . . we have not considered this sufficient to ensure that those who are vulnerable within the system have been adequately obscured. No detainee or refugee in this book is based on a specific individual, however detailed their stories. They are not individuals who are disguised. Their features are not facts. Their identities are entirely manufactured. They are composite characters: a collage drawn from various events, multiple anecdotes, and they are often inspirited by the logic of allegory, not reportage. The details around the two men who died on Manus, Reza Barati and Hamid Khazaei, are in the public domain and so they are each identified by name as a mark of respect.

No Friend
But The Mountains

1

—

Under Moonlight / The Colour of Anxiety

Under moonlight /
An unknown route /
A sky the colour of intense anxiety.

Two trucks carry scared and restless passengers down a winding, rocky labyrinth. They speed along a road surrounded by jungle, the exhausts emitting frightening roars. Black cloth is wrapped around the vehicles, so we can only see the stars above. Women and men sit beside each other, their children on their laps . . . we look up at a sky the colour of intense anxiety. Every so often someone slightly adjusts their position on the truck's wooden floor to allow the blood to circulate through tired muscles. Worn out from sitting, we still need to conserve our strength to cope with the rest of the journey.

For six hours I have sat without moving, leaning my back against the wooden wall of the truck, and listening to an old fool complain at the smugglers, profanities streaming from his toothless mouth. Three months of wandering hungry in Indonesia have driven us to this misery, but at least we are leaving on this road through the jungle, a road that will reach the ocean.

In a corner of the truck, close to the door, a makeshift wall has been constructed of cloth; a screen from the others, where the children can piss in empty water bottles. No-one pays any attention when a few arrogant men go behind the screen and throw away the urine-filled bottles. None of the women moves from where they sit. They must need to go, but maybe the thought of emptying their bladders behind the screen doesn't appeal.

Many women hold their children in their arms as they contemplate the dangerous trip by sea. The children bounce up and down, startling as we jolt over dips and peaks in the road. Even the very young sense the danger. You can tell by the tone of their yelps.

The roar of the truck /
The dictates of the exhaust /
Fear and anxiety /
The driver orders us to remain seated.

A thin man with a dark weather-beaten appearance stands near the door, regularly gesturing for silence. But in the vehicle the air is full of the cries of children, the sound of mothers trying to hush them, and the frightening roar of the truck's screaming exhaust.

The looming shadow of fear sharpens our instincts. The branches of trees above us sometimes cover the sky, sometimes reveal it, as we speed past. I am not sure exactly which route we are taking but I guess that the boat we are supposed to board for Australia is on a distant shore in southern Indonesia, somewhere near Jakarta.

—

In the three months I was in Jakarta's Kalibata City and on Kendari Island, I would regularly hear news of boats that had sunk. But one always thinks that such fatal incidents only befall others – it's hard to believe you may face death.

One imagines one's own death differently to the death of others. I can't imagine it. Could it be that these trucks travelling in convoy, rushing towards the ocean, are couriers of death?

No /
Surely not while they carry children /
How is it possible? /
How could we drown in the ocean? /
I am convinced that my own death will be different /
It will take place in a more tranquil setting.

I think about other boats that have recently descended into the depths of the sea.

My anxiety increases /
Didn't those boats also carry little kids? /
Weren't the people who drowned just like me?

Moments like these awaken a kind of metaphysical power within and the realities of mortality disappear from one's thoughts.

No, it can't be that I should submit to death so easily. I'm destined to die in the distant future and not by drowning or any similar fate. I'm destined to die in a particular way, when I choose. I decide that my own death must involve an act of the will – I resolve it within me, in my very soul.

Death must be a matter of choice.

No, I don't want to die /

I don't want to give up my life so easily /

Death is inevitable, we know /

Just another part of life /

But I don't want to succumb to the inevitability of death /

Especially somewhere so far away from my motherland /

I don't want to die out there surrounded by water /

And more water.

I always felt I would die in the place I was born, where I was raised, where I have spent my whole life till now. It's impossible to imagine dying a thousand kilometres away from the land of your roots. What a terrible, miserable way to die, a sheer injustice; an injustice that seems to me completely arbitrary. Of course, I don't expect it will happen to me.

—

A young man and his girlfriend, Azadeh[1], are riding in the first truck. They are accompanied by our mutual acquaintance The

---

1 Azadeh is a woman's name in Iran that is cognate with the Farsi word for freedom – *āzādi*.

Blue Eyed Boy. All three of them harbour painful memories of the life they had to leave behind in Iran. When the trucks collected us from the place we were staying the two men tossed their luggage in the back of the truck and climbed aboard like soldiers. For the whole three months that we were in Indonesia they have been a step ahead of us other refugees. Whether finding a hotel room, acquiring food, or travelling to the airport, this efficient trait would, ironically, always result in some kind of disadvantage. On one occasion when we had to fly to Kendari, they travelled ahead of everyone else to the airport. But when they arrived the officers there confiscated their passports and they missed the flight for Kendari; and were left wandering the streets of Jakarta for days, reduced to begging for food in the alleys and backstreets.

Now, they are in front again, driving at lightning speed, travelling at the head of the pack, slicing through the strong winds. The trucks' exhausts roar as they travel towards the ocean. I know The Blue Eyed Boy carries an old fear in his heart from back in Kurdistan. While in Kalibata City, during the nights confined in the town's apartment blocks, we would smoke on the tiny balconies and talk about our thoughts regarding the upcoming journey. He confessed his fear of the ocean; his older brother's life had been taken by the raging river Seymareh in Ilam Province[2].

. . . *One hot summer's day in his childhood, The Blue Eyed Boy accompanies his older brother to the fishing nets they had cast the previous night in the deepest part of the river. His brother dives deep into the water; like a heavy stone dropping into the river, his body*

---

2   One of the thirty-one provinces of Iran, located to the west of the country, bordering Iraq and part of the Kurdistan region.

*pierces the water. An unexpected wave comes through and, in its
wake, just moments later, only his hand remains visible, reaching to
The Blue Eyed Boy for help. Still a small child, The Blue Eyed Boy
is incapable of grabbing his brother's hand. He can only cry and cry;
he cries for hours hoping his brother will surface. But he is gone. Two
days later they retrieve his body from the river by playing a traditional
message-bearing drum, the* dhol. *The sound of the* dhol *persuades
the river to give back a waterlogged corpse – a musical relationship
between death and nature . . .*

The Blue Eyed Boy carries this old, morbid memory with him
on this trip. He fears the water intensely. Yet tonight he speeds in
the direction of the ocean to embark on a journey of enormous
magnitude. An ominous journey indeed underpinned by this old
and immense terror . . .

The trucks race on through the dense jungle, disrupting the
silence of the night. After sitting on the wooden floor of the truck
for hours, the weariness is obvious on everyone's face. One or
two people have vomited; throwing up everything they have eaten
into plastic containers.

In another corner of the truck is a Sri Lankan couple with an
infant child. The passengers are mainly Iranian, Kurdish, Iraqi,
and you can see they are fascinated by the presence of a Sri Lankan
family among them. The woman is extraordinarily beautiful with
dark eyes. She sits holding her baby, which is still breastfeeding, in
her arms. Her partner tries to comfort them; he cares for them the
best he can. He needs her to know that is there to support them.
During the whole trip the man seems to try and reassure her by
massaging her shoulders and holding her tight as the truck jolts
violently over the bumpy road. But you can see the woman's only
concern is her small child.

The scene in that corner /

Is love /

Glorious and pure.

She is pale however, and throws up at one point into a container her husband brings over. Their past is unknown to me. Maybe their love brought with it the difficulties that drove them to this terrifying night? Clearly, their love has endured it all: it is manifested in the care of this young child. No doubt, their hearts and thoughts are also marked by the experiences that caused them to flee their homeland.

On the trucks are children of all ages. Children on the verge of adulthood. Whole families. A loud, obnoxious and completely inconsiderate Kurdish guy forces everyone to breathe his ciga-rette smoke throughout the trip. He is accompanied by a gaunt wife, adult son, and another son, a little bastard. This kid has his mother's physical features and his father's character. He is so loud he torments the whole truck, treating everything as a joke, and annoying everyone with his impatient and disruptive manner. He even gets on the nerves of the smuggler, who yells at him. *For sure,* I think, *when that boy grows up he will be a hundred times more thoughtless than his father.*

The trucks slow; it seems we have reached the end of the jungle and arrived at the shore. The smuggler begins waving his hands fervently – everyone must keep silent.

The vehicle stops.

Silence . . . silence.

Even the noisy little bastard understands that he has to be silent. Our fear is justified; we are afraid of being caught by the police. On many previous occasions travellers have been arrested right on the edge of the shore before anyone has boarded the boat.

No-one utters a sound. The Sri Lankan baby silently clings to its mother's breast – gazing but not feeding. The slightest sound or cry could ruin everything. Three months of wandering displaced and hungry in Jakarta and Kendari. Everything depends on silence.

This final phase.

On the beach.

—

At this point I have endured forty days of near starvation in the basement of a tiny hotel in Kendari. Kendari has historically been a draw for refugees because it is a travel nexus, a location where one can easily negotiate an onward trip. But by the time I arrived in Kendari, it had become as desolate as a cemetery.

It is now so highly policed I had to hide in the basement of a hotel. My money ran out and hunger was taking a toll on my body and soul. I woke early and devoured a piece of toast, a slice of cheese and a boiling cup of tea with lots of sugar. It was all I could find to eat – the only thing that got me through each day and night. The police that patrolled the city left no stone unturned in pursuit of us; I couldn't relax for a second. They were throwing everyone they caught into prison, and then deporting them after a few days. Even contemplating that scenario is painful. Having to return to the point from which I started would be a death sentence.

Still, during my final days in Kendari, I ate breakfast and grabbed the opportunity to leave the hotel. In the humid hours before dawn, I was sure that the city was asleep and that no nosy police officer would come along the path I took into the jungle.

I would cross a short, paved road – all the while shaking with fear – and turn into some quiet woods fenced off all around by wooden palings. I think it was private property, I felt like I was committing a crime being there, but no-one ever came. There, in the centre of a huge coconut plantation stood a beautiful cottage. A short man was always there, surrounded by numerous curious dogs wagging their tails. He would smile at me and give me a friendly wave. That kind smile would help me continue down the dirt road through the plantation with a feeling of safety.

A large log had fallen beside the path, next to a flooded rice paddy. I would sit on that log, light a cigarette, take in the natural environment, and put away my tumultuous thoughts and my hunger. By the time I'd finished my cigarette, the sun would be starting to come up and I'd return to the hotel down that same trail through the jungle. The short man would wave to me again with the same kind smile. The tall coconut trees beside the path and the small green rice paddy at the end of the trail, the beautiful moments I spent there, have become for me a divine image.

My life during these last three months has been mainly fear, stress, starvation and displacement – but also those short hours sitting on the log in the divine plantation. Those three volatile months have culminated now, in this paralysing moment when a child's scream could take us back to our journey's beginning.

—

The truck moves a few metres along the silent coast, then switches off its engine. It stalks the beach like a hunter, then freezes still and quiet. My emotions run high. This whole thing could be ruined in one fell swoop.

I hold my backpack to my chest, ready to jump from the truck, ready for a chase, a getaway, on this dark and unfamiliar beach. Even if the police find us, I cannot go to jail. I recall the experiences of other displaced travellers that I have heard over the past few months. *The police never fire bullets . . . When they order you to stop you need to run as far as you can. Don't freeze . . .* My shoes are laced up tight.

The truck moves again, a bit further than before. One more push will take us to the ocean. I am nervous as a child, it torments me. I want the dark weather-beaten man to order us out of the truck. But he is engaged in conversation with the driver and waves his hand to signal quiet. The little bastard keeps laughing mischievously under his breath. He is probably the only one with no fear – for him this is just an exciting game.

The Sri Lankan couple's arms are around each other's waist. They are a reassuring picture, sitting with their heads resting alongside one another.

A comforting feeling /

Two bodies merged; arms, waists and heads /

All merged together /

Their bond is reinforced /

They bond in resistance /

They withstand the anxiety.

With another scream – louder this time – the truck takes off and then halts less than a hundred metres ahead. The motor screams – the truck is a hunter, struggling to catch its prey, it cries out with relish now that it's in its grasp.

The smuggler with the weather-beaten skin orders us to step out. I am at the end of the truck with The Toothless Fool and we don't wait to get caught up with the hesitant exit of the women and children – we jump down from the side of the truck. The babble resumes, the ruckus of men and women and the screams of children disrupt the tranquillity of the beach.

We can't see the faces of the smugglers who walk ahead of us waving their hands to direct us to the ocean. They yell at us to shut up. We are a group of thieves in the night trying to get across as quickly as possible.

The Blue Eyed Boy and The Friend Of The Blue Eyed Boy are – as ever – ahead of everyone. They wait on the shore, their backpacks beside them. The smugglers rush us. The sound of the waves from the roaring ocean muffles other noises. This is the first time I have seen the ocean while in Indonesia, after three fearful months of airports and beach towns.

We have arrived at the ocean /

The insane waves move back and forth along the beach /

They seem eternal /

A tiny boat sits a few metres out from the shore /

No time to delay /

We have to board.

2

Mountains and Waves / Chestnuts and Death / That River . . . This Sea

When humans struggle over territory /
It always reeks of violence and bloodshed /
Even if the conflict is over a location the size of one body /
On a small boat /
And only for a period of two days.

There's a deafening commotion in the bridge. A conflict between frenzied men vying for a place to sit has reached fever pitch. The Toothless Fool and The Penguin have laid themselves down next to the captain's chair leaving one space free for someone else. I place my backpack between their weary bodies and lean back on it. After sitting on the truck's hard wooden floor for hours I am relieved to park my aching backside relatively comfortably.

The younger men have all found places to sit, after a competition which seems pointless to me. They have occupied all the floor space of the sleeping quarters and the families are now forced down into the end of the boat.

The Friend Of The Blue Eyed Boy gets comfortable next to his girlfriend, Azadeh, in what might be the worst spot on the boat. Even though he boarded the boat faster than everyone else, he ends up having to squeeze in next to the families. Of course he's reasoning that Azadeh shouldn't have to lie in the sleeping quarters next to all the ogling young men. The Blue Eyed Boy got to rest in the best spot, right next to the captain on an old piece of foam cushion left over from a chair.

The young men in the sleeping quarters shout and swear at a few families, forcing them too to sit at the end of the boat. Even the Sri Lankan couple are forced out of a sleeping chamber – and this unfair wrangling leaves them without a place. For a long time they just stand there with their baby looking for a place at the end of the boat as others stare back at them unforgivingly.

Down at that end of the boat I can see it's a struggle to find a suitable place to sit. All the women are being screamed at in such a cowardly way; it's totally inappropriate. Every spot is wet and uncomfortable and it isn't clear what all the fuss and yelling is supposed to achieve. Among all the confrontations and quarrels the Sri Lankan family lose out.

In the midst of the fracas, as the women and children try to settle into their hard and uncomfortable positions, the boat takes off; like a heavily pregnant mare cantering carefully across a dark prairie of water.

We are on our way to Australia.

My spot isn't too bad. I rest my head on my backpack. The captain is just a step away from me. I can easily see the direction we are moving in on his compass – south – and the kilometres we are covering, which gives me a false sense of assurance.

The boat travels slowly and calmly over small waves and is getting further from the shore. All the ruckus has ceased and silence falls over the boat. The only thing that can be heard is the rhythm of waves beating the prow of the boat. With the help of the weak light from the lamp fixed above the captain's head, I can see dozens of exhausted people sleeping alongside each other. The long trip through the jungle and the constant jolting of the truck has worn everyone out and they lie there in rows. A mix of tired faces.

The dimensions of a boat /

Unfamiliar waves /

Waves of a foreign ocean.

—

The sky is looking brighter. Little by little, golden glimmers of sun appear on the distant horizon. The captain's assistant shifts back and forth to the engine room, and a few others are standing around.

I can see The Friend Of The Blue Eyed Boy sitting right at the end of the boat. He is like a picture, the pride of youth. Azadeh's head rests on his lap as he looks out at the waves and all the exhausted faces around him. A young guy with a ponytail is sitting next to a kind of window frame in one of the sleeping quarters. His wife sleeps right beside him. He watches The Friend Of The Blue Eyed Boy gripping the edge of the boat with both hands. The Blue Eyed Boy stands next to the captain, busy eating a bag of red apples. A young man – a robust muscular guy – is awake in the stern. His wife and child rest their heads on one of his large arms.

But these are the only men whose bodies resist sleep. Sleep does not seem to take hold of them. Even The Toothless Fool, who always has absurd things coming out of his toothless mouth, is silent, crashed out with his head on The Penguin's stomach. The Penguin's duck-feet spread out even wider than usual. The well-built young guys, who were most vocal and arrogant when aiming insults at women and children while boarding, now just lay there in deep sleep. The Kurdish family are also crashed out. Even their little bastard of a son is drained of energy. He looks like a corpse lying there in deep sleep, although now his face shows signs of childhood innocence.

This is a sleep that transcends ordinary sleep /

It induces unconsciousness /

Pale faces /

Drooling from the mouth.

My eyes are heavy with sleep, but there's nothing like curiosity, adventure or fear to keep me up. My natural disposition keeps me alert and spirited, and it won't let me rest. I can't be constrained to this one spot. I leave the bridge and spend some time wandering through the motionless bodies, from one end of the boat to the other. It's a mess. Bodies are twisted into one another. Even the normal physical boundaries between families has fallen apart. Men lie in the arms of another's wife, children lie on the chests and bellies of strangers. It seems they have all forgotten the shouts and insults of earlier, and all that energy spent establishing gender-based order, because everything is disrupted now. The sovereignty of the waves has collapsed the moral framework. Even the young Sri Lankan family, whose bond is maybe the strongest of all on board, has fallen apart. The husband is in the arms of the man next to him, the wife has her head on the bicep of another man, and their child has ended up across the thighs of a different woman.

It's daylight now and I see the boat has covered a large stretch – more like a small gulf – in a few hours, so far that the shore is out of sight. Only ships and fishing boats scatter the sanctuary of the sea. We are clearly in Indonesian waters, still close to the shore. But the waves are getting bigger and wilder and the boat is beginning to be jounced. The captain manages the waves with skill – his face is dark and sunburned as he guides the boat between the fields of large waves, but his cigarette is always lit. His assistant moves back and forth between the engine room and the bridge. His hair is greying but he seems to receive orders from his young captain and apply them with alacrity inside the engine room.

As we move further and further away from the shore and into the expanse of the ocean, the waves become more belligerent. Then the small motor on the edge of the port side of the boat, the one which pumps water out of the engine room, falls silent. The worst possible occurrence for a forlorn boat carrying all these unconscious people. Immediately, the captain's assistant starts attending to the dormant motor, pulling the starter rope over and over again with all the speed and might his muscles can muster. But the motor just keeps groaning and turning off.

It's all over. I hear the captain suggest we should return. I can't contemplate going back to the coast, a place haunted by home-lessness and the fear of starvation. The danger of being arrested by corrupt Indonesian police and being deported to the place I had fled throws me into a panic. The Blue Eyed Boy, who is standing by the captain, shouts out that there is no choice but to proceed – we can't go back.

The Young Guy With A Ponytail curses at the captain. 'There's only one option: to continue on the same course at any cost!' The captain holds the helm but he mimics cutting his throat – indicating doom. Even though he's young, he has experience of many seas. He is trying to help us understand the perils of the risk we wanted to take. But he can't persuade anyone to his course, not even with all his experience.

The decision is made /

Pursue the adventure /

We feel that we have burned our bridges /

Only one option remains /

Only one way forward /

Advance /

Move forward into the expanse of the ocean.

Those of us men who are awake must now do the work of the small water pump; we have to bail the water out. The boat is leaking, we have to compete against water coming in through a hole in the hull. The captain's assistant supplies two small buckets and goes over to the engine room. The Blue Eyed Boy is standing on the steps leading to the engine room so I position myself outside near the gunwale to make a chain of three. The captain's assistant fills a bucket with water and passes it to The Blue Eyed Boy. He passes the bucket to me. We keep up a brisk pace even amidst the roaring waves that are beginning to surround us.

Water enters through the hole, we scoop a bucketful, pass it through our hands, and empty it out. As soon as the first bucket empties, the second bucket arrives. The captain's assistant is so swift I'm quickly worn out. All I can see are buckets of water, tanned limbs passing buckets, The Blue Eyed Boy's young and frightened face.

Mountains of waves rise and fall.

There's nothing we can do; the water is filling up the engine room – it's half full – we shouldn't have let it rise so high. The Friend Of The Blue Eyed Boy and The Young Guy With A Ponytail are on the other side of the boat, busy with the broken water pump. They are trying to work the oil, the belt and the cranks that won't sound.

And this tough battle for survival takes place while all the other passengers are crashed out on the deck. We bail out buckets of water onto the roaring waves. As they empty, we become hopeful and our spirits rise. But our fortitude depends on the level of the water.

Over the other side of the boat, where The Friend Of The Blue Eyed Boy is, the water pump starts a couple of times, but each time it switches off again. The Friend Of The Blue Eyed Boy and the others dismantle and reassemble the water pump a few times. All their energy is centred on the bits and pieces of this small, horrific creature. Each sound from the pump inspires hope. Each time it turns off, the hideous sound of waves beating relentlessly on the body of our boat dominates again.

All their effort culminates eventually in an enormous screech and the pump is kaput. We're sure now there's no hope for that scrappy pump. Now the frontline of our unjust war against the ocean, our fight to embrace life, is tied up in a single spot: the hole at the bottom of the boat which is expanding by the second.

But as I look, I see the water is reducing with each bucket-load. We are reaching the floor of the engine room. The tables have turned and I feel empowered: we can empty all the water back into the ocean. We are confident that we will reach our destination by noon the next day. Now the water in the engine room has reduced, I have a chance to rest, to walk around the chaotic boat. I want to wake the others up. I want to make them aware of the near-death experience.

—

All over the deck people are piled on top of each other in unshakable sleep. A few of the stocky young guys have left their sleeping quarters and are leaning over the edge of the boat. Their faces are bright red from the intensity of the sun, and as I get closer I can see they are drenched in yellow vomit and seawater. I shake their shoulders and yell at them until they understand the situation involving the waves and our brush with death. But they only respond with groans, foaming at the mouth. They are so weak and impotent that they can't even put a sentence together. There's no sign of those arrogant, insolent youths who had harassed the women and children at the beginning of the journey. Their muscles are no help to us like this.

The families are twisted up together at the end of the boat. I note the Sri Lankans have reclaimed their little baby.

I lift the heavy arms of a mother and father from the sternum of a child who is practically suffocating, and place them on the child's feeble legs instead. I don't want to disrupt the sacred family unit while they are in the depths of sleep, but I don't want the child to suffocate under the limbs of its parents either. I see in this moment that the child is connected to its mother and father, held in the sanctuary of their arms. I embed the image in a corner of my distressed mind so I can visit it every so often.

Tragedy has struck our boat already, but the craft still proceeds at a steady speed, like a song in tune with the highs and lows of the waves.

A caravan of weary bodies /
Stooped and in motionless sleep /
Deep in the expanse of the ocean /
Swept away by those giant waves /
I smell the scent of death.

I feel an amazing sense of dominion and terror equally in my skinny frame and tired muscles. I should return to the engine room.

The water has invaded and is now rising higher and higher again. The captain's assistant is alone, filling buckets of water, climbing up the short flight of stairs, and with all his strength, emptying them back into the ocean. As water is bailed, some spills back onto the deck and runs under those lying there. The Friend Of The Blue Eyed Boy and the others sit in their former positions – they look more bewildered than ever. We are tired and burned out but I think we feel a sense of solidarity, a common cause. We must find the will to stay awake and struggle. Sleep means death. I start to bail out the water again. This is no time to sit around.

I devour one of The Blue Eyed Boy's apples in a few bites and stand on the steps. I exchange my spot with The Blue Eyed Boy, a small change that makes no real difference to my tired muscles. It makes no difference whether I stand on the steps or on the edge of the boat; what matters is that we consistently fill and empty buckets, that we keep them passing between us. The captain's assistant fills a bucket and passes it to me. I grab an empty bucket from The Blue Eyed Boy and pass it into the engine room. Rhythm and acceleration, control and speed – moving hands and buckets with thin handles. One full day of struggle against a hole that keeps widening.

No matter how much water we empty, the level hardly reduces. It has risen up to the waist. The Friend Of The Blue Eyed Boy and the others return to the pump, even though we can all see it has switched off for good. We are like someone falling from a great height, grabbing at anything. In striving to escape death, a belief in miracles arises. Faith intervenes. It would be a miracle to hear the roar of that water pump.

The Robust Muscular Guy exerts all his strength on its cranks – nothing happens, nothing at all. The water pump is a corpse, as unmoving as the bodies all over the deck.

Horrific waves bash us from all sides, they make a dreadful noise. Our poor boat – they are now almost double the size of those earlier – it's almost splitting in two. The boat shakes so violently that the captain's assistant loses his focus – water is dumped on our heads instead of overboard. The sea bashes at us from all sides and the water in the engine room rises higher and higher. The captain's assistant is remarkably swift, he wears us out and puts us out of step. We drop buckets, lose focus . . . and in these short clumsy intervals we fall behind.

The captain jerks the helm left and right without pause – he waves over at The Friend Of The Blue Eyed Boy to fetch his assistant. He goes to the bridge, it seems a new command has come through. That lean and experienced sailor has worked tirelessly for hours. He leaves a huge gap in our line and a feeling of turbulent distress and unnameable fear. Moments later, it seems, the water gains confidence and climbs the walls of the engine room, the waves attack the body of the boat with renewed fury. The Friend Of The Blue Eyed Boy fills in for the captain's assistant in the engine room, but he can't compare in strength, and he's too weak to put up with the smell of burnt gasoline, it's so strong it brings tears to one's eyes. The Robust Muscular Guy appears in the engine room; now he is stronger and nimbler than The Friend Of The Blue Eyed Boy. And The Young Guy With A Ponytail takes my place on the steps. As we swap out, the chain keeps bailing.

—

I want to see the Sri Lankan child; the image of that child draws me to the stern. I step over lifeless bodies with mouths open and drooling. I move towards the families, looking for the Sri Lankans.

The baby's lips are dark and swollen. It rests on its mother's chest, but is breathing more steadily than earlier. Such a feeling of safety, the mother–child bond. Suddenly, The Toothless Fool comes to and drags himself to the side of the boat. He throws up copiously, down to drops of acidic yellow bile. One of the arrogant young guys stands up in turn, stares at the roaring waves, and pisses on both the pile of vomit and his mates nearby. He looks possessed, like someone who has lost his senses after a haunting. The horror of the sea has mesmerised him. He no longer cares where he pisses.

—

The water is full of gasoline from the engine room. The captain's assistant is submerged with rags and a stick trying to find and block the hole in the bottom of the boat. We are useless and can't help him. We can only witness his struggle; anxious spectators of his work. The water reaches his ribs, he dives in again with the stick and rag, his face blacker each time he emerges. He has barely uttered a word this whole time; but his visage holds the might of a warrior whose exploits are lost to the annals of history. The bulging veins on his arms, calves and shins are a message to men, women and the sea. They cover his bony frame like a net. His gaunt and wrinkled face seems to have been sculpted by the sea and its merciless waves. His agility and eerie silence makes me think that for years and years he has been fearless, toying with death and the dark stormy nights as a way to pass time; it is second nature to him.

Shaking his head, The Toothless Fool arrives at the hatchway to the engine room – his face covered with shock. Obviously, he hasn't got his bearings yet after a long, deep sleep; he seems unable to grasp what's going on. The young guy who pissed on the other lads seems to still be undergoing a kind of mental and physical convulsion. I suppose he's also trying to under-stand what has befallen us and our rotting boat. Nevertheless, the captain seems unfazed by all the action in the engine room. He yanks the helm vigorously, and his cigarette remains lit. His authority over both waves and boat is such that his presence is even felt in the engine room, despite that damn hole. An unspoken power connects him, his assistant, the boat and the sea.

The assistant continues to exert himself under the gasoline-polluted water. Blocking the hole could avert the boat and passengers being dragged down into the whirlpool of waves. Although the power and severity of the sea is such that it feels like at any moment the boat could split in half, even if the leak is fixed. Some of the waves are so high and heavy that the boat lifts metres in the air. They bash the bow and sides of the boat and shake us all, especially the kids, with their weightless frames and nothing with which to tie them down. Waves pick up speed and toss us all around the boat's mouldy deck like a carousel; bodies squash up against each other. The edge of the boat is the scariest spot; the impact of a heavy wave could fling anyone standing there off the carousel. Caught up at the top of a wave, the boat dives into a trough, landing with a quake that feels strong enough to split the boat apart. It's being destroyed by these mountains of waves attacking us. It provokes a trembling fear deep in our hearts and souls, like vertigo before impact. The rotten boat is close to capsizing. It finds equilibrium for a short moment, only for another crushing wave to knock into the bow without warning.

The waves pound the bow rhythmically, more severe than before. Even more terrible than the tremors is the horrendous sound each time we're hit, you'd think these giant waves were crashing into seawalls of solid stone.

The captain's assistant finally manages to plug the hole with rags and a stick. Without a word he springs into action, bailing the water inside the engine room. He quickly fills the buckets again and passes them up. The Blue Eyed Boy, standing on the steps, resumes his role.

———

It's midnight. Completely dark. The formidable waves beat the body of our splitting boat without interruption. The smashing waves engender a mixture of terror and lament in our thoughts.

The front tip of the boat ruptures and water bursts out from under the family members, still lying entangled. The sealed hole in the engine room resigns itself to the pressure of the waves, and the water rises again. The other passengers all wake suddenly from sleep, to be confronted with death. We are all damp and numb, but we all continue bailing, knowing we could be dead in a blink of an eye.

This whole mess /

In the darkness of midnight /

Looks like death /

Smells like death /

Embodies death /

The cries /

The screams /

The swearing /

The knocking about /

The sounds of the small children /

The heart-wrenching and painful sounds of the little children /

These sounds transform the chaotic boat into hell.

The buckets speed up and the water is quickly emptied. It seems to me the women are fighting off death even more bravely than the men. Their maternal instincts make of them predatory she-wolves; they stare down the ocean, revealing their sharp teeth.

In the depths of darkness /

On the verge of losing all hope /

One still maintains a little glimmer of hope /

Deep down inside /

A tiny light /

About the size of a speck /

Like a distant star /

Is spotted on the horizon this dark night.

All our hopes are focused on one tiny luminous point in the distance. A common will takes form in solidarity and struggle. What is the connection between our survival and reaching that insignificant bright spot? The far-off light feels vital; a call to war, a call to fight for our lives.

But inside the sleeping quarters, hope seems to mean reaching out for help from above. The ensuing sounds of prayer and recitation make one's hair stand on end.

The musical sound of the spiritual odes infuse horror /

The cacophony of religious recitations is deathlike /

The haunting performance of lament evokes anxiety /

An alarm into the atmosphere, and into the hearts and minds of the travellers /

The harrowing harmony of holy verses brings Judgment Day down to earth from the heavens.

This fear is worse than death I think. Hearing musical odes of faith and ritual chants, the children cling to their mothers. Tears shed by souls from the realm of life-after-death combine with the chanting and supplication.

The Sri Lankan couple seem more afraid than everyone else. The chanting of unfamiliar prayers must be to them strange and foreign sounds. Those odes mix with the children's whimpers until it is like being stabbed by needles; it cuts us all up inside. Their innocent screams override all the other pointless and frightening noise.

The blind will of a wave strikes the sleeping quarters. The blind will of scared people clings to some metaphysical force or illusion in these last moments; they don't dare stare death straight

27

in the face. Like bellowing deer, they forage for their salvation within these eerie harmonies.

The Toothless Fool, who is a Christian fleeing persecution, makes the sign of the cross with his hand with every wave that smashes against the boat. A choir of crosses and hymns, verses in Arabic, in Farsi, in Kurdish and so much more . . . an echo chamber of chilling recitations.

I remember the obnoxiousness of the Kurdish man from the truck – now he holds his little bastard of a son in his arms and sobs. His anguish seems partly for the terrifying waves and partly for his terror-stricken child. I see that in this moment when everything is about to come to an end, his wife is ashamed of his tears. She looks around, confronting the disdain on the faces of the others, and nudges her husband's side with her elbow so he will stop humiliating them both. It's interesting to see how she cleaves to the demands of convention, even now, during this breathtaking crisis.

In the commotion, people weep aloud and in private, but I am silent. Mortality is our fate and I have no choice but to accept and embrace it. I could cry and surrender to oppressive fear, or I can accept its bittersweet inevitability. The path of death and the flow of life are both made manifest in our bodies; the empty vessel is subject to destruction. I imagine myself looking back from an unknown place beyond – myself looking back at me. I see a dead body, but with eyes still alert, struggling to survive.

In that moment everything is absurd /
I search in my unconscious /
For whatever shaped my existence /
In the depths of my mind and soul /

Or the ground /
For belief in a god /
Or a metaphysical force /
I don't find anything at all.

For some moments I exert everything to reach something far down inside the deepest existential places of myself. To find something divine. To grab at it . . . maybe. But I uncover nothing but myself and a sense of enormous absurdity and futility.

Pure absurdity /
Futility /
A feeling similar to living life itself /
The very essence of life.

This realisation makes me brave. So, right at that moment, I light a cigarette, take a few drags, and inhale the smoke into my lungs, into the most abused organs of my body. I have accepted death. Yet immediately, my fear reasserts itself. Feelings of futility and absurdity and an overbearing terror begin to fuse in astonishing ways. Terror reigns, and the absurdity of life usurps it – simultaneously. It is a unique experience; but then, I am undergoing these feelings for the first time. I accept death, and while engulfed in this maelstrom of noise and oppressive anxieties . . .

I drown in the vortex of sleep.

The ruckus of our terrified group /
The sound of weeping in the background /
The beating of waves /

The petrified, silent screaming /

The tormented wailing /

Waves rocking a cradle containing a corpse /

All within a domain of death and darkness /

My mother is present /

She is there alone /

Travelling over the ocean or emerging from within the waves? /

Where is she? /

I don't know /

I only know she is there /

Alongside me /

She is afraid /

She is smiling, and she is weeping /

Shedding tears from years of sorrow /

I don't know /

Why is my mother cheerful? /

Why is she weeping? /

I witnessed a wedding celebration with rituals of dance /

I witnessed lamentations that dictated demise /

Where could this place be? /

Grand mountain peaks covered with snow, full of ice, abounding in cold /

I am there /

I am an eagle /

I am flying over the mountainous terrain /

Over mountains covering mountains /

There is no ocean in sight /

From all ends, the territory is completely dry /

The presence of ancient chestnut oaks /

The presence of my mother /

She is always present.

. . . I am in one of the sleeping chambers, asleep. I can see myself; I am looking from alongside the Sri Lankan woman. No, from the perspective of her embrace. I can see my skeleton smoking a cigarette in the corner of the room. I am sure this place isn't Kurdistan. The location is the ocean, the boat is crumbling, it is filled with empty buckets, and full of punctures with water spurting out . . .

Again, the vision of mountains upon mountains /

There are so many mountains /

A series of mountains together /

Mountains within mountains /

Mountains that carry on and on /

Mountains that are hiding chestnut oak trees /

The mountains are barren /

There is not even a tree in sight /

The mountains transform into waves /

Transform into aggressive waves /

No, this place isn't Kurdistan /

So why is my mother here? /

Why is a war going on in that place? /

Tanks, rows of tanks, and helicopters /

Blades of battle and dead bodies /

Piles of the dead and women's cries of mourning /

A children's play swing hanging from the branch of the chestnut oak tree /

Girls wearing flower-patterned dresses, with musical instruments /

A war is taking place /

Shedding of blood and playing of music /

Mountains and waves /

Waves and mountains /

Where is this place? /

Why is my mother dancing?

. . . I awake in a panic. Darkness everywhere. The distant light had travelled closer. It is larger and brighter. There I am, inside a sleeping chamber. Screaming and wailing can be heard from below. It is a warzone. The whole place is beleaguered by waves. I haven't moved from my spot but notice that the waves are fiercer and more belligerent. I have been all over the boat. In one moment, my soul searches the whole place. Our fears are closer. I am under siege . . .

A scene of valleys /

Valleys full of chestnut oak trees /

In the furthest depths of the valley is a river /

We are surrounded by waves /

The darkness is pitch black /

I am an eagle flying through a frightening dreamlike scene /

Through the beauty of the waves /

The chestnuts are being swallowed into the depths of the valley /

Into the river, into the waves /

One by one they slide down the steep slopes encasing the valley /

They are sliding down the vortex of waves /

The river will swallow, and continue rising /

The river of terror swallows the chestnuts, and rises higher and higher /

The slopes, the confines of the valley, are closing in – narrowing the valley /

I am an eagle flying above the peak /

A river below follows me as I proceed /

I am carried by wings of desire /

They rise higher and higher, taking me up to the heavens /

There are no more chestnuts there /

There are no more valleys /

There are rivers everywhere /

There is a sea /

No, it is an ocean /

There is water everywhere /

We are confronted by the sky /

We are confronted by water /

Why is my mother dancing? /

Why is she crying and dancing? /

The mountains, the waves /

The chain of mountain ranges /

The waves, the mountain ranges . . . /

The boat is a wreck /

Split down the centre /

Caught in the whirlpool of waves /

Calls for help /

The rescue boat is nearing /

Its sails resting over the centre of the sky /

Screams for help . . . /

Help . . .

Help!

I wake in a panic. I have been sweating. It was a nightmare; a nightmare within a nightmare. I can see daylight. The sleeping chamber is full of terrified people. They are screaming deafeningly, screaming for help. There is a ship – standing only a few metres in the distance.

I can't believe it, we are a step away from that glow – we have arrived at the light. There's a ship here, now, full of sailors restless with concern. We have been rescued; I mean we are on the brink of being rescued. Our vague, distant hope has become tangible.

It happens quickly. It has come to this. The whole engine room and the prow of the boat are full of water. In the end the water is victorious; it has raced ahead of the buckets and the captain's assistant, who hasn't stopped bailing. The boat feels extremely heavy. A strong piece of long rope connects us to an Indonesian fishing vessel and the sailors on board I can see looking over at us. The captain and his assistant board the other vessel. The sea is . . . still. Perhaps the fact of a rescue has persuaded it to calm.

They throw a small motorboat in the water and initiate the rescue operation. Everyone wants to board. But they dictate the terms – women and children first. The motorboat does a complete circle around our boat, which I swear is going to sink to the bottom of the ocean at any moment. Eventually, the motorboat sits at the edge of our vessel. Four people – women and children – board. It takes a few minutes for the sailors to lift up the women and children into their boat.

I sense the stress of the fit sailors working to rescue us. We can't wait, this rotting boat is full of holes and at the end of its fight, we're about to capsize. We can't move from our places on the boat even; we can't disrupt the equilibrium. It's a balancing act involving the weight of the waterlogged boat, the calm ocean and our worn-out, pummelled bodies.

I can't believe we have held death at bay – my fear intensifies. I have experienced life with all its glory and had thought death was relegated to the periphery.

Realisation of one's mortality /

Traversing through the mysterious labyrinth of death /

Subsides our fears and conjures up our most beautiful moments /

By embracing life /

Death becomes even more terrifying and horrific /

Death and life are two sides of the same coin /

Death follows on from life /

And death is the sweetest form of life.

Now that death is more remote, my fear of death has increased – it is more horrific, more terrifying.

The small motorboat transfers a few more people to the ship. The sailors pull up the limp bodies of women and children. The Kurdish family board. The husband, that bastard, jumped on ahead of the other women and children.

The Sri Lankan couple reach the edge of our boat only for other families to greedily push them aside. The man has the baby in his arms but he lets the others ahead, maybe fearing that the child might fall. They board after all the other families. The rescue of the Sri Lankan child comforts me and lifts my spirits as if I had been saved myself. The baby is in its father's arms. Its mother doesn't take her eyes off the infant for a second. My eyes follow the child – my eyes, the eyes of a foreigner, together with the loving eyes of the mother, both stitched to this infant's little body. Our concerned gazes are transfixed by this child.

Now, with the women and children rescued, the masculine competition begins. No-one is willing to give an inch. The arrogant young guys jump on the motorboat. I think The Blue Eyed Boy is sick; his lips are extremely dark and swollen. His hands are shaking. He should get on the boat as quickly as possible, but he holds back saying, 'No, let others get on, don't worry. We'll be on board in a few minutes.' For two days The Blue Eyed Boy hasn't even closed his eyes – he looks completely disoriented. He has been working for many hours and no doubt, like me, still sees buckets being emptied before his eyes. I think this scene will be engraved on our minds forever.

The motorboat travels back and forth between our boat and the ship. There are possibly twenty people left on the roof. It pulls up to the port side of the boat and slows. The Blue Eyed Boy, The Penguin and a couple of others prepare to board. But, right at the moment The Blue Eyed Boy is to jump into the rescue boat, our boat flips in the opposite direction. I'm standing on the roof when it occurs; we have come so close to capsizing over the last two days . . . and now it's actually happened, the boat is gone completely in less than a few seconds.

All our dreams, all our fears, all our brave souls . . . /
All drowned /
A massive disaster into a massive disaster /
Sinking into mountains of waves /
Drowning into the darkness /
Sinking into the bitter ocean /
Swallowed up by the ocean /
Swallowed up without mercy.

With the weight of a boulder, the boat bashes us onto the surface of the ocean. I penetrate the water, into the darkness of the ocean, accompanied by the boat, accompanied by its slashed carcass.

Down . . . /
I sink further down /
I sink further down /
The boat is pursuing me /
Trying to catch me /
Catch me and pull me within it /
Death has arrived /

More serious than before /
More horrifying than before.

Death arrives again, exactly at the point when life had gifted us a reprieve. I am alone. No-one else around, just me.

Even more vulnerable /
Even more terrified /
I am just kicking and swinging . . . useless /
I am exerting all my energy . . . totally blind /
I am in the depths of the ocean . . . so scared /
I shut my eyes /
I am too frightened to open my eyes /
Fear of the dark /
Fear of the harsh ocean.

I close my eyes rather than leave them open and witness the darkness of the deep sea. I feel a power watches over me: my guardian watching from above? I can see myself all the way down here, kicking and swinging underneath the boat, the boat that pushes me down into the ocean. Losing control and about to pass out, I have a brief moment of clarity and manage to find refuge by imagining myself elsewhere – away from this boat and all these people who, like me, are flailing blindly in the water. I can sense them – all fighting for their lives. And I can sense the sailors watching as we capsize. I can sense the passengers on board the ship watching the situation that they had dreaded.

I take control again, a new lease of life, and I swim with my body working at full stretch. I have to distance myself from the boat that is bent on taking my life. I get further and further away, using up my last breath in that last moment, breath I have been holding down in my lungs. My guardian watching over me sees a man swimming beyond the limits of his strength. I swim like I am jumping through rings of fire.

I am on the threshold /

Entering the labyrinth of death /

Perhaps the essence of death involves war /

Both living and dying at once /

I swim through my own hallucinations /

All these images /

The constructions of my own mind.

Perhaps the boat *has* sunk to the bottom of the ocean ahead of my small frame. Perhaps I *was* captured within the maelstrom and swim trapped on the spot? Whatever the truth, whatever my hallucination, I resign myself. I must reach the surface, reach for oxygen, reach for the vessel above me.

I am out of breath. Still I swim for the surface and break through a small wave, gasping for air. I open my eyes and a wave smashes over me. Down I go once again, my insides full of water. I am suffocating under the weight of salty and bitter water infused with the taste of gasoline.

I lose control. I'm dazed. I pull myself up to the top of a wave as fast as I can, swimming feebly, my guts heavy with water. I can see the other boat in the far distance. I can also see the maelstrom – the place the boat sank. A bunch of our group are hanging off a long, stray piece of wood. Cries of distress ring in my water-blocked ears. Backpacks and buckets are scattered all over the water, I see shoes drifting away.

I am inspired by this sight of the group of men wrapped around the makeshift raft. My arms and legs are motivated into action, and I plough through the heavy waves. During that moment the balance of life and death vacillates; life comes closer and death is held at bay, it seems.

I swim towards the others; their wails are muted by the grandeur of the waves. I move closer, only to be thrown back by a large creeping wave. My muscles give out; they freeze up. The image of floating corpses passes through my distraught thoughts. But before me is a spar of wood and a group of men all shouting at me, though I cannot hear them. The power watching over me imprints on my mind the sight of corpses caught in this whirlpool of waves. I swim towards the spot where the boat disappeared. I'm caught in the dizzying waves; I reach for my saviour in the form of that spar of wood. I reach for a piece of wood from a boat that has been at war with this sea for two days. A last gift to its passengers.

A battle is taking place /

Waves toss my weary body /

Dying under waves /

Death reigns over life /

A reality too hard to accept /

Totally bewildered.

I get closer, closer to the piece of wood, closer to the group, but every new wave plunges them underwater for a moment. Every time their heads surface, their eyes flick back to me, a man struggling to stay alive. They must feel a sense of safety as they watch me fight against the waves; and hold the wood even tighter. They encourage me, screaming support; urging me to keep fighting. Their backing redoubles my efforts.

Only a few more yards to go. A short piece of rope is attached to the wood. I grab it and yank myself over to the makeshift raft. Hands reach over to me in aid – I'm on the wood, with the others, all of us gripping it and each other extremely tightly. Another battle, launched on another battlefield. I feel I have only just escaped the danger. The waves keep crashing recklessly onto our heads. We drown for a short period, then we fill our lungs with oxygen before another wave smashes over us. We drown under the pressure of that wave, then are free once more for a few short moments.

The waves beat on the crushed and bashed bodies of the damned /
Life comes and goes /
Death comes and goes /
On and on.

Dumped under a merciless wave, there is some relief in the gap before the next. The pressure underwater is so great that I feel ripped apart, ripped away from the group and in danger of being carried off by the waves. Every time I go under, something sharp, like a nail or knife, stabs me in the legs or torso. It cuts and slices into me. Some animus in this wood seems to collaborate with the sea trying to force us to give up and let go. It feels like there are incisions all over my legs. At one point, the onslaught of waves and the onslaught of the spikes protruding from the wood hits me simultaneously. Pain from two places, hitting from different sides, but both with the same aim: my submission – to extinguish my muscles and force me to welcome death.

When our heads rise above the water we keep our eyes on the motorboat. Erratically, it accelerates and circles around us – it manages to pick up a few people floating on the waves. The Toothless Fool is one of the warriors fighting to stay alive, he floats on the water like one of the backpacks. I lost him during the commotion when the women and children were boarding. And now, just when he looks ready to give up and submit to his fate, a powerful arm grabs him by the neck and pulls him out of the water. Like me he has had to battle against the waves, but he is rescued before reaching our raft.

This rescue occurs to me as a series of distorted and broken images. Just like a scene from a film consisting of a few frames, separated from one another but interconnected: hands waving; men on the brink of exhaustion; the dark of the ocean; the presence of the motorboat; the dark ocean; bodies pulled up into the boat, completely debilitated; and finally the sound of the motorboat moving away, and the wake it produces. The waves continue to bash and beat at our bodies; the spikes protruding from the wood continue to stab and cut us from below. Attack from two sides continues. The ripping sensation continues, tearing us away from this spar – the sense we are being pushed to surrender continues. My eyes look for one thing and one thing only: the motorboat.

I am imprisoned for a spell under the oppressive waves. I resist, using all the power my muscles can muster. When my head reaches the surface I look around for the motorboat in a crazy panic. And then an incredible, wondrous vision from beyond imparts to me:

Righteous is the one who can see /
I horrify, like a wayward sensibility /
But, my god, could I ever be a frightening being? /
I, I who was never anything more than a flimsy, stray kite /
Upon the rooftops of a misty sky . . .

The attacks of the foaming waves now seem wilder than ever before. Perhaps with the arrival of the boat, the sea has quickened, intent on swallowing its sacrifice – or its sacrifices. The motorboat seems inadequate. It collects four more people from the group of us hanging off the wood. We are now a disjointed chain. Out of all the passengers, only a few are left – we few who have waited for hours and hours as prey for the black angel of death. We may be wounded, but we are still fighting . . .

The sea seems to have an extraordinary desire to pull down the piece of wood and its distressed and exhausted passengers. The wood has become sodden and starts to sink – it could all be over at any moment. I have nothing left and can't even wave my arms. I black out for a second. But letting go of this spar means certain death.

The motorboat returns suddenly. It circles around us. It adds some small waves to the deadly larger waves assailing us and then stops. Immediately, hands reach out to save me. I feel like a small animal caught in the talons of a skilled hunter.

Moments later a number of young sailors heave my bony, wounded body up over the sides of their ship; their arms smell like the sea. They lay me out on the dry deck. I lie flat on my face and my ears register the wailing and crying of our traumatised group.

The ocean has performed its sacrifice /
That river . . . this sea . . . /
The meeting of both at this juncture.

The Blue Eyed Boy is dead.

3

—

The Raft of Purgatory / Moons Will Tell Terrible Truths

Rescued. Relocated /

A second boat /

Another journey from Indonesia /

Another trial; a test of the will /

Unsure we will reach safety /

Purgatory.

The scorching sun is branded right into the middle of the sky. In the most intimate way possible, that searing sun shrouds the ocean, which resembles a warped mirror extending far away . . . boundless. The waves approach and depart, occasionally rocking our small white fishing vessel which rests beside a grand cargo ship, as massive as a building. Our small craft is like a tiny pebble lying serenely under the shadow of a weighty boulder. The sun appears larger than usual; its radiation streams down, melting skin, smelting us, perhaps the only creatures on that enormous expanse, that wide open sea.

The British cargo ship above us is packed with red and blue containers, arranged so that they reach up to the ceiling of sky, a sky that doesn't host a single cloud. From the deck the sailors aim hoses at our boat and its passengers, soaking us, a people whose scent now embodies the sea. Hairy-chested men compete to take showers – committing acts of stupidity just to rinse themselves under the hot sun. They are all in a frenzy to get one over on another. The women are collapsed on seats on the lower level of the boat, sitting shoulder to shoulder on dilapidated red chairs. Some hold small children in their arms, little kids with bruised and swollen lips.

I can't fully make out the sailors from where I stand on the deck of our boat below. Only their blond heads are visible. It's easy to imagine their eyes; blue eyes, eyes the colour of the ocean. The ocean we have been rescued from. The sailors pull up the hoses and moments later a small platform is lowered down to the deck of our boat with individual packets of biscuits, containers of water, and numerous packages of cigarettes; it descends from above as the men aboard reach out their hands from below. The whole encounter with that British ship has been characterised by extraordinary kindness. We have quite forgotten about the violence, insults, swearing, and tears of our previous experiences with the authorities.

When they saw these offerings, you could see the men's spirits lifting. Each one fights to claim the largest share of the small load. Those married men – men whose wives were left stranded on the lower floor – exert greater effort than the rest. They raise hell until they can clutch a few extra packets of biscuits. They seem to be displaying a form of exuberant masculinity, driven by their over-whelming sense of duty, by a responsibility to fill the stomachs of their families, to feed them at any cost. Wild wolves all of them, hungry wolves, devouring and ripping at entrails. Every now and then they snarl at one another.

After this scrum, the young men immediately light up cigarettes . . . soiling the air with murky smoke, polluting like a dark cloud. The top deck of the boat quickly becomes smothered in it.

They inhale that smoke with deep desire – it journeys through lungs, through stomachs, through dry intestines, through barren intestines – the smoke that is exhaled is infused with the taste of starvation. The flavour of a few days of hunger.

There was no justice, none at all, no egalitarian solution, no morally just outcome in the partitioning of that small haul of goods. Yet, according to the law of the jungle it was a quintessential instance of justice. The stronger ended up with the greater share. I see a pudgy, bald man with a bowed leg filling both his pockets. I watch as he is about to swallow a biscuit, then slips on a puddle on the deck. He nearly crashes to the floor headfirst, but then he skilfully regains his balance. He doesn't even drop the biscuit. With his disabled leg he was able to pack more biscuits into his pockets than someone like me. Righted, he hides a packet of biscuits under his dirty shirt and, red-faced, goes downstairs.

As these tired and angry men childishly vent their frustrations, Our Golshifteh[3] walks up the stairs. She yells at them and grabs biscuits and cigarettes from their hands to distribute among the women and children below. It is as if thunder and lightning have briefly silenced the place. Our Golshifteh is broad of body and face, and her dark eyes are charged with fury. She's

___

3   We selected this name in honour of the Iranian actress Golshifteh Farahani, who now lives in exile. Behrouz respects her a great deal; for him, Golshifteh is a model artist and a profound individual. She is known for her courage in breaking traditional norms, and Behrouz considers her revolutionary.

an Iranian, a mother, she's proactive; a commanding woman. Although we are lost on the ocean she comports herself with bravery and dignity. While many have been prepared to step over their collapsed fellows for a date or pistachio, she tends to the frightened amid the chaos. In our first two days at sea we realised there was no more than one tank of water on the boat, and she rationed it to prevent anyone dying of hunger or thirst. She is as proud, as confident as a lioness. She is brave even to leave the lower floor, which has become a den for more timid women, to confront the men and put them in their place. She has such fortitude that no-one challenges her word. No-one argues with her. There is a special kind of respect between her and the other passengers: everyone knows Our Golshifteh isn't the sort of person to take provisions for only her own two children or her skinny husband. As soon as she leaves, calm descends and we all find a place to sit and swallow these dry biscuits.

I see The Friend Of The Blue Eyed Boy's face is bright red with sunburn. He sits at the edge of the boat, gazing out at the horizon. His girlfriend Azadeh is below with the other women. I know that for more than four months these two have supported and encouraged each other. In Indonesia, they had numerous difficulties. It is not the first time the three of us have tried to reach dry land after nearly drowning at sea. They were among the group on my first failed attempt to reach Australia. But they persuaded one another to continue on this arduous journey. Now they find themselves at an emotional point: one last step and we may reach our destination.

The Toothless Fool passes the helm, grinning victoriously. He looks as pleased as a child with a treat. I remember the basement of that hotel in Kendari, where The Toothless Fool recounted his bitter story. During his youth he was thrown in prison. He told me that he had seen his mother for the last time in jail. She said to him, 'I think this is the last time that I'll see you my son,' and a week later he was told of her death. His father died a mere two weeks after that. When he spoke of them, tears welled in his eyes. You can see the painful imprint of these incidents; he is old beyond his years.

But now he looks like he knows he is on the threshold of enormous happiness, that he can feel his dream becoming true. It's engraved in the lines on his face. That life is smiling on him at last, even as he has come through that period in his life plagued by death. This is the nature of death; even a brush with mortality gives life a marvellous sense of meaning.

Seated all around me, it seems, are people with thoughts full of beautiful dream images – even as they are haunted by broken and disturbing memories. Our hunger had been a barrier to optimism. But now everyone is cheerful. Even those eating or smoking in complete silence are projecting joy into the atmosphere. Our gruelling odyssey has come to an end and – since the British captain has notified them – everyone is anticipating the arrival of the Australian Navy.

Starvation is such a powerful force. It pervades everything. A single pistachio, a single date, might determine whether one lives or dies. This was something I have realised during days at sea, starving. Many times I have seen the others secretly slip a date from their underwear and swallow it in the blink of an eye lest anyone realise, lest anyone notice that their breath smelled of food. Everyone scrutinises everyone else; their eyes searching out a chewing jaw or a shifting throat.

But now all that suspicion has dispersed, it makes way for joy and kindness. We feel blessed by life's beatitude. I feel that all my nightmares are at an end – all because of that cargo ship. I am certain I have escaped death this time, I can bear witness to the fulsome life all around me.

In this state I light one of the smokes that, just minutes earlier, had been such a source of conflict. As I inhale the cigarette smoke, it mixes in my stomach with masticated biscuit.

And yet the nightmare of Indonesia and this ocean still flashes before my eyes.

Wandering homeless /

Starvation /

Battling against the waves /

Almost drowning.

I realise I need time before these fragmented scenes order themselves. But one thing seems clear: at least this nightmare has come to a close, as I finally reach the last stage of my journey.

My poor dry stomach takes over, evicting all other thoughts. I can feel it – I can imagine it – all my focus is fixed on my stomach and on the chewed-up food inside. It's as if I have an extra organ in my body. Starvation and thirst have taken me right up to the frontiers of death; starvation and thirst have turned my every faculty down towards my intestines.

If not for someone like Our Golshifteh, I might not be sitting here at all, on my rear-end, on this hard floor. Instead, I could be like The Blue Eyed Boy . . . deep down at the bottom of the ocean. Of course now the state of the sea is so strangely different . . . totally calm.

A savage law governs all boats destined for Australia. If anyone were to lose their life during the trip, their corpse never reaches dry land. I hear that captains mercilessly leave people stranded among the waves. If I had died on this trip, I'm sure they would've tossed my corpse into the ocean without a second thought – thrown out there as fodder for sharks and strange fish.

Food was the least of our worries on our first trip. But on this vessel, people are alert and vigilant, hungry. Starving. They were in such a state that they were ready for war. And when I boarded, I didn't have a single morsel with me, while the others had stocked up with provisions to last days.

By the third or fourth day of this trip, as we passed the last island that marked the borders of Indonesia, we paused. I was blacking out from hunger . . . I was famished. Fumbling, groping in a crevice beside the greasy engines, I found a single peanut. It was completely blackened, grimy all over. I wiped off the black varnish with my fingernail and popped it into my mouth, and swallowed. Now that a great deal of time has passed, I can assert that one peanut sustained me through all the following days until we reached this cargo ship. Subsisting on a single peanut. When all around me were people with food in their backpacks and pockets.

On one occasion during this trip I was so dazed with hunger that I got up and began threatening other passengers randomly. I recall the exact phrase I blurted: 'Look here, I'm hungry and it's completely natural for me to raid anyone with food . . . I'm about to do it!' A logical statement. Perhaps even philosophical. But uttered at a time when starvation and the fear of death had impaired my equilibrium. Thinking back, the essence of this performance was a parody of power. Just imagine my behaviour, imagine my gestures, imagine me making that pronouncement. Imagine me, whose ribs are protruding from his body. Imagine me, a man whose ribs are so visible you could count them. Imagine me in this state, trying to assert myself in this way. What a ridiculous scene.

And now I consider those days, the seriousness of my hunger and thirst, the unremitting fear of the waves, from this purgatory under the watch of a British cargo ship.

The mashed-up food has become molasses in my guts. The molasses joins with the blood running through me.

I can feel it in me /

I can feel everything /

I can feel how my digestive system functions /

I can feel it with precision /

My body is on the verge of collapse /

I can feel my bones /

My body has become a bone structure /

I am a skeleton covered in layers of sunburnt skin.

But this very body, this debilitated body, is also capable of survival. Before this meal I survived hunger and thirst for seven days. It felt like a form of resistance, a kind of sweet victory. A victory that has rendered my body a crushed and inconsequential entity.

—

A few people are gathering right beside the helm. They are laughing loudly, for all to hear. They laugh at The Penguin, laughing in ridicule. He lies on the captain's pallet, his hands spread wide, like someone surrendering, and his crooked legs splay out to the side like a duck's. His eyes are open but glazed; they reflect the terror he feels. He looks like a corpse.

Last night it stormed. The sky roared and a downpour of weighty raindrops, darting raindrops began – the captain ordered all the men to go below. (This concentrates the weight of the boat low to avoid capsizing. And the boat was in such a state that, in fact, it *was* on the verge of going under.) The Penguin was the only one who defied the captain's orders and stayed right where he was, like a sheet of metal laid out on the floor. A few people tried to lift him, but it was as if he had been nailed to the deck at each corner. So now he has been lying here since last night. Perhaps his mind's eye is still bombarded by images of the storm. He seems completely unaware of his surroundings, unconscious to his immediate environment, unaware of the massive ship that has saved us. It is as if he thinks his fate will be sealed by the tiniest movement.

The Friend Of The Blue Eyed Boy forces a biscuit into The Penguin's mouth and washes it down with water. But still he remains stuck like glue to the deck. He hadn't even shifted under the canopy covering the captain's quarters. No doubt he experienced a harrowing evening beside our weary captain; the rain pelting his body like heavy stones, the wind lashing them fiercely until this morning. He has become a captive to death, locked in his body. Ironically, perhaps if he had unclenched just an inch the storm wouldn't have bashed him so badly.

Now he looks like a piece of pale meat. The men mocking him were pale with fear themselves the night before. They don't realise how brave The Penguin is, the guy they mock now has almost drowned once before. It must be an uncanny and secret quality; the courage that allows him to take on this ocean a second time, to challenge it again despite its gargantuan waves.

Seeing how low he has come, famished and terrified, the others grow bolder and more confident – a wicked disposition. The weak always consider themselves powerful when they see others suffering. But the collapse of others appeals to the oppressor in all of us. The collapse of others becomes a cause to celebrate our own state.

A boy with blond hair whose whole face is beginning to peel sits on the edge of the boat with his bald friend, pointing at The Penguin and bellowing with laughter. Like the others, he tries to ignore his own fear, his own weaknesses; he prefers to conceal them under this cloak of mirth.

A few days ago, when we were docked beside the final Indonesian island, many on board were terrified of the stormy sea and tried to convince the captain to return to the mainland. But The Blond Boy and a few other youths threatened the captain and the passengers, demanding that we head for our original destination. We had no choice but to accept. I admit, I was in favour of continuing on course, but I didn't interfere. Now I am plagued by guilt; no-one else stood a chance against this group of young stubborn guys, which, of course, included me.

There was a moment, during that time, when The Blond Boy fell overboard. A situation that drew its own pointing and laughter. He was frantic then, waving and kicking with panic, a drowning mouse. The Toothless Fool bravely plunged into the waves and dragged him back up onboard. As soon as the boy's feet hit the deck, he was a drowned mouse vomiting sour seawater, shaking and trembling feebly.

So now The Blond Boy finds solace in The Penguin's wretched state, to mask his own fragility and deep-seated fear. He opens his mouth wide, exposing his yellow teeth. Today he is the most powerful human in existence, in contrast to The Penguin who is the weakest and most fearful.

Some people don't seem to care about The Penguin's situation. A tall boy who has been harassing the families and had shouted at the women two nights earlier is calm now. He's eating the biscuit crumbs left at the bottom of a plastic wrapper. A sprinkling of crumbs has gathered around his mouth, and biscuit dust covers the faint hair on his upper lip. He resembles a cat that has dipped its head in milk. He gobbles up the tiny biscuit crumbs and uses his tongue to lick out whatever remains inside the wrapper. The way he lifts his head out of the plastic, then plunges it back inside reminds me of a goat that has had some delicious alfalfa poured into its manger during a famine-stricken winter. He thrusts his muzzle forward, fills his mouth, then lifts his jaws from the plastic container, ruminating. He looks satisfied. And his mouth never stops chewing even though he continues talking. He chews, he swallows, and he spits a series of words into the air. I listen and although his utterances don't seem to be directed to anyone in particular, he is still demanding that those sitting around listen to him. He seems to be justifying his behaviour during the preceding days:

'I told you that we shouldn't turn the boat around . . .'

'I knew that we would eventually reach Australia . . .'

'I knew we shouldn't succumb to the reasoning of these scared women . . .'

'Welcome to Australia . . .'

'One just needs to muster up a little courage!'

And so on, plastering these peculiar expressions of pride, of his arrogance, into the plastic biscuit packaging.

—

The sailors are still looking down at us from the deck of their ship, up there beside their containers stacked to the skies. They look down at our boat and its passengers. At those who were beset by chaos and commotion but who are now calm yet exhausted. A few of the sailors are taking photos; they want to record images of we survivors. They share our anticipation, no doubt . . . we anticipate the arrival of the Australian Navy, they anticipate handing us over, our little boat taken off their hands. The sailors aboard the ship must want to resume their own journey, to get their vessel back on course.

Hours pass /

Sitting there under that scorching sun /

Waiting under that merciless sun /

Waiting in sweet anticipation /

Waiting as we scent the fragrance of freedom.

In the back of my mind, however, a concern is brewing. I worry that the Indonesian water police might even now appear on the horizon. I worry they could turn up and ruin everything for us.

A few of the women have mustered the courage to come up from their den on the lower deck. They have come up to confront the searing heat of the sun; maybe hoping their sweat will evaporate into steam up here. One of them is the wife of Mani With The Bowed Leg[4]; she's holding their two-year-old child in her arms. It's screaming and crying; like one long, deafening canto. The sound of that child crying rings in my ears and cuts through my thoughts. It feels like the noise is gnawing at my brain.

---

4   Mani is the name of an artist and prophet who founded the Gnostic religion called Manichaeism. Mani (216-274 CE) was born in what is now modern day Iraq while it was under Iranian rule during the period of the Parthian dynasty, which was overthrown by the Sasanian empire shortly after. The religion spread throughout many regions and Manichaeans were persecuted for centuries within Sasanian and Roman territories, and later by Chinese and Arab rulers. Mani also suffered a physical disability in his foot or leg and was executed by Bahram I (a Sasanian shah).

With every scream, Mani With The Bowed Leg takes a step forward, tentatively. He caresses his child's face, and then backs away again. With each movement of her husband to and fro, his frustrated wife looks on, critically. She speaks condescendingly to him, in a way that indicates she thinks her husband arranged this whole thing, and is utterly to blame for bringing them aboard this boat, on this sea odyssey. However, her tyrannical stare reflects something else too. It's obvious that she is behind every decision these two make. With her bullying manner, it's hard to imagine this poor cowering man having any kind of say on the issue.

She rocks the crying toddler. She tries to distract the child by gesturing towards the boundless ocean, perhaps the expanse of water will stop the screaming? But the image of these still waters holds no attraction for this little one. The ferocity of the child's wail increases.

Everyone seems distressed by the commotion. And it's clear they'd moved up already from the lower floor after being bombarded with complaints.

The Iranian whose whole life seems to have been characterised by irascibility sits off to the side, growling obscenities under his breath. As he mutters, you can see him prepare himself, slowly building up to yell. His voice rises to a crescendo. Finally, the wrinkles between his eyebrows and on his forehead glow red, and he can't control himself any longer. He shouts, 'If you don't silence that kid, I'll throw you all out into the sea!' The fury on The Irascible Iranian's face and in his tone is so intense that the family retreats back to the lower floor, murmuring among themselves as they descend.

The contrast between The Irascible Iranian and the ashamed Mani With The Bowed Leg is conspicuous. Mani With The Bowed Leg knew very well that he was incapable of defending his wife and child; the veins that popped out of his bright-red face betrayed his fear and embarrassment. He was fearful of the wrath of his wife who now had good reason to dump her misery on him once they got to the lower floor.

Of course today The Irascible Iranian bullies that family, but just last night, during the height of the storm, I saw him cowered in fear on the lower floor of the boat or at the end of the vessel, just hiding in there . . . petrified. He trembled when the massive waves crashed down on us. The rise and fall of the water dictated his breathing. He was so frightened that he leaned into *my* skinny arms and depleted body, with his other hand in that of an Arab boy. Sometimes it takes courage for a man to cry, but this didn't apply to The Irascible Iranian last night. His was no display of bravery; he just sobbed and wept as the typhoon lashed down. He cried deep inside himself, and tried to hide the fact.

The Cadaver looks like a skeleton when he smokes; a bony figure indifferent to his surroundings. He has a callous look, a cold demeanour. On this turbulent boat, The Cadaver seems the least concerned. He sits, one leg crossed over the other, smoking his cigarette. He is one of those who, every now and then, takes out a pistachio or date hidden inside his underwear and nibbles on it like a mouse. He does this over and over again, and then stares blankly around as though nothing out of the ordinary has occurred. He often grabs nearly-spent butts from the captain's hand like a leech; and smokes what remains down to the filter. He acts as if he were seasick and hungry, even though he is actually more vigorous than the rest of us. On a few occasions, he has jumped down to the lower floor to dump his collection of date seeds and pistachio shells.

Last night, before the captain ordered us all below, The Cadaver went down among the women where he fell asleep comfortably. He invited himself into the women's space as though he were married to one of them, and he assumed that not a single person would take offence. His kind is very cunning; in times of crisis they always know exactly how to get the most for themselves from a difficult situation. This morning, most of the men were exhausted by the extremely stormy conditions of the night, but The Cadaver was fresh and lively; he arrived on the top deck with dry clothes and had acquired a supply of biscuits and cigarettes.

A few days ago, I watched The Irascible Iranian realise that The Cadaver had food. When The Irascible Iranian conspires over something, he becomes restless and his wrinkled face is preoccupied. This time he stared over at The Cadaver for an entire day, frowning at him and his backpack, angrily. The Irascible Iranian was looking for an opportunity, waiting for The Cadaver to leave his backpack unattended so he could go after it. The Irascible Iranian is a pitiless, thuggish type – if necessary he *would* throw someone like The Cadaver overboard for the sake of a few morsels. However, he doesn't have the temerity, because The Cadaver is clearly a guy who can take care of himself.

Eventually, with a peculiar urgency, The Cadaver did move away from his backpack to the lower deck. In his haste he even kicked the arms and legs of a few people collapsed on the deck. Not one to waste any time, The Irascible Iranian went for the backpack. He emptied out the clothes and personal effects and searched all the pockets inside and outside. He found a black package. But as he started to open it, The Cadaver re-emerged. The Irascible Iranian promptly stuffed the package back in its place. The Cadaver was no man's fool. He knew what The Irascible Iranian was thinking. He knew exactly when to appear, like a spectre, and when to hide himself in the dark, like an owl.

—

Men are sitting all over the deck of this boat, each carrying their unknown past, each one a survivor of a perilous journey, each now part of this gathering, all brought to this place by a single goal: the aim of arriving in the land known as Australia. The sun is getting hotter and hotter. It feels so close. So close, it makes one think that the enormous expanse of water below us could turn to steam at any moment.

My full attention is on the faraway horizon. I look, anticipating, waiting for the boat to reveal itself. But the razor-sharp rays of the sun illuminate the surface of the water so that, no matter how hard I focus, I can't see a thing on the horizon, that faraway border.

A crystal plain of water encompasses my view /
A blinding white blaze engulfs my vision /
Silence has suddenly enveloped the entire boat /
The surface of the water is bleached white /
The sea is glaring.

Even if a ship were coming in our direction we won't see it in this fierce brightness. I don't know exactly where we are out here – I have no idea how far we are from say, Christmas Island. Who knows? Maybe we're hundreds of kilometres away from Australia, close to the heart of the Indian Ocean. Or maybe we have done nothing but travel in circles while remaining adjacent to the Indonesian shore. I remember that last night, just before the storm hit, my eyes were fixed on the moon. But during this journey I have seen the moon rise on both the left and right side of the sky.

When on the high seas, one is ignorant of geographical location. It has no meaning out there. The eye is too preoccupied with water, water, water as far as it can see. Only the sky is reliable; one can trust the sky, the fixed stars, trust the position of the moon.

So by looking at that moon I knew that sometimes we *were* travelling in circles. At times we have moved towards the moon for long periods. Then hope grows in me. But it crumbles again when we move in the opposite direction, sometimes for an even longer period.

I hate the moon. It tells me we are lost, that we are wandering displaced.

The darkness is increasingly encroaching /
The moon hides itself behind the dark skin of the night /
In the grip of hopelessness I also experience joy /
See, with the disappearance of the moon I feel more secure /
Sometimes ignorance of the truth brings tranquillity.

Recognition of the truth of any situation conjures up a kind of fear or anxiety deep within, inside the secret and innermost places that humans conceal. The truth-telling of the moon, its magical brightness, provokes in me the fear of having gone astray, of displacement. But the truth has another face, a form of comfort, something to be found beneath the surface of terror.

Truth is a contradiction /
Truth is a concoction /
Fear, serenity and anguish /
The moon disappears /
Gloom, despair, murkiness /

The moon appears /

Rhythmic waves, majestic ocean /

Protection /

A luminous sphere, epicentre of heaven /

A radiant orb up in the firmament /

Abandonment /

Opaque darkness /

The sea creeps closer, waves become bolder.

I have always despised waiting. Waiting is a mechanism of torture used in the dungeon of time. I am a captive in the clutches of some overbearing power.

A power that strips me of the right to live life /

A power that tosses me aside and alienates me from the very being that I was supposed to be /

A power that tortures me /

A power that torments me.

Living in anticipation vexes me sorely, it has always vexed me. The sense of cessation and inertia. It's even worse when one's own anticipation is compounded by that of others. At this particular moment we are all staring fixedly at one point, all desiring the same thing.

Things never happen the way you think they will. As everyone focuses on the distant horizon, a large ship appears behind us. We turn around. The Australian flag waves at the highest point on the ship, waving freely in the wind, with a pomp all its own.

4

—

The Warship Meditations /
Our Golshifteh Is Truly Beautiful

The waves have freed us from their clutches /
The waves have spared our lives /
I laugh at them /
I laugh in triumph /
Laugh to express the feeling of victory deep inside.

Dozens of humans with deteriorated and crushed bodies sit in lines of varying length on the deck of a military vessel, making a chain. Azadeh and The Friend Of The Blue Eyed Boy are in the front row, staring wordlessly at a few soldiers who stand there looking like clothes hangers. Mani With The Bowed Leg sits at the head of one of these human chains with his wife and small, boisterous child – they watch the soldiers attending to the others.

The only sounds are waves bashing every now and then into the body of the warship. I have never seen the waves so recalcitrant and unconstrained. They grow wilder, attacking the ship with more ferocity. Yet somehow they appear more beautiful. More admirable.

We can do nothing else but sit. Listening to the waves and following their rhythm is like a fascinating form of entertainment, a good way to pass the time. Until just the day before, waves had inflicted the deadliest sensations. Now the waves are like children's playthings; even the tallest and most powerful wave can only splash a few drops of water onto our heads and faces.

Following days of hardship, it is like a dream /

Night descends, bringing bright skies that contrast the darkness of the previous night /

Serene /

Gracious /

The moon is more beautiful than before /

It has nestled within the embrace of the sky /

It is watching over us /

There is no trace left of that deranged moon, that brutal moon /

There is no trace left of those dark clouds, those prowling clouds /

Everything is calm /

Everything in its rightful place /

Perhaps the sky /

Perhaps the moon /

Perhaps the stars know that it is no longer necessary to inflict violence upon us /

They know that it is no longer necessary to instil terror within us /

They know that they have to transform into beauty, into benevolence /

They must reflect our thoughts /

Our thoughts full of dreams and excitement /

All over the deck of that warship sit human beings /

They are human beings who still wear the scars of dying /

The scars from when death clawed at their faces /

They sit passively on the deck /

But they are happy.

No-one dares to indicate their happiness while under the nose of the stern-faced military. It is as if everyone had arranged earlier that they should hide their joy until they are no longer under military control. Perhaps the idea of expressing joy creates fear in their hearts and minds; the military could very well be averse to it and return them to Indonesia. Perhaps no-one is sure that the deck on that warship is Australian territory; no-one can believe they have really arrived in the land of freedom. Whatever it is, whatever feeling, whatever thoughts are running through the minds of those passengers, they all remain seated in silence throughout the night. Like frightened children, they do not let out a peep.

Even the boisterous child of Mani With The Bowed Leg seems to know this. The heavy silence in the atmosphere has kept the child mute while resting on the father's lap. The child stares restlessly at the father who stays alert to his surroundings. Showing the curiosity characteristic of children, the toddler examines the features of the father's face, following the father's gaze.

The Penguin is laid out flat on the floor just like the night before. It is bizarre, he is still struggling against death, he is still captive to the power of death. His eyes are open in an unusual way and his lips are trembling. His face is paler than before; it has adopted the colour of death. He was the first person transferred from the boat to the warship. When the military personnel arrived to attend to him he was writhing like a snake and moaning. A few officers who had come on board the boat had no choice but to lift him from the floor and struggle to take him on board the ship; they carried him like a sack of hard and dry potatoes. The Penguin's body seemed lifeless and feeble – but when someone went to touch him or move him he stiffened. He tensed; his whole body became rigid like someone having teeth pulled, becoming like a wire or metal rod as a result of the extreme pain.

As The Penguin was taken away, Mani With The Bowed Leg and his family followed, and then the other women and children were transferred. Finally, the men and the youths were also evacuated. We were bunched into groups of four and shifted onto the ship.

While The Penguin was frail and languishing on the boat, all he did was stare at the sky above. Now, on the deck of the warship, he continues to stare at the sky, with lips trembling and teeth chattering.

Our Golshifteh and her family are sitting beside The Penguin's exhausted body.

That woman's face is still exuberant /

Her appearance still beautiful /

Her pride still flourishing /

Her clothes are torn and her body smells like the other distressed people there /

Smelling like the sea /

Smelling pungent /

Smelling bitter /

But Our Golshifteh remains proud /

She remains captivating /

Our Golshifteh laughs at all this distress /

Laughs at all the misery /

Laughing with those dark, alluring eyes /

Those eyes flaming like small suns.

Our Golshifteh's presence within that displaced and wretched community is hard to imagine. She is the kind of person who radiates nobility. No matter what clothes she wears, no matter the situation, no matter if her life hits rock bottom, no matter what; she will leave a lasting impression on her surroundings.

It is difficult to believe that this woman, now sitting here quietly hugging two kids close to her chest, is the same woman who had faced off against the pitiless men exerting their force upon her.

This is the same woman with no tolerance for the heedlessness of the terrified passengers aboard our marooned boat, the same woman trying to instate justice by rationing drops of water and individual dates, the same woman trying to moderate their distribution. This is the same woman who cares about the child of Mani With The Bowed Leg in equal measure to the sustenance of her children, her own flesh and blood. When I encounter a woman such as Our Golshifteh, I feel proud and strong, and all the other devastated and broken faces are relegated to the margins of my consciousness.

The power of Our Golshifteh is a unique form of glory and royalty; she is a representative of our community worthy of standing up to those emotionless and formal soldiers.

Our Golshifteh is truly beautiful.

In contrast, The Cadaver appears soulless and draped in apathy. I cannot work him out no matter how much I examine his face, no matter how much I interpret the jagged grooves and incisions of his anatomy. When I look at his face, I can't even begin to imagine his past. I can't begin to imagine what kind of life he'd led, what his conditions were like. But one thing is clear: The Cadaver is cruel. I am convinced that if he were to open his backpack there would still be a large quantity of dates or pistachios in his possession.

The Irascible Iranian subdues his anger and holds back from grumbling. He has a natural disposition of anger, an anger that has engraved itself into his face over the years. Now he seems to realise that it is to his advantage to keep silent like the rest, and to put on a wretched look.

Looking at everyone's faces /

I realise that the eerie silence has penetrated deep inside /

Looking at everyone's sorrow-stricken and fearful faces /

I imagine a contingent of weary soldiers taken as POWs /

Bodies tainted with the stench of sludge /

Women adorned with the most horrible frowns /

But everything is calm /

Even Mother Nature is benevolent /

The sea is more enchanting /

The waves are caressing us with care /

They refrain from lashing us /

No longer violent /

No longer deadly /

Looking at everyone's wretched faces I also see hope.

As I look into the devastated faces, the virtue that comes to mind more than anything else is courage. Apart from the obvious differences and degrees of kindness and cruelty, and regardless of whatever lay underneath the layers of their personalities, these people have one thing in common. They have conquered the waves and completed an arduous journey. They have endured a whole week of crushing hardship. They have suffered perils to match the most formidable terrors. They have withstood the kinds of torment that are akin to death.

And yet it is extremely difficult for me to consider them as *courageous people*. Understanding the concept of courage requires a form of courage in the very act of thinking. I have never before had the opportunity to delve into the concept of courage with any real intensity because it had never been demanded of me to such an all-encompassing extent. I had never had the chance to realise what it really means to be a courageous human being.

Is courage the opposite of fear? Or is courage a virtue that emerges out of the essence of fear? But that ocean, and those waves . . . it seems that each of them instil a fear and anguish equal to the demolition of a crumbling tower. This experience evokes courage in me; it enables me to contemplate the very concept of courage. For the very first time in my life, that ocean has tested me; it tested my courage in the most intimate way possible; I have been tested within the labyrinths of death.

The ocean has put me on trial /

The ocean has confronted me with a challenge /

The ocean summoned all the theoretical analyses I had formulated in my conscious mind over the years /

The ocean subjected me to conflict /

Positioned me as a blindfolded adversary /

A rival to death.

The odyssey across the ocean on a rotting boat had created the space for a colossal encounter – where the essence of my being could manifest – where I could interrogate my soul – so that I could lay myself bare:

Is this human being who he thinks he is?

Does this human being reflect the same theories that he holds?

Does this human being embody courage?

These are perennial questions. The ocean has examined me with these questions; it has asked me these questions again and again. For years and years these questions have occupied my mind. These questions ultimately propelled me to the other side of the earth, propelled me out into the ocean, an ocean I had only ever seen in geography textbooks.

—

For years I had pondered the mountains /

For years I had dwelt on the war involving occupiers of the Kurdish homelands /

A war against those who had divided Kurdistan between themselves /

An occupation that has devastated an ancient culture /

An invasion that has decimated what was of cultural value to the Kurds /

Destroyed what was cherished by the Kurds /

What was necessary for the preservation of Kurdish identity.

When I was younger, I had wanted to join the Peshmerga. I wanted to live my life away from cities. I wanted to live my life in the grip of apprehension, out there in the mountains, and participate in the ongoing war.

On many occasions we were on the verge of a revolution; a great rebellion was gathering momentum. But every time I was impeded by some kind of fear masked by theories of non-violence and peace. On many occasions I reached as far as the colossal mountain ranges of Kurdistan. However, those theories about non-violent resistance drew me every time to the cities where I took up the pen.

For years and years I contemplated finding protection within the mountains, a region where I would have to take up the gun, a region where I would be among those who couldn't comprehend the value of the pen, a region where I would be obliged to speak their language, the language of armed resistance. But every time I pondered the glory and power of the pen, I would go weak at the knees.

To this very day I don't know if I have a peace-loving spirit or if I was just frightened. I still don't know if I was afraid of fighting in the mountains, if I was afraid of taking up the gun, or if I truly believed that the liberation of Kurdistan couldn't be achieved through the barrel of a gun. This plagued me: maybe I was a coward; maybe my cowardice redirected my thoughts towards a preference for peace, redirected my thoughts to privileging the power of the pen, compelled me to pursue cultural expression as resistance.

But I think that it is only when our theoretical positions are put into practice that we can know their profundity. Only one who contemplates and theorises death to its fullest extent is truly unafraid of death. Theories are theories in the real sense of the word when we internalise them, and only become something more when we embody them.

We cannot practise contemplative and sincere theorising in relation to monumental concepts such as death and life if we choose to be dispassionate.

When we are faced with death or fear /

When we struggle against death or fear /

We acquire deep insights and discover a rich understanding of these concepts /

The ocean provided me these opportunities /

The ocean introduced me to the most intimate relationship possible with death and fear /

Like two wild rams bashing horns /

Like a sledgehammer smashing against iron.

Most of the people sitting on the hard deck of the warship have travelled on the ocean for the very first time. For someone who has mustered the courage to board one of those boats headed in the direction of Australia, there is no way to return, no way at all. Getting on any one of those boats is an extraordinary risk, a massive danger. It is truly a battle against death. Before boarding, most of these people didn't have the slightest impression of the extreme danger that awaited them on the journey. But for me and a few others the situation was different. We had almost drowned once before, and two weeks later we resumed the war with the ocean by boarding another boat. In the two weeks when I was on dry land back in Indonesia, I had an uncanny longing to launch into another odyssey, a passion fused with fear. I confess that the second time I went to board a boat, I felt my legs tremble; an unyielding nausea festered in my guts, a harrowing anxiety took over me.

I threw myself over to the grip of the ocean and its waves one more time, threw myself over to confront the reality, to confront the terror. We advanced for days upon that abyss of water, besieged by waves, until we ran out of fuel and were left marooned along the shore. We were at the point of no return. We had no way forward.

The next day a small boat arrived to meet us carrying barrels of gasoline. Then it was time to make the ultimate decision. Most of the people sitting with me now on the deck of the warship had wanted to return with that little boat. Once the barrels of gasoline had been offloaded, a battle ensued over boarding the little boat. The little boat was floating alongside the edge of our boat. A few of the young guys had been tearing into each other, pushing and pulling at each other's shirts. Even one of the women received a whack right there in front of her husband's eyes; however, that strike influenced the sailors to let her on board. The bashing and brawling had reached a critical point. Three or four of the heftiest young fellows successfully pushed everyone else aside and jumped on the little boat. The little boat drifted away. Seven or eight people had been successful in leaving our boat to return on the little boat, and there went the last chance to go back.

As I reflect on the few months living in Indonesia and the second trip out onto the ocean, I have arrived at a more complete concept of courage, although I still don't feel a deep trust in my theoretical ruminations on the topic.

Courage is profoundly connected with folly /
Battling the waves and continuing on that odyssey would be impossible without foolishness.

A few times something occurred to encourage surrender, something that happened that made us want to quit that dangerous trip. However, I had persevered every time with the help of the recklessness that ran through my veins, that senseless attitude that I harboured. Acknowledging danger is usually a major factor in avoiding danger. But I forced myself to cultivate my innate foolishness until I couldn't make sense of danger anymore. No doubt, if I had applied my rational faculties to understand the dangers possibly awaiting me, I would never have journeyed over the ocean.

This I know: courage has an even more profound connection with hopelessness /
The more hopeless a human being, the more zealous the human is to pursue increasingly dangerous exploits.

During the period I was in Indonesia, and even when I was on the boat, I never had the courage to return to the life I once endured. I never had the courage to return to my point of departure. I felt that I had burned all my bridges. I was condemned to traverse over the ocean, even if it meant giving up my life. I was condemned to battle the waves, to continue the voyage, to arrive at my destiny at the end of this odyssey. When looking back at the situation I had departed, I feel a deep sense of hopelessness. My past was hell. I escaped from that living hell. I'm not prepared to think about it, not even for a second. Considering a return to Iran or return to a life of homelessness and starvation in Indonesia makes me braver, encourages me to move forward.

I am like a soldier caught between crossing a minefield or being a prisoner of war. One must choose. This is the point of no return; I can't turn back.

Perhaps many of those on this warship are like me /
Perhaps they discovered courage /
Discovered it within the valley of dread /
Within minor apprehensions /
Within major horrors /
Perhaps they discovered the courage to combat the waves /
The inevitable war the only way forward.

If the boat were to split in half by a stray wave, we would perish, gone like all the other absurd deaths that take place.

It is wrong to think of our deaths as different from the deaths of millions of other humans, different from the deaths of others who have died up till now, from the deaths that have yet to take place. No. All deaths are absurd and futile. There's no difference between dying in defence of one's homeland, dying for a greater cause, or dying for the sake of ice cream on a stick.

Death is death /
Plain and simple /

Absurd and sudden /

Exactly like birth.

I realise later that the stormy night when the angel of death perched on my shoulders was the night of my nativity; both my birthday and the moment of my rebirth. I realise this only once I set foot on dry land. If I had died, it would have been a fascinating and ridiculous death. Just think about it, a person who dies right on the same day that they were born. This is worthless, the fact that I now want to interpret a counterfactual occurrence; that is, reflect deeply on something that might have occurred in the past – but in fact didn't. Maybe if I had died someone would have come along and philosophically analysed my death using fortune-telling techniques or the movements of the celestial bodies and spheres. On my birthday they would have offered this to many others to digest. Perhaps on my birthday my mother would have constructed mythologies about her son to honour his death; with these sacred and mystifying fantasies she could cope better with her grief. She would spin sacred and wondrous webs around the circumstances. She would associate my death with metaphysical entities and occurrences. But all these sacred mourning rituals wouldn't change a thing.

Death is death.

Either a person dies on the night that marks their nativity, or some other time. The essence of death is reduced to this: non-being. Annihilation during a phenomenal moment. Like a flash of light up in the great expanse of a dark night.

All the remarkable exploits and all the fears.

All the encounters with starvation and thirst.

All now come to an end.

Whatever has passed, we have now reached Australia. Life has shed its love on us.

—

The warship travels all night, so we are obliged to stay seated. They don't even allow us to stand up for a few moments or to take a few steps. We only got to stand for a short time when they sank the boat on which we came. I witnessed them putting two holes into the boat using a stationary machine gun, and watched the boat disappear into the waves. It was then that I realised how modest the boat was in comparison to the ocean. A tiny piece of wood that paled against the ocean's grandeur.

Throughout the night I stay awake due to the pain in my backside, caused by sitting on the hard floor. Bone meeting wood. I remain silent, just counting the waves that beat against the body of the boat. I have become so skinny, and this is the cause of relentless pain, no matter how I try to position myself.

The next morning the warship arrives at Christmas Island. White houses in rows along the slopes of the island, white houses parading through masses of jungle. Happiness has revisited the faces of the passengers; they now dare to smile at each other. The sea is glimmering and radiating up to the island shore; the waves rise and withdraw up to a few metres from the beach. There's no even tenor to the movements of the waves. It seems that some of the waves are gathering momentum from where they begin at the shore and magnify as they shift into the middle of the sea. They are dazed, and sometimes a few waves clash, splashing, disintegrating.

A tugboat emitting black smoke moves up alongside the ship. Weary passengers are transferred in groups of ten onto the island's pier. First they move The Penguin, who is still trapped in the coils of death; they force him off the deck to which he had been cemented. Mani With The Bowed Leg accompanies his wife and child, who cries incessantly. Our Golshifteh and her children are next to The Penguin and moving towards the shore. From afar it looks as if a large community is waiting for us on the pier. It isn't long before it is my turn. I am one of the last, alongside The Toothless Fool, The Irascible Iranian, The Cadaver, and a few other young guys. We board the tugboat.

The only thing I own is inside The Friend Of The Blue Eyed Boy's backpack. On the first trip, my backpack, which didn't contain anything valuable, had drifted into the waves. But The Friend Of The Blue Eyed Boy has kept my book of poetry with him, the book of poetry that I love[5]. I hadn't been sure what to bring with me from Iran. I really didn't have anything of any value.

My lot in life after thirty years /

After thirty years of trying my best in that dictatorship /

After thirty years struggling within that theocracy known as Iran /

After thirty years my lot in life was nothing /

What else could I have taken with me besides a book of poetry?

I had wanted to exit the gates of Tehran airport not carrying anything with me. But I was afraid of the officers. Without a doubt they would have asked why this skinny lad, going overseas, was taking nothing with him. So I bought a backpack and filled it with a bunch of old newspapers and a few sets of worthless clothes.

---

5   The book is by Behrouz's friend and Kurdish poet Sabir Haka, *Fear of Being a Labourer Again in the Afterlife*. Haka is the author of three books.

I departed the airport looking like a tourist. I honestly didn't have a thing that was worth even a cent. If it weren't for my fear of the officers, I would have left like an empty-handed vagabond.

I was probably the lightest traveller in the history of all the world's airports. It was just me, the clothes on my back, a book of poetry, a packet of smokes, and my manhood.

Now I am metres away from completing my long, arduous journey. I have my soaking wet book of poetry in my hands. I have lost my shoes, and my clothes are full of thousands of holes.

The tugboat arrives at the pier. The waves along the shore are tame. A little blonde girl is bathing there, playing in the water; she isn't paying the slightest attention to us. She takes no notice of the weary and worn-out people, no notice of those standing on the pier. The image of that little girl playing is still fresh in my memory. She is laughing, she has drifted into the kindness of the inviting waves. In the world view of that child there is no place for affliction. In her world, there is no space for the hardship that comes from injustice.

She is free /
She is innocent /
She is like the cool gentle breeze on this sunny day /
My first real impression of Australia.

An elevating work platform lifts up the tugboat carrying groups of passengers, its power hoisting them up onto the ledge of the pier. That spot of dry land representing a land of freedom. Moments later I receive my first gift from Australia. A pair of flip-flops, laid in front of my wounded feet and dilapidated body.

A skeletal man with light-coloured eyes /

Holding a soaking book of poetry /

His feet held tightly in a pair of flip-flops /

This is all there is.

5

A Christmas (Island) Tale / A Stateless Rohingya Boy Sent Away to Follow the Star of Exile

A cage /

High walls /

Wire fencing /

Electronic doors /

CCTV cameras /

A cage – high walls – wire fencing – electronic doors – CCTV cameras /

Surveillance cameras gazing at twenty individuals /

Men wearing oversized garments /

Men with loose-fitting clothes hanging off them.

Early in the morning, at six, guards came in like debt collectors and heaved us out of bed. Within a few minutes they took us to a tightly confined cage. It is now almost two hours since they brought us here. These hours have been really tough. It is hard being imprisoned . . . being locked in a cage. We have now been in prison on Christmas Island for a whole month. It is hard being a prisoner.

Since everyone has been separated and confined within new arrangements, I don't recognise any of the people here, although their faces and their manner of speaking are really familiar to me. Iranians who have encountered a dreadful fate . . . cursed . . . damned. They are among the most unlucky. Only one individual among them can be distinguished based on appearance. A dark face – dark, almond-shaped eyes – thin arms, delicate arms of a youth who has just reached maturity. He looks like he could've been a Rohingya from Myanmar. They have separated him from his friends. His silence injects one with a heavy despair, the kind of despair associated with diaspora, a despair associated with exile.

Alienated from home – reflected in the way he stares at those walls of wire /

Alienated from home – reflected in the way he stares at those people whose words he doesn't understand.

The Insomniac and The Hypersomniac are also here. The two Iranians were hauled away from the adjacent room this morning. They were taken straight to the cage, eyes still half-asleep; they weren't even given the opportunity to wash their faces. The plan is to exile all of us to Manus Island on a single flight.

I really want them to take us on board the plane as quickly as possible and just send us wherever they want. I have convinced myself that whatever will be, will be, and now I have sufficient fortitude to accept the outcome. I believe that for me Manus will be just another stage, another stepping stone on the way forward. I can do nothing else but accept the reality. And the reality on this day is that they have determined to exile me to Manus Island, exile me nice and peacefully, somewhere out in the middle of the ocean.

—

My mind has been moulded by the commentary of the Australian officials – they have spent quite some time forming an image of Manus Island in our minds, a savage image of the people, the culture, the history, the landscape. As a result, I think that Manus must be an island with a warm climate and full of insidious, strange insects. That instead of wearing clothes, the people of Manus cover their sexual organs and waists with broad banana leaves. A few days ago, we were directed to information on the internet about the first humans and it evoked these images in my mind. It is exciting – and sometimes scary – to imagine a life alongside people living that way.

The information we had access to explained that the Manusians are cannibals. Rather than striking fear into me, these thoughts hearten me, inspire me. Well, surely it isn't the case that we will be left on our own among the cannibals. Surely it isn't the case that they will cook us into a stew in a big black pot. Surely it isn't the case that they will celebrate everywhere with jubilation and joyous ceremony; celebrate all over the place with their naked bodies, only covered around the waist by banana leaves.

But perhaps they will delight in eating my bony arms, I think. No doubt they would fight over this. The one who is stronger and more brutal than the rest would take my arms away like a wild animal and devour them without being disturbed. They say that cannibals derive more pleasure from eating human arms. Especially if those arms are like mine: little hair, delicate and long.

I am dwelling in these childish imaginings when they finally open the cage. They allow us to go to the toilets. The toilets also have CCTV cameras. It's really hard to relieve yourself when there's a camera staring down at you. Especially if you consider that right now there are a few sets of eyes belonging to unfamiliar people monitoring you, watching you on the screen connected to that camera. Perhaps they are laughing at you and discussing your sexual organs, loudly, for all to hear. However, these immature imaginings are always replaced by even more immature imaginings. Maybe that CCTV camera is there to scare us – so that we won't do anything.

We finish our business and no-one looks at the monitor during that period of time. Maybe the people who are watching couldn't care less about you and the size of your penis. For sure, the camera would've screened hundreds who visited those toilets and their eyes would've become used to seeing the penises of those people.

In that tightly confined cage there is nothing particular to look at, so these idiotic and superficial musings become commonplace. Since I am thinking about the whole situation with such intensity, my mind has grown weary; these thoughts and images condition me to switch off mentally.

This difficult period drags on so slowly. Eventually there comes a change. They move us to the adjacent cage. The Insomniac and some others are taken to a different cage. I see them. They pass through a walkway over on the other side.

When each person's number is called, they first have to strip to be body-searched with a device. Finally, their hair is frisked lest there is something hidden inside. I am also stripped naked even though I am only wearing a pair of underwear. They examine my whole body, even my armpits; they feel right into the hollows. Why should I care, even if I have to take off my underwear?

They are able to see everything with that CCTV camera. So I am prepared for them to do just that.

A grim-looking officer gives a set of clothes to anyone who passes through the strip-and-search stage, even though the clothes don't match the size of the person in any way whatsoever. There is no choice. We have to wear whatever they issue.

I go to the adjoining cage. I have my clothes with me – they are twice my size. Yellow polyester T-shirts – they transform our bodies, they utterly degrade us. We sit on the white chairs there, and again we just gaze at the metal walls. A temperamental young guy is yapping away and laughing. This loud and obnoxious youth, with scabs on his bald head, pulls out a smoke and lights it using the lighter fixed to the wall. It is curious, how is it possible that he kept that cigarette intact through all those body-searches? They even frisked his underwear and that piece of meat contained underneath. Someone asks him how he did such a thing. But he just laughs emphatically and says that he had been a prison warden in Iran. This statement earns him the esteem of the others. It is so reassuring to have a prison warden among us because it means that I can absorb one or two puffs of cigarette smoke into my dry lungs and intestines, and into my drained brain cells.

The Rohingya Boy also continues to look on alarmed at his surroundings, look on perplexed by the strange men, these men who are talking out loud, chatting vociferously. He looks so out of place that no-one feels sorry for him. No-one even offers a puff of the one cigarette that everyone has swarmed on. I also can't be bothered exchanging a few words with him, can't be bothered trying to help him break that mood, can't be bothered alleviating his loneliness, dispelling the harrowing nature of his diasporic condition. I am in no better condition. But the loneliness of the moment is more tolerable for me. For another hour we sit there on those rigid chairs, sit there anticipating the next stage . . . it isn't clear what that next stage entails.

Eventually a bunch of officers show up and read out our numbers one by one. When I enter the walkway I have to strip again. They body-search me with that device. My body is distressed and exhausted from all these inspections. What could we possibly be taking on the plane with us that they are frisking us to such an extent? It is clear that we are the subjects of their securitised gaze. Maybe they are afraid that someone has a razor on them as they board the plane, for instance. Maybe they are afraid that person will put the razor to the pilot's throat. Then the pilot will be forced to change course in the direction of Australia.

So what is the big deal about Manus? What kind of land can it possibly be? Why do they think anyone would want to do something dangerous? The securitised gaze of those officers on our bodies and all that surveillance under the watch of the CCTV cameras is making me worried. I feel that I am a criminal or a murderer who they are planning to transfer from one prison to another prison. Something I have only ever seen in films.

A third cage, where the monotony is broken. A few nurses holding brochures come in, accompanied by interpreters wearing green. They speak about the potential dangers on Manus Island that may threaten our health. They speak about the long-legged, malaria-carrying mosquitoes. And they speak about other mosquitoes I have never seen before, mosquitoes that are completely unknown to me, mosquitoes that are pictured in the brochures. It is possible that one of these mosquitoes is waiting for me over there on Manus. And as soon as I arrive it will insert its sting right into my body. For these mosquitoes, we are alien creatures from alien lands. We foreigners, we are to become vulnerable prey for them, we are to become ideal bait.

One of the nurses, the prettiest of them all, explains the details. She says that we need to take care of ourselves over there: 'At sunset you need to take anti-malaria tablets and apply the special lotion that you will receive while there.' She tells us about the symptoms of malaria and a whole bunch of other crazy stuff, stuff that doesn't concern me at all. The words from that nurse are more like a threat than words of concern for our wellbeing. It is like she is warning us: 'Manus is a dangerous island with tropical and murderous mosquitoes. If we were in your place, we would fill out the voluntary deportation forms and go back to our homelands.'

Their words stir up commotion. Concern and fear are clear in the eyes of the young Rohingya Boy. He looks around the group with his dark eyes, looks around with his almond-shaped eyes, searching for a potential sanctuary in the faces of strangers. But he isn't going to find anything resembling peace and security in our faces. He goes back to staring at the wall in front of him.

When the nurses have left, the guy who had been a prison warden performs a magic trick and produces another cigarette. He pulls it from the pocket of his polyester shorts. It is truly unbelievable. How could he have done that! That single cigarette – it distracts us from the warnings of the nurses and our preoccupation with the tropical mosquitoes. Everyone is amazed by that scabby-headed prison warden; they look on with esteem. And he is also delighted that years of working in Iran's prisons has elevated him to an honourable status – his laughter stretches his mouth from ear to ear, across his face for everyone there to see.

Taking one or two puffs of that cigarette in such unexpected circumstances induces so much pleasure. I really like that guy. I really like the way he is able to transport that single cigarette through all these barriers. He is the quintessential prison warden and he knows very well how to bury a few smokes within the hollows and cavities of the body. He knows very well how to put one over those ruthless officers, those brutes. He can deceive those bastards without a thought.

In these moments I don't know what to do with myself. I stand up from my chair and wander around the tightly confined cage. I still don't know why they pulled us out of the camp so early in the morning. I still have no idea why we had to spend hours doing the rounds of the soulless cages, still no clue why they kept body-searching us. The only thing that comes to mind is that they wanted to torment us at any cost. Sometimes I peer over unobtrusively at that scabby-headed prison warden, just waiting for him to perform another magic trick for us, just waiting for him to pull out another smoke. But he is inattentive and just chats away loudly with his friend; I can't sense a desire for smoking in him now.

I can't believe what is happening to me /
All that hardship /
All that wandering from place to place /
All that starvation I had to endure /
All of it . . . /
So that I could arrive on Australian soil /
I cannot believe I am now being exiled to Manus /
A tiny island out in the middle of the ocean.

My roaming is gradually making my head spin. I also feel that the others aren't impressed by me walking around. I have no choice but to sit back down on that rigid chair again and just stare at the walls. I have always despised waiting, always despised glancing at whatever is around me, staring for hours while I wait for something worthless. I have always despised measuring up people's faces, people who I don't recognise. I hate it. It agitates me. This day we are supposed to be exiled to Manus Island. I want them to place us on that unknown island as quickly as possible. I want the fate that awaits me. I want it to arrive immediately.

I am worn out from all this thinking. Being exiled to Manus is like a club that has been raised above my head for a whole month and is ready to bash down on me. Living with the dread of this looming club is like torture. I want them to put me on the plane as soon as possible. I want to descend onto that island a few hours later. I just want them to take me to that island, the island I have only ever heard the name of. At least I will know where my place is. I will know that I am situated there on that island. And if I have to go, if I have to suffer by virtue of being there, then I will at least feel that suffering for myself. Sometimes experiencing suffering and hardship up close is easier than being terrorised with impending torment. It isn't as though I haven't had to endure adversity in my life.

I have endured so much malice /

I have endured so many uphill battles /

So I am prepared /

I am prepared to be thrown out onto that isolated island.

But sometimes one thinks what reason could there possibly be for a person to have to endure extreme suffering, what reason could there possibly be for a person to have to endure extreme affliction? Why did I have to be so unlucky? Why did I have to arrive in Australia exactly four days after they effected a merciless law? But one can never find a clear answer.

Ultimately, the distressing frustrations of the day culminate in the opening of the next cage. There they don't delay us very much. They take us one by one. They ask a few questions. We have to answer. Then we are loaded into a vehicle. There is a Kurdish interpreter. A woman with large eyes, the colour of charcoal, and elongated eyebrows. When I talk to the interpreter she sometimes smiles in a cryptic and furtive fashion. I can't work out what this means. I think maybe she derives pleasure from the fact that we have been exiled to Manus. However, it is also possible that she approves of the fact that I was speaking with vehemence. Maybe she approves because I responded to that officer from the Department of Immigration and tried to provoke anger in him with my answers. She acknowledges me with that cryptic, furtive smile.

—

They load us onto a bus. A few days ago in this exact area a bloody battle erupted, right in the place where we are now standing like submissive sheep. Lebanese refugees stood up to defy the guards who wanted to load them on board. But the guards smashed them and beat them down. They annihilated them, beat down on the arms and faces of a few of them. The guards dragged their battered and blood-soaked bodies over the concrete. They banished them to Manus Island. No matter how the refugees tried to resist, they couldn't alter the political machinations of a government, a government that had just recently taken power, that had gone mad with the mere whiff of power.

The bus takes off. The path to the airport is surrounded by jungle. The conversation inside the vehicle is about the possibility of a particular scenario: that we will disembark at Darwin Airport and find out that all this talk is nothing but a ridiculous performance, the whole thing just a farce, that this whole thing doesn't involve Manus in any way. However, talk of this kind comes from a place of weakness. At this point, faith in an occurrence that resembles a miracle comes across as ludicrous. We have to accept the reality. Within hours we will be descending on a remote island called Manus.

A few police vehicles follow our bus, and a few travel ahead. It is as though they are attending to our bus like a car transporting a president. We are so disempowered that we couldn't do anything at all, even if we wanted to. Our baggy, cumbersome clothing weighs us down.

Pandemonium breaks loose at the airport. Dozens of police officers stand by the plane in military mode. A few journalists have their cameras ready. All of them are waiting for us. The interpreters are there, also. That Kurdish woman has both her hands clasped behind her back. She just stands there, completely obedient. I can't work it out; I can't understand why they have to securitise that space. I am frightened by the journalists; I am frightened by the cameras they hold.

Journalists inquire into everything. They are always seeking out horrific events. They acquire fodder for their work from wars, from bad occurrences, from the misery of people. I remember when I used to work for a newspaper I would become agitated from listening to all the news about, for instance, a coup d'état, a revolution, or a terrorist attack. I would begin work with great fervour and scramble for that kind of research like a vulture; in turn, I fed the appetite of the people.

The journalists are staking out the situation like vultures: waiting until the wretched and miserable exit the vehicle; eager for us to come out as quickly as possible, to catch sight of the poor and helpless and launch on us –

Click, click /

Waiting to take their photos /

Click, click.

– and dispatch the images to the whole world. They are completely mesmerised by the government's dirty politics and just follow along. The deal is that we have to be a warning, a lesson for people who want to seek protection in Australia.

—

I came across a group of journalists for the first time in Indonesia when I was in an extremely horrible and distressed state, misery oozing from my pores. After nearly drowning during my first attempt to cross, I was weary, I was starving, I was traumatised by the sea. The police had delivered us to dry land. After a six-hour trip we landed in prison, only to escape a short time after. However, it was at the point of arrival, as we exited the police vehicle, that the journalists swarmed us and took photos and film from all angles – from the front and the back. I despised them. I despised the fact that people would end up feeling sorry for me and cry as a result of witnessing me there in that state, and through that medium. What joy could one possibly have in photographing and reporting about someone who had nearly drowned and could hardly walk?

It had been six days. Six days exactly. Six days that we hadn't slept. In that time the scorching sun had gradually peeled away the skin on my face, slowly stripped away the skin on my arms. My clothes were ragged. And my body smelled like sludge. The side of my T-shirt had a tear the size of a hand in it; it was so big that it exposed my bones, it revealed the ribcage underneath my burnt-red skin. My body was on the brink of a breakdown: I hadn't eaten a proper meal for the entire time I'd spent in Indonesia; in addition, there was the stress of being caught by police, the stress of being sent to prison, the stress of potentially being deported to Iran. And due to vitamin deficiency, there were random silly-looking strands of dry, brittle and pale hair in my beard, so stiff that they irritated my face. The ruins of battle glistened in my eyes; the struggle with death three days ago had glazed over my eyes. I was a walking apparition.

I looked so debilitated. I was walking around as though my mind could no longer guide my legs. As I walked, I felt as though I was sitting on a boat swayed by tides. When we disembarked, those nosy journalists and their contemptible cameras bombarded us. I was too weak to put my hand up to cover my face. No doubt, the spectacle of travellers saved from drowning and miraculously reaching dry land was sensational subject matter.

This is the second time in a short period that we have become the objects of inquiry for these intrusive people. The airport on Christmas Island has become a studio for a photo shoot. It seems that they are waiting in ambush, waiting for the time they can see me helpless and fragile. They are waiting to make me a subject of their inquiry. They want to strike fear into people with the movement of my possessed corpse.

—

Exile from Christmas Island /
Exile from Australia /
The airport marks the point of exile /
The airport is completely empty /
The airport is totally quiet.

One lone propeller-driven aircraft stands ready to take us away to a far-off, distant land. I want the officers to board as fast as possible and lead us inside the plane so we can take off. The atmosphere has become really heavy for me. It weighs down on me due to those vultures fiddling with their cameras beside the plane. The officers embark carrying their full backpacks, like soldiers assigned to the front line of the battlefield. Some of them wave at the journalists – there is something going on between them and the journalists. One gets the feeling that they are all in on it together.

The first person to board is The Insomniac. He has to cross a distance of approximately fifty metres from the bus to the aeroplane. They park the vehicles a huge distance away from the plane on purpose – their aim: extreme debasement. Two heavy-set officers wrestle their arms under The Insomniac's arms in a degrading way – they escort him to the plane. Even though The Insomniac is tall, he looks like a baby deer stuck between the two officers. He is reduced to prey for wild lions dragging him slowly towards the steps of the aeroplane. And the journalists exert all their energy so they won't miss documenting the scene. I know they take pleasure from shattering the dignity of a human being.

The Insomniac is struggling against every step, but it makes no difference. The two giants who have him secured from each side don't care, and they haul that piece of meat with a consistent speed. When they get close to the steps of the plane, two others are there to collect The Insomniac. They take him up the steps. Someone waiting at the top of the steps films it all. This is the scenario of that day, a scenario that is repeated again, exactly the same way, at two-minute intervals. The only difference is that the totally conquered piece of meat is replaced with another body.

I reflect, reflect on The Insomniac, reflect on the time he sat on the tip of the boat, on the way he gazed ahead, how he regularly checked the time. I remember how he used to ask the same questions over and over, how he used to ask, 'How many kilometres left to Australia?' Or that night, the last night, the night we were caught up in the storm, that dark night, that harrowing night, the night when he wrapped his arms around me, the night during which he didn't even utter a word. He was terrified. Now all the agony that he has endured comes down to this scene. A scene in which he is more like a dangerous criminal who requires two solidly built giants to contain and relocate him. These incidents occur on Australian soil. The same place The Insomniac was trying to reach, the place he was counting down the seconds to reach, the place for which he had endured this horror.

Now it is The Rohingya Boy's turn. Short. Thin. He looks so much more disempowered. He takes a few steps before his knees buckle. It looks like he is about to fall to the ground. The officers lift him up. It looks more like someone being taken to the gallows to be hanged. I witnessed something similar in Iran. It isn't usual for the boy to express such fatigue and bewilderment. He is a brave human being who has been alienated from his instinct for courage. He has traversed the ocean, there is no reason to fear all this nonsensical turmoil, no need to cower under these ruthless cameras. Maybe he tries to draw on the remnants of courage running through his veins; maybe he tries to be stronger.

After taking a few more steps he turns his head and looks over at our bus. It is as though he has left something or someone behind. Perhaps during this moment of vulnerability he can't find refuge in anything except us. Truth is, throughout this half-day he hasn't spoken a word to any of us. Due to his difference we have ignored him, neglected him to such an extent that we didn't even invite him to draw from a cigarette. But we are the only people he has during this time, even if he only knows us a little. We are his solace. He is on his way to being thrown into a dismal and obscure future. A destiny tied up with being displaced on an island. He is like a victim of a hunt being dragged on the ground. He has no control over his legs and isn't even taking a single step on his own. Moments later he is also on board the plane.

A few other people board. And then they call out my number: MEG45. Slowly but surely I must get used to that number. From their perspective, we are nothing more than numbers. I will have to forget about my name. My ears start ringing when they call out my number. I try to use my imagination to attribute some new meaning to this meaningless number. For instance: Mr MEG. But there are a lot of people like me. What can I possibly do with this damned number? All my life I have despised numbers and maths. But now I am forced to tow this stupid number around with me everywhere. At least I could try to relate it to an important historical event, but although I rack my brain I can't come up with anything except the end of World War II – the year '45. Regardless of who I am, regardless of what I think, they are going to call me by that number. MEG45 now has to cover the same stretch travelled by The Insomniac and the others.

I must admit, I am nervous. The mood in this space is infused with fury, and a little bit of sorrow – furious prisoners under the weight of sorrow. What crime have I committed to justify cuffing me tightly and putting me onto an aeroplane? I would accept this if they would show me the way; I would run to get on the plane myself. But then I am reminded of that poor Rohingya Boy and I think I shouldn't appear weak in the same way, especially with all these eyes looking on.

I have had this experience before; it was a much more horrible situation. At least this time I have been eating and am energised; at least this time I don't smell like sea sludge as I did the last time. But what can I do about my clothes: a yellow T-shirt twice my size that drapes down over my knees; these flip-flops that make a slapping sound when I walk? Until now I haven't seen anyone dressed like this: a short-sleeved shirt reaching down to the wrists – and a yellow shirt at that. An awful blend of colours: a yellow T-shirt, a black pair of shorts, and naked legs reaching down to a pair of flip-flops. No matter who I am, no matter how I think, in these clothes I have been transformed into someone else.

All this aside, how can I pass by all these cameras? In particular, these few young blonde women with a strange enthusiasm for taking photographs – and from such close range, from almost no distance at all. I shouldn't show any weakness. I throw caution to the wind and exit the vehicle. The giants are waiting for me. They immediately lock biceps with my biceps and walk towards the aeroplane. I hold my head high – I take long steps – I want to end this painful scene as quickly as possible.

The first set of people we pass are interpreters. They are dressed in green and are standing there for no reason. Maybe they want to join us on Manus Island, although they don't resemble travellers. I give the Kurdish interpreter the side-eye, the woman who isn't supposed to desert us. Her face is blank. Even her cryptic and furtive smile has disappeared. I can't work her out – her demeanour is extremely ambiguous: indifferent? Anxious? That look on her face makes her seem brooding. I sense pain in her dark eyes.

It is the same affliction that separates me from my past and my homeland. For sure, she is also a Kurd who has suffered. Suffered – because of the stigma attached to her – because of the stigma attached to being a Kurd; because she is a person who dares to dream – because she is someone with roots in the Middle East; because she is always a thorn in the side of others – because she always speaks out of place, speaks about things like liberation, speaks about democracy. Her fate is like mine; she has left everything behind and come to Australia. It doesn't matter on what vessel she has travelled to get to this land: whether on a rotting boat or by plane. I feel that when she looks at me, she recollects her pain. I feel she remembers the days when she was perceived as someone out of place; and it is this that provokes her look of simultaneous disdain and empathy.

We get close to the journalists. One of the blonde girls takes some steps away and kneels down, taking a few artistic photographs of my ridiculous face. No doubt, she will create an excellent masterpiece which she can take back and show her editor-in-chief, and then receive encouragement for showing initiative. That thin body underneath those baggy, sloppy clothes – all from the point of view of someone positioned below the waist. And it really will be a brilliant piece of art. My head I hold up high, dignified, and I try to maintain that as I climb the steps to the plane. But my steps are more like the steps of someone trying to run away.

—

I board the aeroplane. The officers show me to my seat and I am left to collapse into it. There is nothing left of that pretend pride – my head has dropped down low. A crushed person. Someone extremely degraded. Someone worthless. Someone who everyone has laughed at, not publicly but in private, in the mind. Or maybe they shed a tear.

I have been made an example. They gaze at me, witnessing my appearance, witnessing the way I look right at this moment, witnessing the two officers dragging me like a dangerous criminal. However and whatever anyone understands Australia to be, they would despise Australia regardless. I have been degraded in no uncertain terms. The mood infused with sorrow . . . it is weighing down on me. I take a few deep breaths, trying to breathe some dignity back into my spirit.

Moments pass. That young guy who used to be a prison warden is brought on board. There is no trace of his laughter, no trace of that talkative character. There is no trace of the man we witnessed earlier in the day. He sits next to me. The team of officers on the plane equals our number. Two officers sit on the seats next to us. They are monitoring us lest we do something dangerous.

The plane takes off and begins its ascent. We fly further and further away from Christmas Island, the island we risked our lives to reach. The officers give us a slice of cold meat and a piece of cheese for lunch. I don't take a bite. I prefer to sleep. It is tough trying to bring the nightmare of this day to an end. I have to prepare myself for a life on Manus; a faraway island that I know nothing about.

—

Sometime later we are up in the clouds, up as high as we can possibly go. I am entranced by the boundless ultramarine of the ocean. I experience a wonderful sensation, like a kind of victory. I am the same person who conquered this great expanse of ocean on a rotting boat, the same person who crossed this infinite volume of water. I feel a kind of victory because I can now look down at the sea and smile. It's always like that: a powerful force from deep within the spirit combats our weaknesses and moments of hopelessness. I feel empowered. I feel a kind of exuberance. I feel that I am not the same person who just minutes ago was looking for a hole to crawl into, looking for anything to crawl under. I experience an amazing feeling – I repel belittlement and desolation. No, I am not ruined yet. Looking out over the natural landscape, looking out over the grandeur before me, I can erase all the sinking feelings of weakness, of demoralisation, of inferiority. I am able to replace them with hope and joy. I am able to replace them with feelings of gratification. I rest my eyes and succumb to this powerful feeling. A beautiful feeling . . .

I open my eyes. We are still up in the clouds. It is as though I have suddenly entered a divine trance. We have arrived at great heights; there is no bond between heaven and earth. The sky below me resembles a huge white cauliflower. And arranged next to it are pieces of soft cloud – prepared in extraordinary fashion. It encourages one to jump out and dive down into the velvety whiteness.

A desire to tumble over velvety clouds /

A desire to tear off pieces and throw them over oneself /

A desire to swim among them until one cannot swim any longer /

A desire to lie down and rest right there and then /

A desire to find comfort under the velvet . . . /

Forever.

I am up there in a tropical sky, where heavens are always smothered in clouds. And even if those clouds have no intention of raining down, they still elevate their status over the rest of the ecosystem.

The young Iranian prison warden is asleep, his head on my shoulder. I'd always thought it repulsive when someone in a bus or a plane used my shoulder as a pillow, particularly if it were a man I didn't know. On many, many occasions I have experienced this on buses and aeroplanes, and each time I have pushed that sleepy head aside or woken them up, only to have them rest their head on another secure spot. But on this day I don't disturb the sleeping prison warden. He has just endured a nightmarish day; plus, I can still taste those few puffs of cigarette he gave me. This is the least I can do for another suffering human being.

The plane begins to descend and dives into those white clouds. I can tell we are close to Manus Island. I wish I could put my hand out of the window to touch those moist clouds. We pass through them and there it is – Manus Island is in the distance. A beautiful stranger lying in the midst of a massive breadth of water. Where the ocean meets the shore, the water turns white, but further out the ocean wears swampy shades of green and blue. It is a riot of colours, the colour spectrum of madness. Now the ocean is behind us and we are face to face with an exquisite and pristine jungle.

Our aeroplane lowers itself down to the ground, down to that green arena. We descend gradually, we descend slowly. It is now easy to see the tall, thin coconut trees. They are all striving to reach higher, higher up into the sky, all competing for oxygen, all trying to ascend, all trying to breathe. Manus is beautiful. It looks nothing like the island hell that they tried to scare us with. Full of trees, pristine attractions, the allures of nature – an untainted creation of nature.

Moments later our propeller-driven aircraft lands on a stretch of land that looks nothing like an airport. This time there is no trace of all those security precautions, not now that we are at Manus Airport. They just read out our numbers and we take ourselves over to the parked bus. As I walk down the steps of the plane I feel something in my mouth. I wonder if I have accidentally eaten a piece of gravel. It is something round and hard. I roll it around with my tongue and spit it into my hands. I am worried. Immediately, my tongue sticks straight out. It wants to know what has happened. The bottom row of teeth is intact. But that damn tooth from the top row – the one on the right-hand side – has fallen out, totally black inside from decay.

I become angry. Why did that tooth fall out so easily?! How is it possible that it happened without feeling any pain? Why were there no symptoms? It broke off so suddenly! A major incident has occurred in my mouth. Unconsciously, my tongue keeps poking that soft gap that was once the place of a strong, hard tooth. My tongue is shocked by the monumental occurrence in its immediate environment; missing that tooth creates a void in my mouth. It is bizarre: I hadn't experienced any pain in that region.

I always assumed that if my teeth were to fall out it would start from the bottom row with those teeth that were ground down and were already causing me pain. In particular, one that had already turned black. I am agitated by the fact that this tooth has fallen out. I am agitated because it has fallen out for no reason. How weak and useless could a tooth possibly be that it could just fall out so easily – without any notice, without any indication! I want to pick up a hard rock and smash the tooth into tiny pieces. I feel that it has fallen out on purpose, because parts of the roots are still there, some of them right under the layers of flesh of my gums.

What is the reason behind this inauspicious incident? /

Why did it happen right at the time that my feet hit the steps of the plane? /

Why did it happen as my eyes met with the place known as Manus? /

While I sit in the minibus I keep that ominous tooth in the palm of my hand /

I look at it begrudgingly /

Is Manus really a sinister and hellish island? /

Is there some connection between my damn tooth falling out and the life that I will lead on Manus Island?

I am still in shock from this awful incident. I don't want to accept that I have lost one of my teeth. The minibus takes off. I throw that ominous tooth out of the window.

—

The weather outside is like hell. Oppressively hot. Between leaving the plane and stepping into the minibus my whole body becomes drenched in sweat. Agonisingly humid. Suffocating. The kind of weather that alienates you from yourself. Such pure jungle lines the road. All the tropical trees have broad leaves. All the trees rest up against each other; no-one could imagine that a body could pass between them.

The existence of a road through the jungle seems out of place. At some points the road runs adjacent to the ocean and the roots from the trees extend into the water like a large black net. It seems as though the jungle is striving to seize all surrounding areas. It seems as though the grand ocean is taking up too much space. I see a few cottages by the side of the road. A number of scantily dressed women and children are waving at us. Perhaps they know that foreigners are being brought onto their island. Perhaps they have been waiting for hours so that they can wave at us and welcome us.

The jungle scenery and the air conditioning inside the vehicle make everyone feel refreshed. And the prison warden starts to chatter and joke again – he laughs rambunctiously. His words are full of satire and mockery; he is imagining the life he will live here in the jungle. He imagines that he will marry one of the scantily dressed women and bring a few kids into the world – kids of different sizes and shapes. And he will also build his cottage up on one of the tall green trees. He will bring his mother and father over and serve them crocodile meat. Everyone is laughing boisterously at his plan, and they try to match his comedic skill. But the humour masks terror – an undefined terror – a terror cloaked in comedy. The looks on their faces – the kinds of words they employ – it is obvious. In times like these we sprinkle our terror with ironic humour, maybe in the hope of relaxing our exhausted minds for just a few minutes.

The Rohingya Boy stares outside through the window. As always, he is completely silent, totally quiet. His expression is indistinguishable – it is as if he has never smiled before. The nausea brooding within him weighs heavily on the cheerful, yet hollow, atmosphere created by the prison warden and his entourage. During these moments my thoughts focus on him. Silence and gloom are always enigmatic, they draw one towards them. I want to dive into the depths of his imagination and penetrate his visions of the world, visions of a world outside the window; I really want to know his impressions of the women and children waving at us.

———

It is afternoon. The minibus has arrived somewhere that seems to be Manus Prison. A sizeable area with large white tents set up in the centre, and fences that besiege the prison from every side. A melancholic silence. Not even a bird flies past this place. I can't see the inside of the prison, but I can imagine that it doesn't contain many people.

We are the third or fourth group of refugees exiled to Manus. We exit the vehicle and the guards open an open-air fenced-off enclosure. Moments later we are all let into that cage, but they just leave us in there without administering any of the regular protocols. They just shut the gates and secure them with a few strong locks. There is nothing here but a large tent and some powerful metal fans circling at high speed. Even though the sun is about to set, I can't tolerate standing inside the tent and listening to the furious sounds of the fans revolving pointlessly.

Those fans are rusted, but they are robust /
Those fans are all along the sides of the tent /
Those fans contend against the harrowing heatwave /
Those fans fight without respite /
Struggling against the suffocation that besieges the tent.

I am exhausted. I am frustrated. Sweat spouts from every pore. An old woman with an oversized backside moves around quickly, drenched in sweat. She walks around constantly, eyes searching every spot. Her face is bright red from the heat of the sun. Sweat flows through all the furrows and wrinkles on her face and neck. The sweat runs all the way down into a larger trench around her lower neck, and it continues to slide down between her large wrinkled breasts. Her face appears to be the peak of a mountain where water has gathered – the waters are rushing down the slopes like a stream. She brings water for us to drink. Bottles of water, more like bottles of boiling water. The water is so hot that it doesn't quench my thirst at all. I pour one or two of the bottles of water over my head and body, and my tongue tastes the bitterness and salt of my sweat. How hot could it get on Manus Island? Even the fans are burning with the heat.

They bring us a few forms and I sign all of them without hesitation. Two Manusian women are searching our belongings – they are trembling with fear. At the same time they are eyeing their boss, a bald Australian. Moments later, black officials and white officials, wearing completely random uniforms, enter the tent with interpreters wearing green outfits. Straight away those two Manusian women stop searching the bags and bring white plastic chairs. The sunburnt old woman places some bottles of hot water in front of the officials.

The new haughty Kurdish interpreter seems proud of herself; she sits right next to me. She touches one of the bottles of water, and then puts it to one side with an expression of anger. But straight after, she seems to change her mind. She empties the whole bottle of water over her smooth ankles, her glistening, fair-skinned ankles. She begins fanning herself with her hands. She is dressed up and her hair is carefully styled. What reason could this young woman possibly have for dressing like this while we are all in this situation, humiliated by being forced to wear loose-fitting clothes in a mix of silly colours? How idiotic for a person to want to show off to a bunch of poor and helpless humans by wearing those ridiculous clothes. And doing all that while we are fading away in extreme heat. She has a heap of sunscreen all over her face and arms, and I can't breathe from the smell of her. I can't breathe from the mixture of sweat with sunscreen.

Over on the other side is a Manusian official dressed in a baggy yellow flower-patterned shirt, a pair of pants like those worn by mechanics, and raggedy old sandals. He has the responsibility of speaking to us while the Kurdish interpreter and all the others translate. The whole thing is a farcical performance, a stage full of people wearing random outfits, a carnival of different cultures.

The Manusian official reads out a script about Manus and life on the island. He finishes by saying we have to respect the laws of the land. He threatens that if we don't we will be taken to court and imprisoned. An unambiguous threat, right there under a tent as hot as hell. We just stare at all of them in a panicked state. My mind can't fathom life on Manus Island in any way whatsoever. I came to Australia and suddenly ended up on a remote island, ended up on an island the name of which I have never heard before. And now they are trying to educate me about my new place of habitation. Can it be that I sought asylum in Australia only to be exiled to a place I know nothing about? And are they forcing me to live here without any other options? I am prepared to be put on a boat back to Indonesia; I mean, the same place I embarked from. But I can't find any answers to these questions.

Clearly, they are taking us hostage. We are hostages – we are being made examples to strike fear into others, to scare people so they won't come to Australia.

What do other people's plans to come to Australia have to do with me? Why do I have to be punished for what others might do?

But all these questions, all these thoughts, they only exacerbate the mood in here, the weight of sorrow oppressing the prisoners. And all this is going on as my body is being worn out and drained by the climate.

A few Australian officers join our show. After the interpreters and others leave, the officers open a big metal door. They signal to us to go inside. This is one of multiple Manus camps – it is the location where we are forced to reside. Prior to our arrival, nearly a hundred families together with their children were held here for eight months. This is what the Iranian interpreter said. Our ears ring with the noise from the commotion in the adjacent prison. The prisoners there are aware of us. As we enter, dozens of individuals step up to support us. They surround us, each one looking for a familiar person. The whole uproar is just a performance, a ruckus, nothing but a way to pass the time.

I stare at the crowd and I recognise one person who is taller than the rest. Reza Barati is a Kurdish lad who slept on the bottom bunk of my bed for a few weeks while we were on Christmas Island. He is with his friends, and when he notices me he comes right over, filled with joy. Everyone looks pleased and excited to be seeing other groups who have also been exiled to Manus. As the crowds of exiles increase, one feels a greater sense of comfort. Two really different experiences: when a spring flood comes through and only sweeps away one house, the house that belongs to you; and when a flood comes through and destroys everyone's houses. The root of their pleasure goes back to the fear of being alone.

—

The place is Fox Camp . . . that's where we are. Reza describes Manus to me with fervour, the way children talk about things. That has always been Reza's style and character. He tells of how we will starve through the nights; he tells of how the weather is so hot, so oppressively hot; he tells of how the Manus rains are so different to the rain back home in Ilam.

The Rohingya Boy stands over on the other side, next to the metal railings which look like the type they set up in military garrisons, the metal railings soldiers jump off. His bag is next to him, the one with the flower patterns all over it. Unlike me, he is unlucky. No-one is there to hold him in their arms. There is no-one there to show him their room. He looks more alienated than ever before. An Australian officer walks up next to him, takes his bag and sends him to walk along the rooms beside the path covered in dense jungle.

The prison looks like it is in ruins. Four rows of small rooms – they seem more like ready-made containers. It becomes obvious that the tents, which we saw from outside the prison, actually belong to the adjoining prison. Reza shows me a room the furthest away from the seashore. He picks up my practically empty plastic bag and places it in the room. So this is to become my place of residence. An extremely small room with four beds in two sets of bunks. Large metal fans, their necks turning, barely make the suffocating air inside tolerable.

———

The sky has suddenly become cloudy. We can finally breathe in some fresh air. It seems that the tropical sun is waiting for the slightest cracks to appear so that it can sear through and incinerate the earth. And the clouds seem to be the mother protecting the earth. They cover the ceiling of the heavens lest the merciless tropical sun violate the earth. However, sometimes these same clumpy clouds become careless and the sizzling sun takes advantage of the neglect. It burns the earth. It scorches the earth.

It is only through the murderous heat that I come to understand the cultural differences. You see, the sun presiding over Kurdistan was the most tender element of nature. During the year's colder seasons, this sun graced human skin and the entire ecosystem with the most pleasant heat.

The sun radiates over the beautiful mountain slopes /
It generates heat over the beautiful mountain tops /

It is this sun that everyone eagerly awaits /

It is this sun that everyone longs for /

And this is why this sun graces the centre of the Kurdish flag /

But the tropical location of Manus has the most ruthless sun in the entire world /

As soon as it gets the chance, it cremates everything /

In the absence of clouds, the sun reigns supreme /

The sun goes on the hunt.

Reza sits on the bottom bunk, and speaks of the time on Christmas Island and the few memories we share. He also speaks of his mother and little sister. I don't know why Reza always speaks about his family.

After he leaves, I wander around the strange prison. A few large water tanks are constructed behind the rows of bathrooms, and they are connected to the bathroom ceilings through plastic pipes so that they collect rainwater. Beside the large water tanks is a massive metal tunnel, which looks more like a chicken coop. Between that metal tunnel and the water tanks is a pristine and cosy area, like a magnificent garden, with yellow and red flowers as solace for the eyes. A strip of wood from a coconut tree has fallen there, and long flowers that resemble chamomile have grown around it. I sit there on that strip of tree, sit there among those flowers. I feel full of life.

This soul-destroying prison is made with a mix of lime and dirt. Everywhere, fine white sand sticks to one's feet, particularly to the plastic flip-flops. From one end of the camp to the other drain pipes protrude from the kitchen and bathrooms. They create a potion of rotting excrement, the perfect fertiliser for the tropical plants growing around those drains – so good that the plants grow to double their normal height. The stench of sludge, a multicoloured spread laid out for both microscopic and mammoth mosquitoes which linger regularly around the troposphere above the drains.

Where the hell is this place?

What kind of prison is this?

The prison is besieged by fences encircling its outer rim. Fences cordon off the bathrooms, and through their wires are tied numerous small pieces of cloth. These pieces of cloth look like ribbon and are remnants from the people who were held here before us. The ribbons of cloth are withering away due to the intense sun; each one represents a memory, the ribbons are a series of recollections, all of them hark back to another lamentable time.

Countless pieces of cloth are tied there. A number that could all too easily ruin a human being, a number that could all too easily destroy a soul. How could they have possibly endured this run-down filthy prison for all that time? But the ocean and its tides are up alongside the camp; a ten-metre distance separates us. We can find comfort that we are in the company of the sea every day. It is easy to connect with the sea that lies beyond our reach.

The distance between these fences and the ocean is under the cover of tall coconut trees, a whole variety of shrubs with broad leaves, and interweaving weeds. The coconut trees are even growing inside the camp. It is easy to imagine what a massive and pristine jungle stood here before the prison was built.

The prison is like an enormous cage deep in the heart of the jungle /

The prison is like a grand cage next to the tiny gulf of water /

A body of water that merged with the ocean /

*The tall coconut trees that line the outskirts of the camp have grown
naturally in rows /*

But unlike us, they are free /

Their grand height allows them to peep into the camp at all times /

To know what is going on in the camp /

To see what is happening in the camp /

To witness the anguish suffered by the people in the camp.

—

I return to my room. It is so tiny. I feel as if I am suffocating
inside it. The thin wooden walls are full of little memories, full of
monumental memories, full of memories written here by families.
For sure an Iranian family has lived in this tiny room. On the ceiling
and on the walls are written 'Khosrow', 'Susanne', 'Shaghayegh' and
'Nilou', and the names are accompanied by dates. Glancing over
the list of names and the way they are arranged it is easy to imagine
that they were a family of four. Khosrow: the father of the family.
Susanne: the mother. Shaghayegh: the eldest daughter. And
Nilou: the youngest daughter, the most adored. The structure of
a traditional Iranian family. From the father down to Nilou, from
the head of the family down to the smallest member.

Khosrow is the name of a shah from ancient Iranian history.
And Susanne, Shaghayegh and Niloufar are names of flowers,
all as beautiful as each other. The family used the cuter, more
endearing name Nilou for the youngest daughter.

I don't know why my mind is preoccupied with them. I think
about where they might be now. I think about what they might
be doing now. No doubt, they lived hard days on this bleak island.

The wife and her little girls would have been incarcerated here for eight months. For sure, they were also told that they had to end up living on Manus. For the long period of time they were here the thought of settling on Manus must have loomed over their heads like a heavy club. Perhaps now they are in Australia. Or perhaps they were forced to return to Iran. The date they wrote related to their fourth month of imprisonment and I can't tell where they ended up.

The rest of the writing is Persian poetry which everyone uses to interpret their destiny, to interpret their future, to interpret their lives. These poems are probably the work of the mother of the family, Susanne. I guess this because Iranian men are too proud to break down emotionally in front of their wives and children; they hide their humiliation, they do not reveal their sorrows or dreams by writing fragments of poetry on the wall. Those poems must reveal the innermost and pure emotions of Susanne and Shaghayegh. They were scribbled up on the walls at the peak of hopelessness and fear, during the gloomy darkness of the nights on Manus.

Being the youngest, Nilou wasn't able to find solace in writing on the walls. Maybe she asked her mother in her childlike tone, 'Mummy, what are you writing?' or 'Mummy, can you also write my name next to Daddy's name?'

I don't know why I feel the presence of that family when I read the poetry /
I don't know why I feel the presence of the wife and her daughters when I read the poetry /
I feel their presence and their beauty /
They were lively and active /
They were living life.

I imagine that Nilou would play every day in the dirt among the multicoloured flowers, the flowers that grew between the family's room and the side of the small tent that was probably a church or a mosque. Or she would talk to the butterflies that regularly flew around those flowers. She loved those butterflies. Or she would make homes out of the dirt under the flowers for the crabs and frogs. In the end she would get mud all over her clothes, causing her mum to reprimand her. Her angry mum would wash her little arms, legs and face inside the filthy showers.

Behind one of the beds they also drew some pictures. I'm sure some of the pictures were drawn by Nilou. She drew a small house that looked like a cottage, two windows, a daddy with a thick moustache, a mummy with large dark eyes, and two daughters, one smaller than the other. She drew beautiful trees surrounding the cottage. None of her trees look like the trees on Manus; none of them look like those haughty coconut trees. She also drew a high mountain that looks like the summit of Mount Damavand in Iran. And a sun rising behind the mountain – the sun looks happy. Two eyes, a little nose, and a beautiful smile grace the face of Ms Sunshine. That sun was no doubt a compassionate sun in the mind of that little girl. Its heat was a source of comfort. It was distinctly different to the sun above Manus that day, the Manusian sun trying to stifle us all, the Manusian sun trying to incinerate us.

Daddy's moustache is a symbol of his strength /

The strength of a father who could protect his family /

The strength of a dad who could take his helpless little daughters under his wings /

The strength of a dad who would never let anyone harm them /

A dad who certainly didn't have any power inside that prison /

A dad who is now unable to protect his family /

A dad who is held captive /

A dad who is rendered weak /

A dad who feels ashamed in front of his family /

A dad who feels humiliated in front of his little daughters /

He is so disempowered that he feels he had made his family captives with his own hands /

He feels that perhaps he has caused his children pain and suffering /

He feels that perhaps he had spoiled the dreams of childhood /

A dad ageing rapidly with anguish.

I lie on my bed. I have a headache. Maybe it's because of the sun. Or maybe it's from dehydration. The water in those bottles is warm and can't quench my thirst. I am wondering about Nilou and her family; I am pondering all the little children who are now on the island of Nauru thousands of kilometres away, the little children all the way in the middle of the massive silent ocean. I am pondering the fate of little Parnya, who was Firouz's daughter, Firouz With The Hazel Eyes. A family that had come over on the same boat with us, suffering seven days of starvation and thirst, reached Australian soil and were immediately exiled to the island nation of Nauru and are now incarcerated there.

Parnya was a little Iranian girl of about six or seven years old who tied her hair in pigtails. Her hazel eyes were just like her dad's. That little girl was so polite and sweet. There was a time, between our first and second attempts to reach Australia, when we were confined in a residential accommodation building near Jakarta, and kept there before we had to move on a few days later to reach the water. She accompanied her mum, Shokoufeh, her dad Firouz With The Hazel Eyes, and her big brother Pourya. While we were there she brought me a glass of water and asked politely, 'Uncle, when will we be going to Australia?' I can still hear her voice. She was so innocent, so little.

On the final night the weather was stormy. The rain was coming down hard, the rain was heavy, bashing down on top of our little boat. Darkness, darkness everywhere. I saw Parnya. She was sleeping in her mother's arms. Her mother, Shokoufeh, had also passed out. I saw Parnya's face under the yellow light from that damn lamp, that weak lamp, the lamp hanging from the ceiling, knocking back and forth. I saw her face, which seemed bluish from where I was standing. It seemed she had fallen into an eternal sleep while in her mother's embrace. The violent waves had besieged us; they were bent on pulling Parnya into the sea, pulling her together with her mother and her brother, who was also sleeping on his mother's lap, pulling all of them into the abyss of that dark ocean. The boat was shaking violently. Firouz With The Hazel Eyes was a thin man, unable to assist his family . . . terrified, he looked over at them and said, 'My children are going to die.' He just cried.

Now they've been imprisoned on Nauru. I'm sure Parnya can't fathom this life of affliction in any way, this life she finds herself in, a life that could break the will of the most macho of males. She has no idea what that prison was built for, she has no idea why a harmless child has to be there, why a child with no bad intentions has to be held there. She has no idea why she has to be locked up.

The mood of sorrow that has tormented us all over the last few days emerges again /

Once again sorrow bears down oppressively /

Once again the questions smash against the rim of my mind /

Why does the Australian government have to exile little girls of six or seven years old? /

Why does the Australian government have to incarcerate them? /

Where in the world do they take children captive and throw them inside a cage? /

What crime are those children guilty of? /

And thousands more questions that have no answers /

Thousands more questions that cause me more headaches /

Even greater headaches.

That damn fan keeps spinning pointlessly. My whole body is drenched in sweat. I take my clothes off. Whatever position I lie in to try to sleep, half my body becomes covered in perspiration. If I turn my back to the fan, my stomach and chest become soaking wet. If I turn on my back, the fan has to dry that sweat that sticks to my body. My body has lost so much fluid, so much perspiration has been dried up, all the pores of my skin have clogged up – I feel that I am suffocating. The roots of my long hair are soaking wet and have begun to itch. I have scratched my neck so much that it hurts, and I'm sure the lint that has built up has turned red, kneading with grated skin.

Always /

At these times /

When one has a headache /

And sorrow rears its head /

When the mood is filled with sorrow /

It weighs down mercilessly /

The scent of nightmares wafts in.

—

I am on a large ship /

A ship that resembles a British tanker /

A ship like the one that rescued us and brought us here /

In the middle of the ocean is a small, vivid, green and bountiful island /

Encircled by dangerous waves /

It is rocking /

The waves are shaking it /

Exactly like that rotting boat from that stormy night /

The boat that was captured by the belligerent waves in the ocean /

There are little children on that island /

They are terrified /

Their arms are raised /

They are pleading with me for help /

There are tall coconut trees growing on the island /

The children wrap their arms firmly around the tall, smooth tree trunks /

I get closer /

Nilou is there /

She is wearing an outfit patterned with many, many flowers /

Yellow and red, like the flowers growing next to the coconut tree /

Parnya is also there /

Standing there with her hair in pigtails /

118

And there are other children I don't recognise /

The island is getting smaller and smaller /

The waves are getting higher and higher /

The waves are swallowing up Nilou and the other children /

I can only hear their voices /

No matter how I try to dive into those waves, I can't move /

Like a stiff nail, I can't move at all /

That island submerges into the spinning ring of waves /

The children are still on it /

The island sinks into the abyss of ocean /

The coconut trees have linked hands, but they too drown.

I wake up in a panic. My head is pounding. And the fan spinning continuously has dried up the sweat covering my body. I turn on the lights. I have to light up a smoke. I read one of the inscriptions written on the wall next to my head. It is Nilou. She has written something up there in a child's handwriting.

'Oh God, do something, take us to a nice place. Kiss, kiss.'

6

—

The Wandering *Kowlis* Perform /
The Barn Owls Watch

Days without any plans /

Lost and disoriented /

Minds still caught up in the waves of the ocean /

Searching for peace of mind on new plains /

But the prison's plains are like a corridor leading to a fighters' gym /

And the smell of warm sweat everywhere is driving everyone insane.

One month has passed since I was exiled to Manus. I am a piece of meat thrown into an unknown land; a prison of filth and heat. I dwell among a sea of people with faces stained and shaped by anger, faces scarred with hostility. Every week, one or two planes land in the island's wreck of an airport and throngs of people disembark. Hours later, they are tossed into the prison among the deafening ruckus of displaced people, like sheep to a slaughterhouse.

With the arrival of newcomers, the prison reaches peak tension; people stare at them like invaders. They are mainly taken to Fox Prison because it is large and tents for the newcomers can be assembled in that isolated corner. On the western side, two prisons stand opposite each other: Delta and Oscar. But from Fox Prison only Delta Prison is visible. It looks like a cage, like a hive full of bees. There isn't the slightest room to move within these two adjacent prisons. The prisons are a confrontation of bodies, a confrontation of human flesh. Friction from their breathing, breath that smells like the sea, smells like the deadly journey.

In Fox Prison nearly four hundred people are kept in an area smaller than a football field. The spaces between the rows of rooms and the corridors are streams flowing with disenfranchised men, coming and going from all directions. The atmosphere in the prison is made up of scenes of famished people, provocative and deafeningly boisterous. No-one knows anyone else. It is like a city in which a plague has sent everyone into a frenzy. The crowd is frantic. It seems that if one stood still, one would be carried away by the motion.

—

Appearances reflect extreme nervousness, gazes perpetually examine the faces and eyes of their counterparts. Among us is a group of men who, far from their days in the busy markets of their homelands, still reduce everyone to commodities – objects worth barely anything. The prisoners wander in all directions, lost. Time will be necessary, a long time, before all these male bodies, all rooted in their particular homelands and cultures, can get along together.

The prison is like a zoo full of animals of different colours and scents. For a whole month these animals – these men – have been crammed side-by-side in a cage with dirt floors. There are so many people in the prison that it feels like they are sitting and talking on tree branches and on the roof of the toilets. People are in every corner of the prison – even near the small slough behind the toilets. At sunset, when the weather cools and the coconut palms begin to dance, the prison compound becomes a good space for meandering. Most prisoners prefer to leave their rooms. During these periods there are always some young lads looking to build credibility by dominating the noise in the enclosure by chatting and yelling. It is a jungle full of people who band together in peculiar ways.

The simplest way to gain status is to identify with a group. That is, to affiliate yourself with other individuals who you think share your identity; people who are going through the same set of circumstances as you. Just one motivation: escape from the void and the horror that has the power to crush and pummel you. Depending on a group or a collective identity masks loneliness. It's a kind of escape route, a shortcut. This sort of collectivism first took shape through the shared experience of the boat journey. The fear and pain from a difficult journey affects those involved so much that they instinctively link themselves to a group identity with their fellow travellers. With time, this group identity based on the boat experience shifts towards other identifiers, such as language and nation. After some time, groups become based on a single criterion: where one is from. Afghan, Sri Lankan, Sudanese, Lebanese, Iranian, Somali, Pakistani, Rohingya, Iraqi, Kurdish.

Room swapping begins after a few months; prisoners are drawn to their compatriots and those with whom they share a common language. A kind of internal migration takes place in our tiny prison. Slowly, gradually, the significance of the shared boat experience gives way to the importance of shared language.

(However, in all the years in the prison, people who experienced the boat journey together will insist on their bond. They constantly remind each other to not forget the brotherhood created by the experience: 'remember that we are GDD, MEG or KNS'. The collective trauma from the journey is in our veins – each of those boat odysseys founded a new imagined nation.)

At times the creation of these communities leads to bad fighting, but usually reason prevails, tensions are quashed, and everything returns to normal – things never get too intense or dangerous. The delusions and anger from the dangerous sea trip still plague the prisoners and a wild aggression still runs through their blood when interacting with each other. Conflict is mainly between Iranians and Afghans; the roots of the feud between them originated a long time ago and run deep, carrying a lot of history. The Iranians express a form of nationalistic superiority, and Afghans won't put up with being patronised. The developments over the months slowly but surely prove to everyone that the principle of The Kyriarchal System[6] governing the prison is to turn the prisoners against each other and to ingrain even deeper hatred between people. Prison maintains its power over time; the power to keep people in line. Fenced enclosures dominate and can pacify even the most violent person – those imprisoned on Manus are themselves sacrificial subjects of violence. We are a bunch of ordinary humans locked up simply for seeking refuge.

---

6   The term 'kyriarchy' was first coined in 1992 by Elisabeth Schüssler Fiorenza to describe a theory of interconnected social systems established for the purposes of domination, oppression and submission. We have applied this term for the purposes of labelling the complex structure underlying Australia's detention regime. The technique of capitalising the phrase is employed to personalise the system and give the impression that it exercises agency. Refer to the translator's note and supplementary essay for more in-depth description of the meaning of the phrase and its significance to Behrouz's thought.

In this context, the prison's greatest achievement might be the manipulation of feelings of hatred between one another.

Over time, the incidents that occur in Manus Prison prove to everyone that a prisoner is a being with no solace other than brotherhood – a brother in whom to confide one's pain. The more time that passes in the prison, the deeper this feeling becomes – it is a pillar of the prison. Here, people are subject to more intense scrutiny. A prisoner notices the tiniest change like a blind mouse that has only its sense of smell.

We are four hundred people /
Four hundred lost souls in a tightly confined space /
Four hundred prisoners /
Anticipating the nights /
. . . so we can leave /
. . . and enter our nightmares.

We are bats in a dark cave that react to the slightest vibrations. Every day we repeat, overcome with fatigue, an aimless walk of approximately one hundred metres. It seems that they are forcing us to traverse the length of a putrid, foul-smelling pool by repeating only one impractical and futile swimming stroke. Hopeless visions worse than monsoon winds blow away our dreams in the nights and everything becomes tainted by bitter nightmares.

In addition to the torment produced by the oppressive enclosure of the prison fences, every prisoner creates a smaller emotional jail within themselves – something that occurs at the apex of hopelessness and disenfranchisement. Most prisoners evaluate their health and vitality through regular close examination of their bodies, developing fragmented and disrupted identities, and a warped sense of self, that makes them cynical of everyone else. This is the objective of the prison's Kyriarchal System, to drive prisoners to extreme distrust so that they become lonelier and more isolated, until the prison's Kyriarchal Logic[7] triumphs with their collapse and demise.

—

During this period in the prison, there is nothing to occupy our time. We are just thrown into a cage and made to wear ridiculous loose-fitting clothes. It is even prohibited to play cards. In Corridor L, a few people were able to get hold of a permanent marker and draw a backgammon board onto a white plastic table. They began to play, using the lids from water bottles as counters. Almost instantly, a group of officers and plain-clothed guards entered Corridor L and crossed out the game. They wrote over it in bold letters, 'Games Prohibited'. It seemed that was their only duty for the entire day: to shit all over the sanity of the prisoners, who were left just staring at each other in distress.

Imagine a community of four hundred people, neglected in a boiling hot and filthy cage, still traumatised by the terrifying sound of waves ringing in their ears and the sight of a rotting boat fixed before their eyes. For how long can they simply talk to each other? How many times can they walk up and down the same hundred-metre distance? An unwritten law: whoever enters the prison has all their belongings confiscated. There is no chance of

---

7 The logic of the system is capitalised as well as the system itself, again to grant agency. The aim here is to give an identity to the operations of structural violence and systematic torture – a form of anthropomorphism. Refer to the translator's note and supplementary essay for further details.

getting a notebook and pen. It is extremely distressing for people who have not experienced prison before – it drives you to the edge of insanity.

The heat is debilitating. By noon our bodies begin to show signs of the impact of the sun's rays as they sliver through the open passages of the prison. The sun seems to be in cahoots with the prison to intensify the misery of the prisoners . . . it uses its rays like shafts to violate us. Sometimes the intensity of the heat increases so much that even looking at the prison fences is frightening. One can sense how hot the metal has become. However, the mind has the power to leave the prison and imagine the coolness under the shade of a bunch of trees on the other side of the fences. One can even feel the pleasant, cool temperature. All the while, I can feel sticky sweat running down into all the deepest crevices and cavities of my body.

Sweat that creates small rivers /

Sweat that has a mind of its own /

Sweat that flows naturally and aimlessly /

Sweat that enters cracks and gaps around and within one's backside and joints /

Sweat that keeps running /

Everything winds up in your ass and in your head.

For me, isolation and silence are the greatest gifts I could ask for. Faced with prisoners who reach out to their mates by yapping, yelling pointlessly and laughing loudly, I long to create, to isolate myself and create that which is poetic and visionary. I realised early that I was a stranger in this community, an alien community

I have to put up with, and this feeling sparks my retreat. It is a conscious decision to leave them. They get on my nerves.

Years later, I will look back at this time, and I will see myself like a coconut tree with roots deep in the ground and my hair taken by the wind.

I am alone /

Surrounded by human traffic passing in all directions /

Arriving . . . departing . . . and over again /

A cycle of absurdity and bewilderment /

Totally lost /

I am like a wolf that has forgotten it is a wolf /

I retain only a perspective /

That tender sense, that tranquil intuition /

That flame within my being /

When someone violates my solitude, I carry the hatred in my veins.

I have reached a good understanding of this situation: the only people who can overcome and survive all the suffering inflicted by the prison are those who exercise creativity. That is, those who can trace the outlines of hope using the melodic humming and visions from beyond the prison fences and the beehives we live in.

What else could a prisoner desire other than a moment of silence, solitude, and to feel as though one were standing stripped naked in the middle of a lush jungle?

What else other than to have a cool breeze pass through the thousands of nets made up of knotted hair?

During these days, this is my greatest dream.

One place where I hope to be alone for a moment is in the toilets. But even there some bastard always appears in the adjacent stall, singing with his awful voice. Or there's someone at the front of the queue, on the other side of the toilet door, waiting to trade places with you. And no doubt there are others among them waiting for you to finish, waiting to dump their filth on your quiet moment of peace. Sometimes someone bashes the toilet door with punches and kicks, holding on to his penis: 'Hey man, get out, my guts are exploding!' There is no escape, not even one moment without sensing the presence of another person. But I learn over time how to stand alone, like the coconut trees inside the prison – how to exist in seclusion like them.

In the first days, there was always a gadfly getting in my ear, some person annoying me. They'd get in my ear, do a round within my quiescent mind, exit through the other ear, do another round outside, then re-enter through my ear to circle my mind again. Numerous gadflies would perform their rounds continuously – this form of torture was always present. When I'd put my feet up on the prison fences, one of these gadflies would immediately jump in and interrupt my quiet time. Like sharp thorns, they'd tear my dreams apart. Perhaps these kinds of people become unnerved when seeing someone sitting on a chair and they feel that they have to plonk themselves down and shatter the beautiful moment of solitude by saying pessimistic things. With time, the others have come to understand my way of thinking and my temperament – my need for isolation.

In the final hours of the evening the prison disappears into the darkness of the jungle and the silence of the ocean. A terrifying, awe-inspiring woman from the East shrouds the prison compound with her hair.

We are all transformed into dark shadows scavenging for scraps of light. I discover freedom in the ember of my cigarette. When the darkness of night sets in, I walk the hundred-metre distance to the prison fence, put my feet up on the barriers, and from behind the prison fences dream of freedom while engulfed in my cigarette smoke. Sometimes the liberation in a cigarette involves imagining a woman with almond-shaped eyes to counter the violence of this militarised jail. These kinds of illusions come from nowhere and have no purpose but to occupy my mind as I sit around freezing, my body drenched with cold sweat. I look upon these stupid thoughts of physical gratification with disdain, kicking them aside. I throw myself again into my own world of introspection – a world full of mystery and joy that takes me by surprise.

I am stuck in a balancing act, existing between two different worlds. The violence of the prison is bizarre and novel. We have been thrown onto a remote island. We are still plagued by memories of the traumatic boat journey that stank of death. We are distraught and can't do a thing to recover. I feel that I am being taken over by multiple personalities: sometimes blue thoughts parade through my head, and sometimes grey thoughts. Other times my thoughts are colourblind.

I feel that the only thing I can count on is the calm, melodic sound of chanting, the quiet singing of folk ballads that absorbs me back into the cold mountains of Kurdistan. The amazement and horror felt during the nights on Manus has the power to thrust everyone back into their long distant pasts. These nights uncover many years of tears deep in our hearts and open old wounds; they plough into every dimension of our existence; they draw out the bitter truth; they force the prisoners to self-prosecute. Prisoners are driven to crying tears of bitter sorrow.

Since his daily routine is a meaningless cycle of repeated struggles, a prisoner has nothing else to do but recollect his childhood. This searching and battling immortalises the dusty remnants of the past. These forced conditions of loneliness make everyone endure scenes of an internal odyssey that would ruin any man. The odyssey summons dark angels and secrets relegated to the unconscious; like a magical curse it positions before every prisoner's eyes the most long-standing issues and bad blood tied up in the soul. Difficult pills to swallow that would be too much for any person, let alone taking them on a stomach suffering with heartburn.

More than anything, prison makes one terrified of loneliness /

This is the most shocking paradox in the life of a prisoner /

Time dissolving before you /

And perhaps the wedding of eternity with the thousands upon thousands of faces /

Smiles, sobs, tears /

And bitter dreams.

The prisoner is a piece of meat with a mind that is always moving between the darkest, dullest and most worn-out scenes. In some moments, a particular image will suddenly emerge from his mind's most profound labyrinths. At this stage he must face this both strange and familiar scene and clarify things for himself. At this very point he begins a battle that may take months to settle down, for the vision to be subdued or eliminated. The mind of a prisoner is a brew of images that are sometimes contradictory; scenes constituted by his own philosophies and histories. The prisoner is captive to his own life history, and all these isolated occurrences take shape in the unconscious during periods of solitude and silence. However, they also destroy his sense of self.

Probably the life most worth living is a solitary one /

A quiet life, a lively existence, and a glorious one /

But what a bitter life that is /

Life is such a magnificent thing /

Life is such a terrifying thing /

When a prisoner steps onto foreign territory and sees loneliness reflected on the fences of a forlorn prison /

He sees himself . . . the one who is alone /

The world with all its beauty and marvel comes crashing down over his head /

Perhaps the world stands still then /

And the prisoner must determine his destiny /

Come to terms with this life and the thousands of faces and images before his eyes /

Loneliness creeps under his skin /

Until he suddenly realises that it has enveloped him /

It seems he represents the last human being /

Naked and laid bare /

He must answer the difficult questions of life /

He must reveal who he is, what he is /

He must answer why he is lost, why he is bewildered /

Why he is silent, why he does not answer /

This realm of the mind is itself a prison /

His existence is splintered like a dry piece of wood /

Bashed on the ground of a barren and vast desert /

He is a small and rotting boat /

A frightened boat – without a paddle and unmanned /

He is a boat on the silent ocean /

An ocean the colour of milk /

Millions of stars dispersed into the depths of the universe /

All over the sky /

They glimmer /

They challenge him /

The horizon is the colour of blood /

It's a landscape full of wonders /

Full of mystery, questions and challenges /

It's a place that seems to move the prisoner unconsciously /

Till he finds sanctuary with others who have shared the experience of suffering.

It's a case of safety in numbers and producing noisy, ear-splitting nonsense to escape the solitude and, more than anything, to distance oneself from the horrors that few have the strength to absorb or come to grips with. Fear persuades people to hide beneath commotion and noise. They themselves know all too well how fake it really is. It is prison, and coming to terms with its paradoxes requires solitude. There is no solace in yelling, screaming or distraction. What we yearn for are the joys of childhood, for mystical movement, for freestyle rhythms, for liberation through dance.

On these nights there is always a stage set up for dance

performances at the end of Corridor L. Most nights after eating his dinner, an Iranian guy in his twenties – Maysam[8], known as The Whore – gathers a bunch of his friends together and dances for hours. He plays a *tombak* drum made out of a piece of wood, and he sings upbeat songs. He has acquired his moniker 'The Whore' from being a farceur and dancing around and showing off his physique. It is like a badge attached to him by others, people we don't know.

Maysam The Whore has a special talent for gathering people around him. I think his spirit could be part of a legacy, inherited from the soul of the *kowli* peoples of Iran, peripatetic people who conduct street performances and dance along the roadsides of strange cities. His friends drag a large white plastic table from the corner of the prison until it is in front of his room in Corridor L. This announces to everyone, scattered, bored and wandering all over the prison, that tonight the stage is ready again for dance and entertainment. Like professional circus performers, or the sidekicks of a street theatre troupe, accompanied by clapping and eccentric but sometimes comedic antics, they invite everyone. All are welcomed to what is happening at the end of Corridor L. All gather around the white plastic table. In this format, performances are directed with extraordinary skill. The performers know exactly what sounds to produce, on which part of the table, with which part of the hand, and which point of the drum to hit to make the most raucous and loudest sound.

These people are born into the world to make others suffer. I'm sure they are the kind of kids that would smash the neighbours'

---

8 Maysam is an Arabic name, and also the name of a famous companion of Imam Ali (first Imam for Shi'as). It has strong religious connotations and is usually given in religious families.

windows with rocks for no reason, or would ring the doorbells of homes along the street during the heat of summer and then run away. But in prison this unique and boisterous spirit acquires them a kind of amicability and provides inspiration to others. Their creativity increases until their ear-splitting and polyphonic sounds reach throughout the forlorn and isolated prison. They have only one duty: to drag out the communities from all of the prison corridors towards Corridor L. Everyone knows that the only purpose behind all the ruckus is to set the opening scene for the entrance of Maysam The Whore.

Their main style is original: a combination of clapping and rhythmic beating on the table, then crying out and proclaiming. It is a collaboration between three or four people, all whipped up into a frenzy. Then they perform that same quick rhythm on the table and, finally, one or another of the members announce, using the language of the street, 'Gather 'round my people, my prison-mates . . . hurry up, hurry up and . . .' They repeat this a number of times in unison.

In the space of a few minutes, a significant crowd gathers in Corridor L. They look on enthusiastically, all eyes on the three or four individuals. Whenever the crowd gathers around, a kind of competition begins of who can show off the best. It ends up such that the harmony of the group during the initial part of the performance falls out. All members try to project their individual style and become the star of the show. The sounds fuse together – we can't distinguish one voice from another.

There are even some moments when the passion involved in this fooling around also takes hold of the audience, inspiring some to jump up with the performers and start beating the table, or to try to draw attention to themselves with hilarious dancing. People fool themselves by drowning in the joy of these situations; they lose control of themselves and their behaviour is like that of people at a party who've been drinking too much. It is as though they are conning themselves into thinking this is a real festival, set up for a real purpose. Prior to the performance, everyone with the desire to visit Corridor L had been Iranian, but now others have arrived. Many develop the courage to join in the partying and dancing, and with these experiences they realise something – they start to see the show as a reflection of themselves.

Some Sri Lankans or Sudanese people enjoy the events and show keen interest; they follow what is going on as they stand at a distance. They are like people standing at the end of the street watching a family celebration that has spilled out of a house. They don't appear to feel a close personal bond until they are involved in the action up close.

In the meantime, the Australian officers watch over the excited community with contempt. This is the social dynamic between the Australians working in the prison and the imprisoned refugees. The Australians' perspective is a mixture of abhorrence, envy and barbarism – the crowd is aware of that. At times this even encourages the audience to cheer louder. For them, this pretend celebration is a good opportunity to get on the officers' nerves, to mess with those who hold them captive, a kind of childish spite that expresses a desire for revenge. This is one of the only forms of power available to the prisoners.

The Kyriarchal System of the prison is set up to produce suffering. These celebrations are a form of resistance that says, 'It's true that we are imprisoned without charge and have been exiled, but look here, you bastards . . . look at how happy and cheerful we are.' But this is the same old simple trick habitual to all humans – escape from fear by lying to oneself. The performance plays out so naturally that the prisoners themselves forget that there is no logical reason to celebrate.

Humans always find any excuse to gather together; these celebrations are enacted in relation to marriages, birthdays and graduations to such an extent that they have been crystallised in everyone's collective consciousness. They are almost mandatory.

In the minds of the prisoners it is unnecessary to explain why they are happy and why they want to celebrate; it is unnecessary to answer to anyone. Maybe, if someone came up to them and yelled, 'You idiots, why are you so cheerful? Why are you dancing and why are you singing at the top of your voice?' that person would get no answer other than, 'We are celebrating for exactly the same reason that others celebrate.'

The prisoners dance because they have to dance, to spite those people who exiled them to the prison. This infuriates the Australians. Sometimes the officers chatter through their communication devices, confused because they don't know why these imprisoned and humiliated refugees are partying and dancing. What infuriates them more is that they have no excuse to break up the festivities – ruin them just like they did with the back-gammon table, spoil them by writing, 'Games Prohibited'.

Everything is interconnected: joy, fear, hate, envy, revenge, spite, and even kindness. All these moving pieces revolve around Maysam The Whore, and he revolts against everything. There is no secret underlying his popularity other than an accumulation of suffering endured by all the prisoners, which shines through his rhythmic movements. Like a mirror, the prisoners see themselves reflected in him. Someone who is so brave and so creative; he flexes these attributes through his muscles, muscles he uses to challenge The Kyriarchal System of the prison. He employs a beautiful form of rebellion that has enormous appeal for the prisoners. A man with boyish features who uses them to peddle poetry and to satirise all the serious aspects of the forlorn prison. The spirit of Maysam The Whore contrasts with the desert of solitude and horror of the prison. This is like a reward for the prisoners; a gift in the form of a collective response, a collaborative effort among men who have been banished. A gift that is grasped at, a gift they will hold onto.

When the spectators reach a climax of enthusiasm and anticipation, Maysam The Whore appears in supreme fashion like an epic hero, completely confident in the power of his muscles, as though he has previously crushed and bloodied his opponent in a stadium in front of an amazed audience. He is a popular tightrope walker or a magician, mesmerising all who watch. He comes out of the last room in Corridor L and into all the pandemonium, into the ruckus that is transfixed on him and only him, to dance until he wins over the hearts of the crowd. He knows exactly when to appear, and in which style – he is a master at work. He dances with such artistic prowess that with each step he draws louder and louder cheers. He is the spirit of the community, a heartwarming and appealing enigma.

Every night he wears a different style of costume. Clearly he contemplates all the production aspects of his performance, including costume design. And no doubt, the few other individuals in charge of livening up the party help out as his artistic assistants. There are messages of joy and excitement glowing on their faces; and when Maysam The Whore enters with gestures and expressions he merges into the vibrant camaraderie among the troupe; they all encourage him to let loose and perform in more liberated ways.

One night he is in character as a religious leader, adorned with religious headgear. He enters the set wearing a long *abā*[9]. Using a blue bedsheet, the troupe has designed this *abā* with a few beautiful slits down the side. He also has a white *amāma*[10] made of the same material and wrapped around his head. It is a total caricature of an *ākhūnd*[11]. But in contrast to a religious leader who usually has a long beard and elicits fear of hell, Maysam The Whore's face is smooth and hairless like a real-life angel.

The place erupts with cries and cheers. The chaos is extremely powerful; the audience can hardly make sense of the way his body is moving and dancing between the room and the table, which stands in the middle of the crowd. Even though he is mostly covered with that ridiculous yet amazingly beautiful outfit, we can still see parts of his body. Maysam The Whore's artistic method involves dancing beside the table with amazing speed. He shakes his hips and backside with skill. It is clear why Maysam The Whore chooses to dance to a fast-paced song: to bring the audience with him and conquer the hundred ills they have suffered. Three or four individuals in the troupe embody all their talents in their hands and voices till they are one step ahead of the audience; that is, closer to Maysam The Whore's movements and in closer collaboration with him. They improvise and contribute to the song; they even attempt to take control of it. They try their best to harmonise, to share the limelight, but Maysam The Whore is the star of the show. They follow him by beating on the table or by singing. Once he has the audience completely in the palm of his hand, The Whore suddenly jumps on the table in one move. The scene of a religious leader dancing on a platform, surrounded by

---

9 An *abā* is a cloak worn mainly by religious scholars in Iran.
10 An *amāma* is a turban of choice for clerics in Iran.
11 A religious cleric common in Iran.

an enthusiastic audience whipped into a frenzy, is full of nuances and contradictions.

After a few minutes of dancing, Maysam The Whore takes on a role resembling a preacher requesting silence from a congregation. He proclaims, 'Because we are incarcerated men and there are no women in this prison, from this moment on I hereby ordain gay sex completely permissible[12].' This sentence hits like a typhoon and the scene erupts with laughter and cheers. Joy reaches a peak and once again Maysam The Whore dances at a fast pace, and the audience follows, clapping and cheering.

The performance is not over yet. Maysam The Whore slowly removes the *amāma* from his head with a flourish and tosses it into the crowd. Then he throws the religious *abā* in the corner and leaves everyone looking in amazement at his near-naked body. On this particular night his underwear is particularly spectacular. He is wearing men's underwear, red, with the sides cut out. Like a style of women's underwear, he wears them tucked between his buttocks. This move sets the place off and raises the roof. This is how he becomes known as The Whore; he carries the moniker with him for the whole time he is in the prison. He is a man who ridicules everything, and his presence, his dancing, his singing, helps us forget the violence of the prison for a moment. He is the superstar of the prison.

Doing night-time shows isn't enough. You can also find him in the long mealtime queues in the role of his *ākhūnd* character, which he enacts so beautifully. He can be seen preparing hilarious props and making the prisoners burst with laughter. Just imagine

---

12 Same-sex relations and practices are criminalised in PNG and punishable with up to fourteen years in prison. In Iran, people engaging in same-sex relationships and activity are imprisoned, forced to undergo various medical procedures, or subject to corporal and capital punishment.

a religious leader, beardless and wearing the clothes of a cleric, standing in a long queue. He doesn't even need to utter a word. Just being there like that is enough to engage the others. More than anything, he diverts the attention of the detestable officers towards himself. He stands in direct opposition to a system that wants to fatten up lambs for slaughter. With just one word spoken by him, we experience the essence of life.

—

In addition to prisoners bustling between the fences and the hallways, others prowl the prison. Parts of the prison are under the surveillance of a group known as G4S, a security company with the responsibility of keeping the prison secure. The officers of the company keep a number of prisoners under close watch. It's better to refer to G4S by its real name: Bastards' Security Company. I could think of so many ways to refer to the officers, but this one is most apt. Perhaps I could refer to them as watchdogs or attack dogs. Each one of them has a walkie-talkie on his waist. Every now and then, these nosy officers write things in their notebooks, which they always carry in their pockets. They note things about everything and everyone. Their approach to work is based on being a bastard. You need to be a total bastard to work in a place where you detest everyone.

From the very first day their work is valorised: 'You're an army here to protect the nation, and these imprisoned refugees are the enemy. Who knows who they are or where they're from? They invaded your country by boat.' The situation is completely clear to them – here, in their sights stand their enemies, rounded up from all over the place. My god, you should see the look in their eyes: cold, barbaric, hateful.

They sit around in groups at the end of the corridors or along

141

the fences opposite the ocean, just passing time and ruminating. No doubt they are discussing every one of the personalities in the prison. A large number of them witness the festivities put on by Maysam The Whore. They don't interfere, though. They sit on chairs at a distance from the community, making sure their presence is felt. The areas they have to monitor are determined beforehand and each one sits on a plastic chair and scans the perimeters for hours. All the pockets and corners in far-off sections of the prison are dominated by their gaze – eyes tracking us down and committed to pursuit.

After nightfall, the prison compound eases back into its natural state. During these initial months there are only two large lamps, one on each side of the prison distributing light to the surrounding areas. The lamps are there to illuminate the space, but the light loses its brightness before reaching Fox Prison. The enclosure is like a horror scene on these nights. The shadows are at war, and people can only rely on their intuition to find their way to the bathrooms.

In the darkness, the presence of the officers makes the prisoners feel more captive than at any other time. The strong, heavy-set men seem much bigger when their shadows emerge in the darkness. There, in every section of the prison, they keep watch like hostile animals. Their gaze ploughs through and it seems that there is no chance of avoiding its pervasive scope.

G4S prison guards (in the prison we just call them 'G4S' for short) are mostly overworked and have spent most of their lives working professionally in Australian prisons with different kinds of criminals. Without question, crime, criminal courts, jail, prison violence, physical violence and knife attacks have become part of their everyday routine and mindset. Many of the guards are ex-servicemen who have served for years in Afghanistan and

Iraq; they have been waging wars on the other side of the world. They have killed humans.

A killer is a killer . . . plain and simple. I read somewhere, or maybe I heard it from someone, that a person who commits murder becomes younger. Or they age slower. These people have no concern for others. A killer is a killer; violence oozes out through their blurred, diluted pupils. I'm convinced that the soul of a killer is reflected in their eyes.

I come to this understanding by watching many of the G4S bunch. In one instance, one of these G4S guys is standing in front of a bloody situation; a young guy has slit his wrists in the toilets. The guard turns to me and says, 'Sorry – I can't understand you and this petrified young guy. I've been a prison guard for most of my life . . . Sorry.' This is the extent of his compassion. What can you expect from a man who has spent his whole life immersed in the violence of prison? The belly of this man is so huge that it is disproportionate to the other parts of his body. It seems his skinny legs are just hanging off his massive gut, a disgusting pair of limbs stuck onto his body. This is a man who admits that he can't comprehend ordinary people.

Clearly, he has exerted a lot of pressure on himself thinking about this, and tried to squeeze something, anything, out of his heart. Perhaps the difference between him and his colleagues is that he actually recognises that he has become a heartless machine. Maybe he concludes his lack of sympathy has come from living a life as a prison guard. He may never find an explanation other than the fact that he is a veteran of the system and is therefore different from ordinary people.

During each shift, the number of G4S guards on duty in each prison climbs to fifty. At seven in the evening dozens of G4S guards gather between Delta Prison and Fox Prison so their supervisors can talk with them for a few minutes. From that distance it is unclear what the lively discourse is about. Just men in the same uniform behind the fences. That is all that is visible: passive guards squashed together in a garrison-like environment listening intently to a man standing on a chair. The supervisor finishes speaking and they become like a platoon of soldiers just starting duty. They approach the prison and spread out from top to bottom. They head directly to the areas they have been assigned.

Like robots following orders, they enforce every prison rule – rules for both micro-control and macro-control, and rules for the most trivial things through to the most pivotal. There is also a large proportion of G4S guards who are Manus Island locals or are from Port Moresby. When the prison opened, they were summoned to work, men who until then had been busy spear fishing, sawing wood in the jungles, or picking and selling tropical fruit in the island's local market. The agreement between the government of Papua New Guinea and the Australian Department of Immigration stipulates that a large percentage of local people must be employed. Therefore, the prison is forced to employ people who, until then, were the freest humans I have encountered. But now they are absorbed within The Kyriarchal System, absorbed into the prison structure, absorbed into a culture of systemic violence. The Australians have tried to graft them to the corporate culture of the G4S company but, unlike their Australian colleagues, these people are free spirits. They are indomitable, and have little care for maintaining order by following the prison's rules and militarised logic. They are polar opposites to The Kyriarchal System. But the Department of Immigration has no choice but to tolerate them. They cannot be constrained by regulations and organisational structures. They wear the scent of the jungle and remind me of the fish swimming in the ocean. The fruit pickers with their extraordinary calves have climbed the tallest and wildest tropical trees and their feet have touched the sand from places most humans will never get near.

The enormous differences between the local guards and the Australian and New Zealand officers are conspicuous. To me, it seems that G4S and the Department of Immigration assign duties based on these distinctions. Without exception, the local people and those from other parts of Papua New Guinea are at the bottom of the pecking order. Every Papua New Guinean officer working in the prison is expected to follow orders from the Australians without any thought or question. At the end of the month, after all their hard labour, their monthly wage is only equivalent to five days work of even the most overweight Australian officer. This encourages them even more to ignore the rules of the prison, at least as much as possible.

The contrast between the locally employed officers and the Australians is even represented in the colour of the uniforms. The locally employed officers wear purple uniforms and their duties involve scouring the prison in groups from end to end. Kyriarchal Logic has imposed this . . . a message to all: 'Let it be known that in this prison local people are nothing. They simply get instructions and follow them.' This configures the relationships among the three basic elements in the prison: the prisoners, the local people, the Australians. The result is that the local people form alliances with us. This relationship includes some kindness and empathy. At times, the local people smoke in secret the cigarettes they receive from the prisoners; they smoke at the end of halls, in dark and hidden corners of the prison, out of sight from the Australians, and shaking in fear. Sometimes they chew on betel nut and get high; then they talk gibberish with grainy voices.

Betel nut, from the tree by the same name, is grown locally. It is the size of a small tomato, and is chewed by locals as a natural stimulant. They crush them on the ground and then chew on the substance inside. After chewing the seed for a few minutes, they spit it out with a mouthful of saliva. They spit out onto the ground all the bits and pieces without any reservations whether they spit onto the grass, in a rubbish bin or on the concrete floor of some office – this is a custom.

When an officer gets high on betel nut, their mouth is stained red. When someone uses betel nut regularly, their teeth are always red, so practically all the local people have red teeth. This is a customary part of the Manusian culture. Blood-red teeth, like a predatory animal that just moments ago lifted its head from devouring its prey. The first time I sat in a group with local people I felt I was in a blockade of real-life cannibals. Faces mapped with wrinkles, curly hair, mouths laughing and filled with blood, the Australians hoped they would scare us.

Is it possible that such kind people could be cannibals? The locally employed officers are particularly kind and pleasant. Their hearts reflect special traits that can be traced back to their liberated nature and a behaviour unconstrained by laws. Their presence in the prison creates a better balance; however, with their arrival the space becomes more constrained, numbers increase, and the environment becomes suffocating.

In the prison, the sense of awe and domination is strong, and these haunting feelings penetrate everything. In the dead of night, at the peak of darkness, one is reminded more than ever of the power of the fences. The prisoners exhale a raw horror and deep hopelessness; they hold onto their nightmares – hold the nightmares in their arms, deep inside, as if they are trying to hold back strong winds that would engulf the corridors. A heavy and all-encompassing silence lingers at the ends of the prison; this is the only sanctuary for an emaciated prisoner.

So there I am, silent, puffing on a cigarette. During these periods even the old crickets are asleep. I can see the coconut trees that stand above the prison, that seem in flight, that seem like prisoners' hair released in the cool breeze. But the crabs are following the long fence in search of food.

Maysam The Whore, with his hook nose, is worn out from the show that took place when the sun set, and from hanging out with his eccentric friends. He is now sleeping in his sweat-drenched bed. The guys are possessed by nightmares that rise out of the pit of their being.

Toads from the ocean have found a warm and humid spot under the fence. The toads lie with their eyes closed, in a state of meditation, in a marvellous state of peace.

In a dark corner of the prison, under the downpipes of Block P, an officer with a red face and white hair looks straight ahead, standing completely still, like an old barn owl watching over the prison. At this time of night, the Papus[13] have finished what they were doing, and are hanging out, sitting on plastic chairs, their eyes bloodshot and weary. They are waiting for the morning to come, waiting for the company buses to pick them up and drive off in various directions to their bungalows in the jungle.

Over the following months, the pretend celebrations and partying prove to be no match for the oppression of the prison,

---

13 'Papu' is an age-neutral honorific for males particular to Manus Island. Refugees incarcerated in Manus Prison use the term in a gender-neutral way to refer to all locals.

for loneliness and hopelessness. As days go by in Manus Prison, even Maysam The Whore becomes more secluded and starts to deteriorate. We must find another way to cope with exile.

—

Rumours have spread in the prison that a group of lawyers plans to visit Manus Island the following week. The sole purpose is freedom for everyone. Hope begins to take root throughout the prison.

A team of men with powerful saws are in the western side of Fox Prison cutting down trees and clearing the land. What is it they want to construct? Maybe a swimming pool.

7

—

The Oldman Generator /
The Prime Minister and His Daughters

Fox Prison has six main corridors. Each one of these corridors consists of the following:

Two open entry-exit points /

Twelve small rooms, approximately one-and-a-half metres by one-and-a-half metres /

Flyscreened windows /

Four imprisoned individuals, in bunk beds /

Forced to adapt to each other's sweaty bodies and the elimination of personal space /

Twelve rusted fans facing the same direction /

Forty-eight individuals /

Forty-eight beds /

Forty-eight foul-smelling mouths /

Forty-eight half-naked, sweaty bodies /

Frightened /

Arguing.

Inside the rooms seem clean, even though they are extremely stuffy and cramped. Wooden flooring, difficult to see with the large fan that stands in the centre of the room. Apart from the prisoners in rooms within the corridors, there are other prisoners who have to endure horrible circumstances, relegated to a distant corner of the compound, among the sound of dreary and monotonous fans, reduced to living like dogs.

Between the main corridors and the large tent erected near the main gate and used as a dining area, construction seems to have been going on – a metal structure is covered in rust. This strange building is called 'P'. One end reaches into the compound and the other end is along the fence adjacent to the ocean. A dark and narrow tunnel sixty metres long, three metres wide, two metres high, and damp like a wet barn. In fact, it is more suffocating than a stable for mules, filled with half-naked bodies, stinking breath, stinking sweat.

It is hard to believe anyone could live there, let alone the one-hundred-and-thirty individuals packed into the place by force.

Dark /

Two-hundred-and-sixty dilated pupils /

One-hundred-and-thirty rotten smells /

All together they stink like a fast-rotting corpse /

Sixty fans /

The sound of an old tractor perpetually polluting the atmosphere.

Metal is ubiquitous there; so is human flesh and skin. The ceiling of Tunnel P is shaped like a dome; it looks like a real tunnel or an enormous tube.

What's important is the affliction of the awful smell of bad breath, circulating the room. For every two beds there is a fan; a fan that whirs incessantly. It blows a hot vicious kind of air, so it is useless. The air flows over the bodies, bodies that are always exhausted.

The fans are waging war, always on the job. But the sound of the old tractor prevails in the end, ploughing up through the inclined clearing. Again, the unrelenting smell.

It isn't clear why the architect designed this disproportionate and strange building. According to what line of thinking was this ugly masterpiece created? Inside the tunnel, two rows of beds are arranged opposite each other. Between them is a tight walkway, wide enough to let only one body pass. To go from one end of the tunnel to the other, someone has to bother the others a number of times. For instance, someone who wants to reach their bed at the far end of the room has to calculate first while at the beginning of the tunnel whether anyone is going to come in the opposite direction. Or they have to determine whether someone might want to come down from their bed and come towards the exit. Organising bodies so they will not brush past each other takes effort. Because the space is so small and always filled with people coming and going, one can anticipate rubbing shoulders, and this shoulder-bumping and the interaction of your body with the sweaty, near-naked body of another is disgusting.

The floor of the tunnel is concrete, worn out, and covered with holes, both tiny and wide. The atmosphere is humid and warm, an ideal environment for all kinds of tropical insects to nest and lay eggs. The stench of hairy men's foul breath and sweat, sleeping alongside each other – this is more disgusting than the sewage gathered outside the tunnel. Like the smell of a dead dog, this stench sometimes combines with the smell of shit.

—

On some days when the clouds are thinner than usual, or the sky is filled with only sparse pockets of cloud, the heat in the tunnel reaches temperatures that could cook a human body. Prisoners are like pieces of meat in a metal pressure-cooker. During the day almost no-one dares sleep or lie down on their beds inside the tunnel. No-one even feels like sitting down inside because every second spent in there means experiencing heat that sears eyeballs.

There is an alternative. The prisoners find sanctuary under a single old tree with wide leaves that stands between the dining area and the small room erected for no clear purpose at the top of the compound. This thick tree generously spreads its branches across the whole area. Like the cool shade of an umbrella, it comforts many of the distressed men from the tunnel. The shaded space is filled with plastic chairs. The prisoners sit there, leaning back on the chairs.

Killing time involves a simple trick /

Reach out and hold another sunset /

Another one of the thousand-colour Manusian sunsets /

Then, reach out and hold another night /

Another one of the dark island nights /

A futile cycle . . . /

Night and day revolving /

Under the shade of an old tree.

In some periods during the middle of the day, not even a bit of water-bearing tropical cloud emerges in the sky. The temperature reaches its peak.

Two suns are in battle /
One descending from the sky /
One ascending from earth /
Searing /
Extremely bright /
Reaching total domination.

When the sun and the earth come together as one, places of shade become rare and the prisoners gather under the shade of the old tree, like baby chickens sheltering under the wings of their mother. The Papus and Australian officers work incessantly and monitor back and forth, all throughout the prisons. The faces of the Australians: bright-red faces . . . blood-red faces. Australians with fat asses . . . sweaty ass cracks flowing like rivers. It seems that even sunglasses are defeated. And the mosquitoes . . . what intelligent creatures! They have disappeared. Living beings that evade the light. Precise and quick in the dark.

Does anyone understand the strategic operation of mosquitoes? With the first sign of the retreat of the sun, they return in full view. They are bizarre creatures. Once they sense a human body they jump into action in amazing fashion. They certainly possess a kind of reasoning or a capacity for strategy, even though they are supposedly brainless. How is it possible that they form a special alliance characteristic of any disciplined and mighty army in order to attack bodies? This occurs at particular moments when one wants to sleep or when one's eyes are drifting into sleep. They have an unusually keen ability to sting places it's hard to defend with one's hands. The war zones are the deepest section of the lower back, behind the thighs, behind the ears, and all the far-off and deep corners of the body. When bitten in the tropics, the spot or mark itches for weeks.

Unconsciously scratching /
Fingernails digging deep into skin /
All over the bitten region /
Ploughing, ploughing /
Sometimes so relentless /
Sometimes until there is nothing left /
Leaving no skin /
Leaving open wounds.

Acquiring these wounds is annoying, even more annoying than the itch. The atmosphere of humidity and heat is so oppressive that it transforms every little wound into an infected clot of pus. After each wound heals, a permanent black scar remains. The deeper the wound, the darker and more ingrained the scar.

Enormous suffering /
Little black tokens of memory.

I will carry a few of these beautiful, black souvenirs with me for life – on my ankle and two or three in the dip of my lower back.

The mosquito remains a potential threat always. We believe that at any moment it could confine a prisoner to his bed for weeks.

Every day at sunset a number of nurses dressed in orange and carrying boxes of yellow pills enter the compound. Immediately a long queue develops opposite the little room near the main door of the prison. Futile struggles to defeat the malaria-carrying mosquitoes, these murderous creatures, their figures constituted by long flimsy legs – terrifying and unbelievably cunning. I say futile because basically it is all just a game; what I account here came straight from the nurses' mouths and spread through the entire prison.

The Kyriarchal System of the prison exaggerates the threat of malaria-carrying mosquitoes so that fearful, clueless prisoners come from everywhere, with no choice but to stand in a long line so that they can take pills. These kinds of pills are distributed to villages for cows bloated from overeating. Fear is an extraordinary force for motivating people; it pushes people to hurry up and determines their direction. Fear: a mountain of ice that has almost completely disappeared under water – the mother of all tortures.

The motherfucking nurses enter the prison with their ridiculous clothes, their spotty faces and their particular kind of arrogance. Immediately, they enter the tiny room without looking over or offering any other form of acknowledgment . . . they are just disrespectful. They position themselves behind the table and quickly start working.

Meanwhile, one of the Papus is engaged in a duty ordered by an Australian. He is emptying a box of bottled water right there next to the nurses so the prisoners can take the pills on the spot, in front of the nurses. A group of idiotic prisoners are in the middle of stirring things up as only they know how. The nurses settle in and the prisoners feel they are well-placed now to engage in something important. Before the nurses arrived, some people were sitting on the ground, and now they stand up and give the queue a more orderly form. Others group together, chatting randomly and, suddenly, they check themselves and get in order. The enthusiasm of those in line for taking the yellow pills is a combination of fear and stupidity. Fear of mosquitoes in love with human blood and, subsequently, that other much greater fear: that is the fear that drives one to stay alive, and the stupidity of the prisoners trusting in these unrighteous nurses and The Kyriarchal System of the prison.

Perhaps when the drive to stay alive is more prominent, the prisoners have no choice but to put all their faith, naively, in the pills and the nurses. Zeal and faith resides in the few people positioned at the head of the queue, and a false sense of pride. In haste, they quickly snatch the bottle of water from the hands of the Papu and swallow the pill. Straight away, they distinguish themselves from the crowd and look back at the others self-importantly. What they feel is this: 'I'm not going to die tonight. It's guaranteed that tonight I won't be dying of malaria. From this moment until tomorrow sunset – when we have to endure the stench of this morbid line again – I won't be dying. And you all have to wait until you reach the position I enjoy right now. Your sentence involves continuing to stand there until you get to feel the way I do now. I mean, it's certain, I'm not dying . . . you see how lucky I am . . . I'm victorious. Tonight, I'm not going to die. Tomorrow, I'll see you back here again. Right here with the nurses, the Papus, the yellow pills, and these bottles of warm water. My god, I'm so lucky that I'm not going to die tonight. I'm so astute, I managed to get one of those ghastly pills into my stomach. I'm clever because I was one of the first ones.' And the others bunched up at the end of the queue eventually take their pills, one after another, and exit the queue.

156

Standing in line induces the feeling that death is just around the corner. That feeling of imminence . . . even the family networks of malaria-carrying mosquitoes occupy a space in that corner. That imminence, atop the coconut trees. That imminence, watching the community from the bushes behind the fences; selecting its prey so that it can have its way once night falls. The deception is obvious. The queue is pointless; there is no reason to be there . . . it is all in vain.

With time, with the changes experienced over days and months, the evidence is clear – it has been a lie. Everyone is convinced: there is no basis to the notion that the mosquitoes carry malaria. It's not that malaria isn't in and of itself dangerous. No. But there haven't been enough reported cases to justify such a horrible queue. It becomes clear that no-one in Manus Prison has died due to the malaria-ridden sting of this mosquito – this long-legged, thin, adorable mosquito.

—

Away from Tunnel P, over on the eastern side and near the fences that border the shore, some more building is going on. There is a decaying construction, with walls full of holes and cracks. The holes look like they were made with an iron mallet, bashed until the holes cracked through the disintegrating wall. It appears to be a grid of concavities. The structure has a gabled roof and four rooms within it.

Inside the rooms and all over the outside walls, cartoons are painted. It seems that it was designed with the intention of attracting little kids. The image of a cow with black spots. A playful elephant with a trunk so long it spreads all over the surface of the disjointed sections of the wall. A grand lion, its tail buried under one of those holes. But with a little bit of focus, and by following the lines, one can tell that the tail passes through the hole. A few crooked trees with broken branches, but full of bright red fruit and apple blossoms. A number of faces, filled with the smiles of a mummy, daddy, and children with school bags. Mummy has glasses. Daddy has a disproportionate moustache. There are letters of the English alphabet in different colours. And a scene of birds flying above all the other pictures, near the roof. A tall white stork that is now becoming darker in colour. It seems that it was a place for teaching classes for the kids from the imprisoned families who have been here at a previous time. But now a new group of Sri Lankan prisoners live there.

This space is part of Australia's legacy and a central feature of its history – this place is Australia itself – this right here is Australia. One always feels an astounding nostalgia for abandoned legacies. The source of this feeling is uncertain; it's like the feeling evoked in an abandoned cemetery – a graveyard surrounded by weeds, drawing the old crows, all huddled around the place. One only need live a short time in these large, dark rooms. Just look around, at the ceilings and dark corners, until you accurately understand its architecture. The paintings are decaying, they have a kindergarten character – they still contain sentimental feelings. A feeling of past lives. A feeling that is weak in comparison to the architecture, but nevertheless undeniable. A feeling of life that is weak in contrast to the tremendous feeling of death.

The architect of the building certainly did not create it for a group of humans to occupy. At most, it looks like the small guard-rooms of a garrison in a battlefield. It's reasonable to say that it, like Tunnel P, is a barrack-like warehouse. During the 1950s the Australian Navy seized a large piece of land that back then was a dense jungle. They destroyed the jungle and established a large garrison. Long before this area was transformed into Oscar Prison, it was an entertainment ground for Navy officers so they could play baseball. These rooms were built in a hurry in one or two days by a company of a few dozen soldiers back in the '50s.

These rooms are like an ants' nest – besides the four main rooms there are a few other rooms in the other sections, haphazardly constructed. A few rooms, narrow wooden doors, sleeping space fit for one person of medium height, coffins embedded vertically into the wall, without a window, without the regular wall height towards the ceiling. Perhaps these few rooms contain mysteries of their own – they have been completely locked up. Perhaps bitter memories are buried in them forever and the last person who locked them took the key and threw it into the depths of the ocean behind the fences – the restless ocean beyond the fences, amid the sound of immortal waves.

Room of the dead /
Room of darkness /
Numerous coffins /
The smell of decay /
The smell of dead dog.

The rooms are part of a series. Their fences are adjacent to the sea and there are smaller areas cordoned off with blue bedsheets. A few Sudanese men have wrapped many bedsheets around two pillars that hold up the new makeshift roof connected to the original structure; they have made a room like a pen for a herd of sheep or goats. Inside it smells like sludge because the cement floor is full of potholes and the soil is moist . . . that smell of putrid soil mixed with the smell of the prisoners' horrible breath. A chemical brew of two disgusting smells, together with the stench of the sewage trough that passes alongside the room.

The atmosphere is suffocating. It's better for one to live among the rubbish than to live in a place that smells like this. At least on a mountain of rubbish it's always possible for a fresh breeze to blow. Or for new rubbish to bring different smells. But in a pig pen the smell is rotten. It decays. It's intoxicating. Dizziness and insanity settle into the mind.

Due to the lingering smells, the army of mosquitoes has congregated – mosquitoes with nothing better to do than stand around at the regular gatherings. But for me, I prefer the sanctuary of my room, rather than looking at the magnitude of microscopic yet brutish mosquitoes, and inhaling what is essentially the smell of shit. At night, inside the protection of my room, I hug my pillow tight.

A few metres over is the toilet complex, constructed with gabled roofs. More precisely, they are small ready-built rooms made of wood that were abandoned here years ago. A complex of maybe ten small rooms, a few of them without doors or, rather, a bunch of them that have just rotted away over time. It has become a region of humidity and cultivation, a lab for algae. The whole lot has turned green.

The floor is always in the same state: piss up to the ankle. These toilets are so filthy that the toilet space has extended along the ground for a few metres. The toxic water has seeped into the surrounding area, penetrating the space where various species of plants are growing. It is such that anyone who wants to enter has to first go through a dense mass of weeds – weeds that reach up to the waist.

On many occasions I see prisoners whose rooms are in that region pissing among the plants in the dead of night. They prefer to piss right there in a comfortable spot among the bushes. Pissing quickly in a few motions in the middle of night. An empty space, a determined trek to those small rooms, standing, taking their spot, a quick look around. When certain that no-one is around, pissing there among the vegetation. From the time they piss to when they pull up their pants it is important to check all around them with caution lest someone notice. The neck has a really tough job: keeping adequate watch in this situation involves turning the head three-hundred-and-sixty degrees. While turning, the neck muscles have to pause for seconds while facing different directions.

This style of pissing – I mean pissing during a dark night, in the middle of nature, in a busy prison with filthy toilets – could be a blessing. The feeling of joy evoked by freedom and, at the same time, stress. The sense of liberation fused with draining the tubes. One aspect of this minor feeling of liberation pertains to that gratifying feeling of the actual act of pissing. Another aspect is connected with defying the prison's designation of space, forcing people to relieve themselves among difficulties and obstacles. Pissing on the plants is no worry at all except working the neck and muscles, acting quickly, and concentrating when directing one's stream into an open space and away from one's pants.

This great sense of liberation is enough to lift the spirit of an individual – he returns to bed with peace of mind. In this stretch of distance all is good if the prisoner knows no-one will suddenly appear from behind the small rooms. But things are different if the eyes of an officer are peering at him – one look is enough to ruin the tranquillity. In this situation, someone self-assured may continue taking a piss, just letting it out without really paying attention to his surroundings. However, someone who becomes embarrassed will have to terminate the whole project. It's difficult for one to make up his mind to end an activity such as this; it's hard to do that in less than a second.

One night, I am smoking along the fences when I notice a skinny Sri Lankan lad with a moustache – like the moustache of a cat that has grown curiously in two different directions. It makes him look somewhat comical. His moustache always gets my attention while we are queuing up for food. For this reason, as soon as he exits his quarters this night, I notice him straight away. He is walking fast, straight ahead. He is like a youth who only has minutes to steal an apple from the neighbour's garden and run away. His movements reveal that he aims to do something unauthorised – from behind the wall he looks around with suspicion. Actually, he is scanning three-hundred-and-sixty degrees from the very start, scanning around until he finds the spot he is looking for, scanning around for the spot where he can offload in peace.

When he is certain no-one is around, he steps between the bushes and drops his pants halfway so that his ass can enjoy freedom. His back is to the kitchen. But this way of pissing is not common among the men. Usually only kids drop their pants halfway when pissing. An adult just pulls out his penis. He wants to piss in the direction of where I am sitting, along the bottom of the fences. I am right in front of him. What an idiot! I say idiot because if he were a little more attentive when looking all around he would have noticed me sitting in the dark. Even my smoke is lit. I am surprised he hasn't seen me – down go his pants and out comes his penis, right in front of my eyes.

I think if he were any more careless he would have pissed on me without noticing. He would've finished the job with ease and probably with pleasure. If he were more careful, or less careful, the situation afterwards wouldn't cause trouble and problems for both of us. His movements are so well crafted that the scene looks constructed. He is positioned right before my eyes, ready to piss right on me, and then suddenly sees me as he is about to let loose, sees me sitting there in front of him with a smoke. As soon as he lays eyes on me – I mean when he notices someone is watching him – he becomes so disoriented that he immediately shoves his penis in his pants and, like a hungry stray dog that comes across a piece of meat or steals something from the neighbour, he flees back to his bed with incredible speed.

On the morning of the next day I see him in the queue for food. He is hiding behind a few others. Hiding there with that moustache . . . scared. He doesn't have it in him to face me. Clearly, the incident from the previous night has embarrassed him. No doubt, part of his feeling of humiliation is due to the way he ran off. He is embarrassed not necessarily because he was pissing in the bushes; that is, not just for doing something that was unacceptable according to common norms. He understands completely that he shouldn't have fled in the way that he did. It's not that he should've just continued what he was doing. But he should've left the scene in a dignified way.

Over days and months, this incident plays out in both our minds over and over. I mean, every time our eyes connect we both develop a sense of embarrassment. This is something that annoys and troubles us considerably within the prison. This is peculiar to prison: one can't harbour animosity towards another for a long time. This principle is also true when it comes to friendship. Prison is no place to tolerate a feeling of misery for long, and the same even goes for a feeling of joy. During waking hours, the prisoners lock eyes dozens of times. Tolerating these feelings for a long time is torturous; every time we see each other this feeling of misery resurfaces.

I try a few times to approach The Sri Lankan Lad and look him straight in the eyes and say, 'Brother, for me there's no problem with you pissing in the bushes. The toilets are so filthy that you had no choice but to relieve yourself outdoors.' Either that or even lie by exaggerating and say, 'I despise the filthy toilets here and also piss on the ground sometimes.' But these kinds of dialogues are too explicit, and would create awkwardness and increase the degree of shame. It would be like an admission or reaffirmation of the incident, and for this reason I give up on every occasion and prefer to put up with the miserable feeling.

He is really embarrassed when confronted with me. This is out of my control. He rightly feels vulnerable and ashamed in front of me. Only god knows what is going on in his mind every time he sees me, what form of disruption is taking place. Maybe he tries to communicate with me in his mind and structures many reasons to help explain the incident. But it never happens. We never find the strength to eliminate this miserable feeling, or replace it.

In the prison even saying 'hi' is a massive headache.[14] There are always people in the queue for the toilets, for food, inside the corridors, the enclosure. In fact, in every corner of the prison, people are always watching. One is always in their crosshairs. When gazes meet, replying with the word 'hi' is a quick way to get away from the people who have been forced to be a part of one's life. In the beginning, maybe a few instances don't induce stress, but as time in the prison increases, slowly but surely, the very act of saying 'hi' is transformed into a source of affliction – the same act that was once an act of kindness. Similar perhaps to family

---

14 The common greeting in Iran is *salaam*. These passages in Farsi highlight fully the paradoxical nature of greeting another inside the prison as the author describes; saying *salaam* in this environment resonates with a particular rancour because of the reverence and spiritual connotation associated with the greeting.

members who have to greet each other all the time, or are forced to issue fake smiles.

The distress caused by saying 'hi' is so intense that when prisoners pass each other they pretend that they don't see anyone. It is like shadows, just passing each other. Cars with foggy windows in which one can only see directly ahead. This kind of behaviour, not saying 'hi', is relatively easy as long as people are not obliged to look at each other at all. If miserable feelings develop between individuals, the disturbing situation is intensified. Between the Sri Lankan Lad and me a particular mood develops – we even divert our paths when we see each other from a distance. I don't go near the fences opposite the rooms occupied by the Sri Lankans as often as before.

—

The atmosphere in the prison is constituted by micro-level and macro-level disciplinary measures designed to create animosity between the prisoners. Hatred runs through every prisoner. In the prison, hatred makes prisoners more insular. The weight of hatred is so intense that the prisoners will suddenly collapse on a dark night and give up resisting . . . surrender to a system that induces and amplifies hatred . . . and accept refoulement. This basic aim reflects The Kyriarchal System of the prison: 'Returning the refugee prisoners to the land from which they came.' The only time the power of the fences can bring the prisoners to their knees is when it joins forces with those very people inside it. The prison is designed to breed hostility, animosity. Maybe if the toilets had been designed in a way that piss-filled water didn't reach up to the ankles we would never have had to face that experience that night and, subsequently, the two of us would not have felt as miserable about it.

The Kyriarchal System of the prison instils in prisoners perverse habits and sordid and barbaric behaviours. Just these filthy toilets had caused this youth, and many others, to piss wherever they wanted; pissing in the bushes, big clusters of plants covered with yellow and red blossoms. People pissing on flowers is repulsive. And this is just one example.

The main toilets in the prison get so busy at times that prisoners have to wait in long queues. A wretched state: the prisoners eat together at fixed hours so, naturally, they pour into the toilets at a similar time. The floor of these toilets is decaying concrete full of tiny crevices – tiny yet deep – tiny yet full of accumulated grime and semen. It is a place where prisoners masturbate and ejaculate into the cracks running through the ground – the putrid smell from these crevices is suffocating. The shower tap is just a hole in the wall. You see, the toilet and shower are in the same little room. Down low, the drain for the showers is actually a grimy canal, flowing with the filth from the neighbouring showers, transferring the dirt to the next one.

Sometimes these dirty canals aggregate masses of hair that has been shaved off that very day. The flow of water, which is always cold, gets blocked. When the prisoners form long queues to get razors with blue handles, bunches of hair soon accumulate. Razors are not replaced more than once a month. This is because the authorities think that if prisoners have access to razors they will be more inclined to commit suicide or self-harm. So the prisoners often have faces full of hair. Dozens of prisoners with long beards, waiting in line for food, waiting in line for the toilet.

When a razor breaks, a prisoner is forced to use his friend's razor, or just wait for weeks. The chances of missing out on a razor are great because the queues form suddenly and supplies dissipate in less than an hour. The queue for razors is the most controversial and chaotic queue in the prison. The prisoners become violent, so much so that sometimes the tension results in throwing kicks and punches. In this situation, there are also prisoners who have each other's backs, prisoners committed to brotherhood. They share one razor and shave off their excess hair. As part of The Kyriarchal System of the prison, supplies are withheld; this is clearly a strategy for conditioning prisoners, forcing them to behave badly.

—

At the end of each night a group of Papus enters the prison with cleaning equipment and large buckets. Just youth with fuzzy hair and yellow uniforms with black bands around their legs and around their waists, uniforms that suffocate their naturally muscular physiques. As they enter, right there at the main gate, they separate into groups and then spread through the prison like obedient soldiers on duty. Groups that seem better skilled at faster cleaning techniques are sent to the bathrooms. Without speaking a word to the prisoners they mop up all the filth in the bathrooms in one or two hours. They pour it into large plastic buckets and dump it behind the fences into the ocean.

These young Papus always have a look of fear when they encounter prisoners. The origin of this fear lies with the Australians, and it forces the Papus into silence. The Australians gossip to them that this prison, in which they are supposed to clean the bathrooms, is for dangerous criminals and terrorists; at any moment they could initiate something dangerous and attack. These are expatriated prisoners and it would be better not to become acquainted with them. This is enough to create an atmosphere of fear, especially for those who have little experience of people from another hemisphere. This kind of introduction creates an impression that will probably take years to reverse. And this fabricated impression imposed on the minds of the cleaners is just like the false image of the local people that the Australians imposed on the prisoners before exiling them to Manus – of primitivism, barbarism and cannibalism.

The engagement of the local community with the refugees is conducted through fear. The imprisoned refugees feel that they are in a nightmare; their feelings about the locals are transformed into a nightmare.

A nightmare turned into a reality /
A nightmare within the prison /
A nightmare with the sound of locals /
A nightmare drumming with their footsteps /
The Kyriarchy produces terror /
Inhibitions of terror /
Foundations of terror /
Two groups living in terror.

The Papus behave according to this fear while they are working. For instance, say one of them has exerted a lot of energy lathering up all the washing detergent in the toilets, and now wants to rinse them with water. And then a prisoner wants to enter. The local can't bring himself to request that the prisoner wait a few moments. In these kinds of situations, the Papus just stay quiet. They just wait until the prisoner realises and stops for a little while until the Papu washes away the foam. On the rare occasion that the prisoner enters and closes the door behind him, the Papu is made to stand waiting, scratching his head.

These same fuzzy-haired Papus that keep completely silent as they are busy cleaning the toilets, are amazingly happy and cheerful as they clean the area behind the fences. On many occasions, in the area between the Fox Prison and Delta Prison – when it is time for a noon break – they burst out laughing really loud and chase each other, broom handles in hand. They have a tendency for getting physical when joking around; I mean, they take any opportunity to chase each other; they hit each other with water bottles, or kick each other in the ass. Friends kick each other, yet their relationships overflow with sincere kindness. Every blow from a kick or punch is equal perhaps to a kind embrace, or equal to sharing good times in conversation. Sometimes, the joking around and chasing becomes so intense that it seems like they've forgotten the rules and regulations of the prison. The thing that usually stops them in their tracks is a reprimand from the Australian officers. With the first indication that the Australian officers are looking on with disapproval, the Papus suddenly realise that now they are working for a company with complex regulating structures. They realise they have to rein in their ways of engaging.

In under one hour, the futility of the sanitation measures becomes clear. The cement floors full of crevices attract grime. The filth seeps deep within; it is always in the same state. The cleaning is only a charade, just to reassure us that the bathrooms are regularly tended to. With all the filth accumulated in these bathrooms, they are still probably the only place in the prison where the prisoners feel liberated, if only for a few minutes. It is a region where the imposition of prison regulations is lessened. The prisoner can imagine himself outside the prison compound and away from the invasive gaze of the officers . . . if only for a few minutes. For this reason, a few Australian officers are always assigned to prowl around that section. Every now and then, they shine their flash lights in the direction of the toilets. They want to exert their authority, make their presence felt. In this way they announce: 'It is true that we don't have access to the toilets, but from out here, standing by these fences, we're in complete control of what goes on in those cubicles.'

At any moment, someone may slash their wrists with one of those razors, the ones with the blue handles. Self-harm is a regular occurrence. This is an excuse to monitor the toilets. For some, at midnight, these cubicles become places where lovers can fulfil their desires. However, some young men are also vulnerable to exploitation. But this is of no concern to the officers. They are there to govern the place, to remind everyone that they are enforcing the rules and running the system of surveillance. One can't enter the toilets without sensing the looming presence of the officers seated just outside. Their overbearing presence makes sitting on the toilet seat an anxious moment. It is as if their gaze has the power to penetrate the wooden doors and pollute the space, disrupting the degree of freedom experienced within the cubicles.

Day after day, encounter after encounter, moment upon moment . . . recording memories of these encounters within the toilets. The place is a chamber that encapsulates history. The pain inside the prison seems to pile up in these isolated spaces, here within the toilets. The toilets are a cache for all the suffering spawned from other parts of the prison, suffering that culminates in incidents, incidents within these toilets. Perhaps unhealed wounds from long ago are opened up again in here.

A horrified youth with a face pale with fear /

Trying to protect himself for hours on end /

Fighting as he was cornered in different parts of the prison /

Fighting hopelessly /

Fighting till he can't think straight /

Fighting till he loses control /

But the fighting finally stops /

It all stops /

It eventually stops right here /

It finally stops /

Here in this desolate cubicle.

The place can be a sanctuary where people banish the daily psychological struggles and turmoil of all the other places in the prison. But in the end, at sunset or during the darkness of midnight, someone takes hold of one of those razors with the blue handles, chooses the most appropriate toilet, and over there, in the moments that follow, warm blood flows on the cement floor. The cubicles are places for screaming out. Or they are marked as chambers of devastation, the devastation of youth who have lost their innocence, a devastation constituted by absolute hopelessness. A location of the clash between terror, hopelessness and outbursts of deep anguish. For this reason, the location embodies an uncanny sense of awe, an eerie spirit.

—

When the prisoners' frustrations reach their peak, during those sensitive hours when the sun seems to poke its finger directly into the eye of the prison, the generator that creates the electricity switches off. The prison finds itself in a crazy state and collapses. It is as if a hot iron hammer has smashed down into the centre of the prison. Within minutes the prison is transformed into a living hell.

Even the prisoners undergo a bizarre metamorphosis; consciousness is completely altered. The prisoners are stunned on all levels – right down to their basic instincts – struck with jolting surprise and heightened anger. A massive charge of half-naked men spills urgently out from inside the rooms and containers and amasses under the shade of the corridors. The uproar reverberates in remarkable fashion. Together they are like a flock of seagulls that recognise the scent of a storm and flap across and into each other with no control. At these particular moments the prisoner has no way of expressing his frustrations besides bombarding the confined space with pointless profanities.

Usually when the prisoners are swearing, some of their attention is directed towards the crowd. With each word that leaves their mouths they anticipate the reaction of the group; they wait to see the response. The one who swears anticipates praise and validation. The atmosphere is such that the prisoners utter the most vulgar profanities, competing against each other with their expletives, swearing as though they have abandoned everything else. The rationale is that the one who swears the loudest is the bravest – giving the impression that he is braver than he actually is.

This is a feature of some of the prisoners: in times of crisis when prisoners huddle up in one spot, they parade their masculinity and bravery by bellowing for no particular reason. However, when a situation escalates into a serious conflict, these kinds of people just crawl into a corner and behave as though they are not even there, so they don't have to take responsibility. There are others who stay at the entrance to the rooms. As they scratch their heads and bodies – sitting there confused – they shake their heads over and over in disapproval.

Different emotions mix in their reactions. A sense of weakness, of helplessness, of misery, of frustration – all these emotions cascade down their faces. People are like that, whether they are prisoners or whether they occupy any other position. Their behaviour is always linked to their environment and to the people around them; they calibrate their behaviour accordingly. This space is a meeting point for emotions, a space where emotions meet to negotiate. In this space, there is no solace except the face of brotherhood looking back at you, there on the face of a fellow inmate. A solace invoked by the face of a fellow prisoner who himself is at the last frontier of helplessness.

Under these circumstances, in the midst of all these bleak and unbearable emotions, a feeling close to joy stirs beneath the surface. As suffering becomes normalised, people experience this particular feeling of joy. A twisted satisfaction in chaos and destruction.

—

In the distance, Australian officers hold their notepads, dripping with sweat, and every so often noting something down. The managers talk to their superiors via walkie-talkie. They regularly monitor the corridors from one end to the other and issue orders to their subordinates. With clenched fists, the prisoners collaborate to create a deafening ruckus in response; they whip up a fracas. After some moments an officer appears on the scene. An interloper in the crowd, he enters and approaches the group as soon as some other officers join him. He politely and earnestly apologises and explains that it is not their fault . . . that 'the generator has broken down'. From the other direction an abrupt announcement states that the water in the bathrooms has been cut off.

Within a few minutes a zigzag of naked men forms in the narrow sliver of shade behind the corridors. The setting in the prison is like the front line in war: men all over the place, all moving around in frustration. The officers are completely useless and provide no assistance; they just mill around. They do nothing to help the situation, but their numbers multiply. They are also fitted out for war. A group of officers escort the managers; they emerge in the midst of the crowd. Another group of officers gathers in a corner, but they remain motionless. They simply communicate with officers in other locations through walkie-talkies.

The prison becomes a hive of killer bees, and someone has disturbed the tranquillity by striking the hive with a stick. Prisoners are running around confused, wandering around confused, looking around confused. It is as though they feel that if they remain put they will have relinquished something, and as a result many swarm into the bathrooms. The stress that besieges them makes their guts difficult to control. Within a few minutes the toilets cease to function and the smell of shit and piss sweeps, the whole space from end-to-end. As time passes, the foul smell of human excrement worsens, contaminating the area with intensity.

An unusual tension develops among the prisoners, affecting their interactions. The prisoners have become wolves, a threat to everyone else. As though they are on the threshold of a bloody battle, the prisoners size each other up, and they also size up the officers who try to make themselves appear calm and collected. For someone who comes across as physically weaker, this is particularly alarming. Furious prisoners with straining guts are looking for somewhere secluded, and looking for any excuse to rain down a barrage of profanities and insults – usually on the weaker inmates. In such circumstances, those prone to losing their tempers – people with little tolerance – can just snap. The simplest and most basic thing can trigger an attack on a puny body, a powerless being, a defenceless figure. With every minute that passes, the more one's mental energy turns from the heat to the toilets. When one is in urgent need of a toilet, the mind has little control over the body. All nerves are pulled in the direction of one's guts.

What a scene, looking on as a group of people lose all equilibrium. In this situation, one realises the extent of human frailty and helplessness. Those in charge of the generator are acutely aware of how easy it is to dominate the prisoners, simply by pressing a button. Everything is reduced to the generator – a mind made of machinery and wires. No-one knows its whereabouts in the prison, or maybe its location on the island – no-one knows where it is installed.

What is driving things? The Kyriarchal System of the prison? Is it the highly intelligent 'high-ranking' officers governing the generator, and then subsequently governing the minds of the prisoners? It's as though they know exactly at what time of day or night to hit the switch. Exactly the time when tolerance levels have sunk deep down. At any moment a serious fight might break out between the prisoners, or the prisoners against the officers – and right at that moment the power and water issue is resolved.

The prison is in the middle of a clenched fist /
Now loosening, now tightening /
On the verge of exploding /
Then, all of a sudden, balance is re-established.

In the midst of all this, some officers are reporting regularly through their walkie-talkies, sending accounts to their superiors, to those behind the scenes, to the ones receiving the final decision. The decision about when the electricity and water are to be restored.

As midnight draws closer the prisoners retire to their foam mattresses, return to sleep after a day of commotion. Suddenly, the generator quits again. Another hammer clobbers the head of the prison. Everyone's hopes and dreams manoeuvre in tandem with the unbearable intensity of heat . . . seeping alongside each other into the tapestry of nightmares.

Startled out of sleep, the prisoners wake. Sweating, heads bursting as though in a furnace. Not to forget the mosquitoes. Now, without any fans operating, the mosquitoes venture more ruthlessly into the rooms. Within minutes prisoners escape the rooms and drop directly into the black of night, unleashing a monsoon of profanities. The swearing echoes through the abyss of darkness that restrains the prison.

The prison evaporates into the darkness, evaporates into the horror. Even the coconut trees become silhouettes of terror. Bodies transform into dark shadowy figures under the moonlight, transform into what seem to be unknown marauders setting up a blockade. Yelling and screaming, people cry out, sounds emerge out of the unseen, sounds sweeping through every area in the prison.

The stray dogs respond to the volume of noise, the hounds that always prowl the outside perimeters of the prison and the edge of the fences. They bark . . . they bark in a way that rings with the mystifying depths of the dark jungle. The Papus are also frantic. They stick close together, sitting curled up on the floor against the walls. They are preparing for the worst.

Before darkness falls, however, the Australians flee the prison. They always exercise this tactic. Before nightfall they exit in waves. They manage to do this without anyone noticing; they are really sly. Their instincts smell danger, and the officers try to contain a justified fear. They are hyper-alert in case out of nowhere someone strikes them on the back of the neck under the cover of night, delivers a blow out of revenge. The prison landscape is so violent that it is likely that out of a few hundred there could be at least one angry and disenfranchised prisoner who could decide to commit a violent act – and enact it during the night – in the dark, behind the bathrooms, or alongside the obfuscating coconut tree trunks, next to the coconut trees that can completely hide a person. This is a possibility and certainly occupies the minds of the officers. It also plagues the system, even though it is The Kyriarchal System that determines these conditions. In this environment every individual is a security risk.

The fear of the officers results in getting the generator up and running a lot quicker this time. When the lights go out, the prison transforms into a dangerous beast. At any moment an uncontrollable situation could emerge. The generator has a face with the following features:

A device resembling someone of old age /

Constituted by an intricate system of deteriorating wires /

Poles and pipes of rusty metal /

Probably within a dingy space /

Somewhere worse than the prison /

Covered by an old cloth /

Under the protection of a rag /

A rag that is withering away /

The generator is withering away.

During these moments I want to believe the generator is a living being, with a soul, an organism that takes pleasure in throwing the prison into disarray whenever it feels like it.

The prison is inoperative, and after a few minutes it regresses even further, regresses into horror. The yelling and screaming finally cease. Just the sound of random, muffled barking can be heard coming out of the depths of the jungle. It seems that the sounds are migrating deep down into the darkest of places, travelling further and further away to the rhythm of some never-ending music, to an eternal rhythm. The sounds continue to drift until a heavy silence creeps in to hold the prison captive. Only the cry of birds remains; they know what is going on around them.

In the dead of night, the prisoners' pupils increase remarkably in size. The prisoners are left with itchy bodies, they are left rubbing their sleep-deprived eyes. Fear plants itself into the landscape of hopelessness, and then, suddenly, in the midst of these phases, the lights come back on in the rooms. Now with the lights back on in the compound, the prisoners return to their rooms without hesitation, return to standing in front of fans buzzing with delight. The prisoners return to their rooms in haste; the transition is rapid. They feel that they have lost time; they now have a limited period in which to sleep.

Whenever the prisoner rests his head on a pillow for a stretch of time, excruciating stress comes over him, stress over The Oldman Generator. At any moment it could decide to shut down again. This occurs on some occasions, right when some prisoners are sleeping. The prisoners can never predict when the electricity and water will cut out.

The generator is operating with a higher level of logic. It has more agency than the prisoners because there are periods when, technically, it shouldn't shut down – but it does. Sometimes early in the morning, sometimes afternoon, sometimes during periods when the sun completely dominates the prison . . . at times when the sun goes hunting for the skin of prisoners. This irregular functioning is a reality. So much so that sometimes during the days and nights it switches off a number of times. Sometimes it functions continuously for a whole week without a hitch. Then right on the day when the prisoners think the generator has been repaired or maybe replaced, it suddenly turns off again.

The generator manipulates our minds to such an extent that it has morphed into some kind of agent; it has developed human motivations. Sometimes the prisoners select adjectives that ascribe human qualities to it: 'That stupid generator', 'The generator is a cunt', 'Generator, you bastard', 'You asshole of a generator'. And in the times when not a peep of trouble emerges after a week, some better terms are used: 'Mr Generator'. But Mr Generator could shut off at any second. He could shit all over everything and mess with everyone's heads. He quickly reverts back to 'Bastard Generator' or something similar. I swear, Mr Generator displays a more cunning intelligence than the prisoners.

On days when the problems with water and electricity extend for longer than usual, the bathrooms become useless. Within the first hour, all the cubicles fill up with empty bottles of water and the toilet bowls flood with human waste. That place becomes so filthy that there is practically no way anyone can bring themselves to come close. So there is no chance anyone is going to sit on one of the toilets, close their eyes, and dump. When the toilets are in this state the prisoners are forced to find new locations. Their search leads them to the area behind the water tanks, behind Tunnel P, and even in the sewage canal. These places pile up with rancid faeces, seeping deep into the spaces. The smell is so vile that one feels ashamed to be part of the human species.

—

There is a trained engineer, a short man just beyond middle age with a round, bald head. His flat face is bright red, and greying hair grows out from both temples in an orderly manner. He is possibly the most respectable man in Fox Prison. This expert in engineering is known throughout the prison for being an honourable person, a true leader, a businessman, a bankrupt merchant – in general, a skilled expert who knows exactly what he is doing. We call him The Prime Minister.

He is a respected family man whose role in the family and among his kinfolk is a blessing from above. He has unconditional love for his daughters, a love more extraordinary than I've ever known or witnessed. He has a compassionate smile and he continues to express his fatherly instincts in the prison. He usually bestows this sensitivity on the younger prisoners. His kindness is unconditional and he is generous. He is a man of virtue.

He belongs to a special category of humans; for instance, one would feel ashamed to defeat him in a game of chess or backgammon. When such a special character enters the community, most people don't lie around as usual or spread out their legs in front of him. People are in most cases careful not to say something ill-mannered in such a person's presence. Even though he is so very righteous, having someone like him locked up in prison can be a nuisance; it is hard to behave oneself in the presence of The Prime Minister.

His incarceration is a contradiction. In the chaotic and conflicting landscape of the prison, he is a man in search of routine and formal behaviour – in a prison that does not tolerate any sense of collective responsibility or propriety, not even a scent of ethical order. Inevitably, the presence of a principled individual, like The Prime Minister, someone disciplined in enacting his principles, becomes hard to bear. The Prime

Minister, our esteemed intellectual, himself becomes intolerable. The other prisoners become so fed up with The Prime Minister, this educated and orderly personality, that they dedicate more attention to the younger guys among them.

The Prime Minister has a face distinguished by sagging grooves; they seem to reflect some bad events, things he has had to live through. One can tell from his skin and his physique that he is a man who has led a privileged life. For this reason, some wrinkles seem out of place. Grooves on his face, the result of a series of incidents he had absolutely no control over. Tracks on his face, that have unwillingly and unknowingly appeared. He has lost everything he worked for throughout his life. Completely out of his power. A downfall that drove him to traverse a path, a journey with untold dangers . . . dangers unfamiliar to a man of his status. There is a pronounced contradiction between his character and that needed to endure a sea odyssey full of tribulations.

A distinguished man inside a harsh prison: The Prime Minister and Manus Prison exist as opposites.

The Prime Minister finds himself in an environment where he now has to wait in line for hours to get food. Or he has to endure a great deal of hardship just for a simple visit to the toilet. For sure, it is hard for all the staff and management to comprehend seeing The Prime Minister, a respected figure, standing in the toilet queue wearing his baggy clothes; it is hard to reconcile this scene with someone who once commanded respect from his employees. This is a truth that his daughters must now contend with – the fact that their father is incarcerated in Manus Prison. You see, their love for him was always associated with his status, when he occupied a position of dignity.

It is even possible that he finds those around him intolerable. The room directly opposite his is occupied by Maysam The Whore.

Two personalities, two complete opposites. At the same time, he still maintains his aura of superiority and gravitas, even though in reality he is a failed manager. He maintains that image, so much so that even Maysam The Whore remains respectful towards him.

The Prime Minister, an eminent person, doesn't seem the type to migrate. It seems as if he popped up mistakenly in Manus Prison. So this honourable Prime Minister has shy and habituated guts and has to shit right at a certain hour. Sometimes he calculates and plans with precision, as he is used to doing, so he ends up shitting out two days' worth. His shitting routine is well calculated and he is conscious of all the relevant details around him. But there are times when disciplined and organised people make computational errors and wind up stuck right there in a spot with no way forward and no way back – like a rock climber left hanging on a cliff face, where one slight move might result in a fall. And such a dilemma could occur on an overcrowded day . . . hot . . . at the height of tensions. One such case stands out: our noble figurehead The Prime Minister feels the full brunt of it. It is the worst possible situation for someone who has been granted the utmost respect.

He needs to go to the toilet right at the moment when the empty bottles of water and filth have piled up mountain-high inside the cubicles. A group of prisoners are standing along the walls hoping for the water to turn on. Our distinguished fellow, The Prime Minister, is in a lot of trouble. On the one hand, he can't enter one of the cubicles in front of dozens of sets of eyes watching the toilets – even if he decides to go ahead, there is nowhere to relieve himself. On the other hand, his guts are under so much pressure that he becomes frantic, like a wounded animal. Perhaps at that moment he is cursing his calculated plans. Perhaps he has controlled himself over a two-day period so he wouldn't need to journey over to the cubicles. However, when he absolutely has to go, the water cuts out. Perhaps he has eaten too much. It is also possible that he has acquired diarrhoea due to drinking bad water.

But all this is meaningless at this moment – it makes no difference to his situation. It is important that The Prime Minister, our respected intellectual, finds a place to do his business and then pull up his pants before anyone sees. Sometimes a particular area becomes too full of people, so much so that the volume is too much for the eyes to bear, so much so that all the restrictions of social etiquette fly out the window. The Prime Minister, our important intellectual, shouldn't lose the opportunity. He loses the opportunity even though he is moving through and searching every remote spot of the prison.

Maysam The Whore describes all this afterwards with a lot of flair and pomp to a group of prisoners. That bastard . . . the whole time that the distinguished Prime Minister is running around like a chook with his head cut off – running everywhere in a panic – Maysam The Whore is chasing him around. People like Maysam The Whore always have a strong intuition for these kinds of things. So the moment when the prison falls into crisis before our eyes, he goes out searching for the most spectacular and unique subject possible: in this case, the respected Prime Minister taking a shit in an isolated corner. No doubt, Maysam The Whore engages in this cat-and-mouse game with great enthusiasm. This is clear when he narrates the scene using all his talents for those other prisoners; he gets so worked up that he is crying tears of laughter.

Maysam The Whore says that in the end our renowned expert finds a spot behind one of the tanks, drops his pants with no regard for any set of norms, with no regard for any social customs . . . at that moment, with no regard for anything that he has until then identified with . . . and he shits out two heaps of dark, rotten faeces. Maysam The Whore tries his hardest to describe the scene in all its details; he even goes to extremes to describe the colour of the stool. The audience of prisoners listening to Maysam The Whore are left with feelings of discomfort as they sit on their seats. It is a mixed atmosphere, an atmosphere of shame, of laughter, and of humiliation. One or two can't tolerate the extent of the ridicule in the satirical account. In anger they leave the gathering. However, others don't feel the same and don't object to Maysam The Whore. Respect is replaced with pity, but the other prisoners can't stop thinking about the scene. They put up with the profound inappropriateness of the whole thing because the tale is particularly entertaining.

The reputation of the esteemed Prime Minister is completely ruined; it is as though his dead body has been laid out on the ground for the community to walk all over and pummel with kicks. But in reality this scene is, purely and simply, a profound humiliation, a demoralising degradation not exclusive to our educated role model. Once again, Maysam The Whore has become a mirror for the suffering in the prison. Covered by the theatrical mask of satire and comedy, the prisoners try to avoid facing up to the realities of overwhelming humiliation. There is no refuge, no sanctuary available except faith in Maysam The Whore and his ludicrous mockery. This is possibly the simplest method for confronting the humiliation.

The prison dictates that the prisoners accept, to some degree, that they are wretched and contemptible – this is an aspect of the system designed particularly for them. An objective of The Kyriarchal System: no-one has the right to express the very human feeling of munificence. This is in contrast to the character of someone like our dignified friend, The Prime Minister.

The prisoners feel a kind of masochism: a joy as a result of the humiliation. By joining in with Maysam The Whore they belittle The Prime Minister, our noble thinker. In reality, they are acting in accordance with The Kyriarchal System, and they are also demeaning themselves. The prisoners unconsciously identify with the shattered character of the distinguished Prime Minister – their sense of self re-imagined in another. As a result, the ridiculing and joking coincide with humiliation and shame. On the one hand, they feel a kind of liberation in the defamation of the renowned expert. Yet Maysam The Whore's antics and words destroy something precious. Without having a good grasp of their own emotions at this time, the prisoners derive even more enjoyment from that which Maysam has decimated. They have become tired of having to revere the distinguished Prime Minister every time they see him or to watch what they say around him.

Under the aegis of Maysam The Whore, they kick the corpse; payback for making them play out long periods as obedient subjects, and for the incursion of a superficial etiquette into their social interactions. The Prime Minister, our important intellectual, and his behaviour, are instantiations of lawfulness, and this has to be destroyed. The prisoners can only tolerate one set of laws: The Kyriarchal System eliminates any other code. The soul of the prison won't entertain ethical norms that pertain to a society beyond the prison; norms are shoved aside, and it is Maysam The Whore who pillages them.

Maysam The Whore tears apart all the barriers that restrict and guide social engagement. For the weary prisoners this is a breath of fresh air. As the months go by, the prison establishes a principle: it makes no difference where a prisoner is from, what he has done for a living, his social status, or his age. In terms of the social dynamics of Manus Prison, life in this environment is uniform. Ultimately, everyone is reduced to one social standing.

The prison is a region of repetition and uniformity in which the tiniest diversion from routine becomes the talk of the compound. In a short time word will get around the whole prison. Even those in the next prison will hear about it. Following up on the news in the prison is a simple way to pass the time. If these kinds of events involve a disciplined and principled person like our own honest Prime Minister, they will spread all over at the speed of light.

On ordinary days no-one ever really sees the respected Prime Minister going to the toilet, but on this day a new story emerges, an unprecedented and novel tale. This narrative circulates within the prison, a place that is usually monotonous and morose.

In the imagination of the prisoners, the honourable Prime Minister not only shits all over his principles but also shits all over the identity he has established in the prison. The incident is so profoundly incongruous with their social conditioning that the prisoners interpret it as the virtuous Prime Minister turning a large sector of the prison into a cesspool. The next day he looks like a toad struggling among frogs inside a stinking swamp of filth.

Two weeks later the news hits the prison like a bomb. The kind and gentle Prime Minister has left the prison. He requested a transfer to Oscar Prison. Everyone is surprised that the authorities accepted this – it is the first and only time it has ever happened. Then one day, after a short time at Oscar Prison, he left early in the morning, without saying goodbye to anyone, without saying goodbye to the young guys he had befriended. He had to go back, he had to accept refoulement – his family was in danger, they could not survive alone, they needed protection. One of the officers smiles as he relays the news, and says that, just before leaving, The Prime Minister had said that he wanted to return to his daughters.

—

Still no word from the lawyers who are supposed to visit Manus Prison. But some anonymous Australian individual has told one of the prisoners that there will be no need for a lawyer or a court hearing. He said the prisoners will be freed in less than two months. A wave of happiness swells through the prison.

The jungle behind the fence on the western side of Fox Prison has been razed. A team of labourers continue working under the heat of the sun. Shovels and picks have now reached the main field. The land seems to have been flattened. Over the other side, labourers are causing a ruckus and changing the position of large metal containers – white containers – and moving them towards the clearing. What are they in the process of building? Maybe a dormitory for the officers. Maybe a runway. Maybe . . .

8

—

Queuing as Torture: Manus Prison Logic /
The Happy Cow

A twisted, interlocking chain of hungry men /
Bodies mutate under the burning sun /
Heads in an oven fired by the sun /
Undergoing sickening transformations /
A long line of men of different heights, weights, ages and colours.

Days in the prison begin with the commotion of long queues – long,
pulverising queues. Hungry prisoners rush out of their sweaty, sticky
beds early in the morning, and like bees they swarm the tent that
makes up the dining area. In this instance, hungry actually means
starving. Once dinner is over, no-one can find anything else to eat.
In the dead of night, the smell of hunger wafts through the entire
prison. No-one is allowed to take even one potato from the dining
area. Anything that can be eaten has to be eaten right there under
the tent. It is the last chance to fill their stomachs, stomachs that take
over from the mind, stomachs with full authority over the body.

At the front of the dining area always stand a few grim and brainless G4S guards. They focus their gaze in a way that feels like a stop-and-search on anyone who exits the tent. If a pocket shows the slightest bulge, the guards order a Papu to frisk the prisoner. Part of the strategy to totally control the body. The Papu shakes his head in disapproval while he searches all the pockets, the lower legs, the torso and then under the arms. At times this activity results in the discovery of a single potato or a crushed piece of meat. When the Papus find something, they pick it up as if it has come out of the rubbish bin. The Australian G4S guard reminds the prisoner again: 'Taking food out is against the rules.'

Young men stand in the sun for hours, queuing for dirty, poor-quality food. The meat is like pieces of car tyre. Jaws struggle to chew the badly cooked meat.

The prisoners are aware that at the start of the queue in front of the tent, a few G4S guys sit on chairs and order groups of five to enter the dining area. The Manus Prison Logic is about domination.

Domination: five people need to leave the dining area so that five people can take their places. The community has to wait until five people leave, and then the officer can control the next five with his finger, giving permission to enter. We are like puppets on a string, put in motion with the flick of a finger. Every mind is caught up in a process, a process that has become normalised. *A domesticating process.*

The officer himself doesn't have any autonomy or control over his own fingers, not even over the way he chooses to sit. Everything is micromanaged and mechanical. The prison regulates the quantities of things and limits the time. A totally mechanical and prescriptive process has been put in place:

The logic of five /

Five people follow on from five people /

Then the officer turns to five people on their way out /

Next, five people /

The automated finger signals five people /

Another five enter /

Five people to replace five people /

Five enter, sitting on five chairs at the beginning of the queue /

The number five /

Five chairs /

Five chairs prepared at the beginning of the queue /

The rest wait, standing in line /

Everything is reduced to the number five.

Sometimes the officer in charge of entry, instead of signalling with a single finger, signals with all five fingers.

Human agency is subdued by the number five.

The queue is a replica of a factory production line. Total discipline. Calculated and precise. The first stage is at the end of the line – a place covered by an awning, a place from which no-one can tell where the queue ends. The queue makes a turn behind the rooms occupied by Sri Lankans. After at least half an hour, one arrives at the bend and realises that the queue extends for another thirty metres.

Five individuals with full stomachs /

Five individuals leave the tent /

Again, the logic of five.

The queues are a series of trucks loading up as they work inside a fiery excavation site, inside the inferno of a strip-mining pit. Empty, then full.

At the bend, hungry prisoners experience a mix of significant emotions. Joy and pain, hope and hopelessness. Arriving at the bend is an achievement, but the prisoner leaves the shelter of the shade and enters the section under the burning sun. This means preparing to face the sun, a sun that penetrates each cell with its stinging rays. Like thousands of hot needles pricking into thousands of interconnected spots. Witnessing the queue from the point at the head of the bend reminds the prisoner of the difficult path still to be endured.

Arriving at the bend, however, evokes a little feeling of celebration, a little feeling of hope. The prisoner realises that he is there, realises that position right there and then, realises that the stage involving the bend has passed. He is one stage closer to food. A thirty-metre trip ahead, but now the prisoner has no choice but to move along, stuck to the wall.

The queue forms parallel to the wall, in total sun. Hot and merciless. But there is a small overhang that stretches out to cover a medium-sized person's shoulders. It projects a narrow shadow just over the heads of the prisoners. The prisoners are forced to protect themselves from the heat of the sun by moving up close against the wall. In this position, if they move a little, the sun will bear down on their bare heads and necks. Parts of the shoulders are still exposed to direct sunlight, still exiled across the other side of the border of sun and shade.

The problem doesn't end here because the queue forms over a concrete surface of thirty centimetres, a surface that stands half a metre above ground level. It looks like a step positioned high and extended, a step on which the prisoners climb, standing up there, stuck up against the wall. A high, extended step, thirty centimetres wide, half a metre high, with groups of men standing on top. Fear of the sun's heat, scrambling just to stand there under a narrow piece of shade – this causes the queue to form straighter than any other. Other queues, in other places, outside the prison, form like a chain, loose and lax, possibly a small curve, possibly a large curve. But this part of the queue takes the form of a straight line. The queue is cramped. The desire for food causes people to push towards the front, extremely hungry people just reacting instinctively. Bodies are grafted together here, much more than in other queues.

Groups of men are up against the wall /

Groups of men are embedded into the wall /

The spectacle of the prison queue is a raw and palpable reinforcement of torture.

Throughout the line a few G4S guards supervise. These G4S guys are distinctive, unlike the others at the front of the line or those with other duties in the tent. These few people stand in the shade of two tanks of water opposite the queue. They do nothing but stare at the queue, a queue moulded into the wall. They do absolutely nothing. The purpose of their presence is simple: to announce that the queue has a master. They are like shepherds guiding a herd of sheep down an obvious path, a path they are following anyway. At times the guards take notes in their little pads, probably out of habit. Or they communicate through their walkie-talkies. However, some of their actions are relatively kind. For instance, there are times when one of them carts a box of bottled water from the dining area and places it next to the queue. The bottles of water have become so warm that drinking them troubles the stomach.

At the same time, there are always those among us who are like stray dogs looking to pounce and steal a piece of meat; they try to jump to the front of the queue from behind the tanks. They have a strong sense for this kind of skilful leap and know exactly when to execute it, at a time when few will notice. Even if people notice, they are so quick that there is no chance, for instance, that someone at the end of the queue could recognise them – or, in any case, have the opportunity to register and recollect. The direction of the leap is calculated. It is carried out so the face remains anonymous. From the end of the queue, they appear to be phantoms – dark figures that pass by for just one moment.

The leap occurs in a spot at the head of the queue. Like hopping up on the rung of a ladder. When the leap is performed successfully, the perpetrator stands up in a way that signals that nothing out of the ordinary has occurred. The shoulders, the face, look exactly like everyone else in the queue. This is an outright deception. It requires artistry.

There's a massive difference between someone who simply lies in words and someone who lies convincingly. Those individuals work their bodies to convey impressions, for example: 'I'm just so exhausted', or, for instance, 'That sun is such a bastard' or 'What a long line', or 'Oh god, I'm exhausted, I've been waiting in this queue for ages'.

These guys are so skilful that one can hardly tell the difference between them and the others who have been standing under the sun for a long period. And separating them from the queue usually results in physical conflict. They don't respond to verbal protest, so someone needs to approach them at the front of the line, identify them, and then kick or punch them out of the line. For a prisoner standing upright and already exhausted, engaging in such an act requires double the energy. Every now and then it ends up in a brawl.

Interestingly, most conflicts end without interference by G4S guards. A bit of swearing and some harmless kicking and punching, and the whole thing is over in a few short minutes.

One interesting point is that the violators themselves also accept that they are low-lifes and immature individuals, juveniles with no honour.

Behaving like a juvenile is a successful way to acquire food quickly. There are others who get food to their mouths, but are respectful and just in doing it. These people wait hours before the food is distributed. They occupy the head of the queue, the starting point of the line. The only superior quality they have over others is their ability to wait for hours on end with their chunky asses, wait for hours without moving, sitting on stiff chairs or standing in the sun. They are people with nerves of steel, indifferent as mules.

Imagining this is difficult: how can a human stay put and wait for hours without leaving that spot? How can he just stay there, not moving an inch? I always imagine them with the features and forms of domestic animals. It's bizarre how their personalities are reduced to gluttonous pack animals. The personality of each one reflects heritage with the mule; it is all over their faces, no integrity, no dignity. Cows. Greedy and gluttonous cows. Leeches. Hanging like leeches. Behaving like professional beggars.

I admit that I don't feel comfortable with their presence in the prison. I see them ahead of me and a desire for violence erupts inside me. If I had more confidence in my muscles I might make my way through to the front of the line to beat them up. It isn't as if I am scared to fight with those who stand way down the front of the queue. No. It just isn't worth the trouble. Also, I am sure I don't have the strength necessary to sort things out, to assert myself, to completely beat them down.

So instead I imagine a man with powerful muscles. Calm and collected, he steps from the queue and announces to all the men that he will be enforcing justice. The men – even those at the front of the queue – look on with curiosity.

But this performance is not for them. Not even for The Mules. It is designed to grab the attention of the officers standing in the shade of the tanks. They huddle together, looking on keenly. I imagine the powerful man walking purposefully to the front of the queue. His strut entices and intensifies the curiosity of the onlookers. When he reaches the front of the queue, The Mules stare at him with confusion.

The officers by the tanks start to relax, reassured that they are not the target. Their huddle loosens. Yet all focus remains on the powerful man. Suddenly he takes the neck of the first person in the queue. And lifts him off the ground. Then, with one well-placed kick, he sends the first Mule flying to land behind the tanks. The powerful man works his way through the line methodically, casting out individuals one after another . . .

But this is just a fantasy, something I draw from the depths of my hungry guts. I am no such powerful man. I accept that the other men are heftier than me. I accept that they are thieves who have taken everything from me. At times, my imagination even makes them out to be lions, whereas I'm a lowly fox, frail and weak, waiting to scavenge their leftovers.

This is the reality of the situation. The system is designed in such a way that people who enter the dining area ahead of the others can eat more desirable food, and sometimes even treat themselves to a piece of fruit. But the people at the end of the line find nothing but junk left to eat. The cooks follow instructions from the head chefs. Right at the beginning they open a box of beautifully coloured cake along with trays of fruit for the first comers. When the first groups leave the dining area, the cake disappears and only fruit is issued. As time passes, the better fruit is replaced with poor-quality fruit, and the quality becomes increasingly worse. Finally, people in the second half of the queue are left with only black pieces of meat and rice that seems to have been made using seawater.

The queues have agency and they establish something: any person in the prison who behaves in a more despicable and brutish manner has a more comfortable lifestyle. As the period in prison increases, this kind of justice transforms into a principle and more and more prisoners try to coordinate themselves with the culture of these individuals, the few people at the front of the line.

Certainly, the cooks could distribute the food in a way that the pieces of cake reach everyone. Or at least reserve some for the first group and some for the last group. And perhaps keep some for those in the middle. Or, for example, the cake could be allocated to those in front and the fruit for those at the back. Or the other way around. Or even nothing at all for anyone; that is, the same situation for everyone. Or reserve some for the front group over a few days, and then for the last group over a few days. Perhaps the best, the most complete, form of justice would involve no-one at all determining who gets what. But this is not the case. The best stuff always goes to the first served – The Mules, that is.

By adding a few extra staff members, they could speed up the distribution of food. Or if they were not willing to do that, at least they could erect another tent so that the queues wouldn't be so agonising. But the prison system means that the one who desires food has to suffer.

Someone like me is always the last to enter the dining area, and month after month I miss out on getting any fruit or dessert. There I am, just a frail fox. This is the most precise description. Yes.

Just one frail fox /
Staring at that queue /
From afar /
Staring at that queue /
Over and over /
And over again.

I circle the prison and then stare at that queue again and, finally, after coming and going a few times, I position myself at the end of the line, which has reduced by then. I fill my stomach with whatever is available, and then follow with another cigarette.

Starvation is a drill /
It drills down into the stomach /
Then it drills down into the mind /
It drills down into all the nerves /
It drills down and makes holes /
In the end it just drills all the way down.

During these days I realise that I am being worn out. I realise this with all the cells in my body. At times I ask why my brain is unable to use the forces of my body to acquire something sweet.

My body has an extraordinary burning desire for dessert. I need something sweet.

Being so hungry, completely starving, one loses sight /

My eyes are two violet orbs with swollen veins /

My vision is opaque /

I can see only black /

I visualise my whole body as a skeleton /

My being embodied as bone /

A skeleton left wandering /

Taking feeble steps /

But I visualise a community /

A community of people standing at the front of the queue /

A community of flesh /

A community of satisfied guts /

A community the sight of which I can't digest /

A community of people whose mouths are always open.

—

Competition arises, but competition always ends in the victory of a single individual: the person known as The Cow. This man is always the first person to enter the dining area, and this is the reason for his nickname. He is thirty-something years old, with a big head, a skull like an old hyena, a short neck like the rough stump of a chestnut oak tree, and lascivious eyes, broad and elongated. This is a guy whose suppressed libido is redirected to his guts and, ultimately, between his jaws. It is remarkable how he accepts the nickname The Cow without protest, in fact with pride; he doesn't show the slightest resistance.

Some of us wake up really early and, after a short stroll through the toilet complex, we go straight in the direction of the queue. He sits on the very first chair. He locks his arms together and sits there passively, staring directly ahead for hours without moving from his spot. Other prisoners slowly and calmly arrive at various times to occupy the chairs lined up after him. The first seat in the queue has become reserved just for him – the competition among the others does not affect him. This individual seems to transcend the queue. Every day, at the same hour, he waits. There he is with his disproportionate body, wearing his ill-fitting and ridiculous clothes, sitting on his regular chair, looking like a huge torso, waiting for hours, listening for the cooks to announce meal-time, listening for the lids lifting off the pots.

The officers give orders and the queue begins to move. Then The Cow goes into action and invades the dining area. Every day, he holds this record. His attention is occupied with the movements of the cooks and the arrival of pots of food, and he also observes the way the G4S guards settle into their positions. He gobbles up his breakfast, and then a few hours later he appears back in that same spot. This ceremony of feasting is repeated in the same fashion at dinnertime. The presence of this guy and his extraordinary appetite causes bewilderment. But in the end he just audaciously withstands their contemptuous gazes. His daily plan of action is tenacious.

As time passes, all the others get used to the presence of The Cow and acknowledge the significance of his place. His persistence, determination and tenacity in maintaining this routine, and his resistance to the hurtful jibes deriding his reputation, gain him a special kind of notoriety and even a kind of popularity among the prisoners. Everywhere he goes, the prisoners taunt and mock him even though they know he won't react. The Cow's feelings can't be hurt, nor does he react violently; he even plays along with them so that they can ridicule him more skilfully. He seems to actually take pleasure in the way a word can be moulded into mockery. It seems that the more insolent and contemptuous the words used to caricature him, the prouder he becomes. This is why I always use 'The Cow' to describe him; I call him The Cow without hesitation and without reservation, because he really seems to accept the role.

His behaviour in other areas of the prison is a sight. He ambles around the rows of bathrooms, his towel wrapped around his naked body. His legs are chunky, hairless – his lower legs have a particular kind of sheen. Like a toad in winter, terrified of the cold, he is compelled to hunt for somewhere inviting. Distrust in his eyes, a battle between fear and stress in his eyes, glances of suspicion from his eyes, glances in all directions. Sometimes it is as though he is a blind mouse, acting with speed and agility. He is everywhere, every smell, every corner, everything that attracts his fancy; he is everywhere. He seems to be suffering from an inexplicable shortcoming, an unconscious struggle, trying to fill a void. It is as if this existential emptiness is concentrated in a second faculty for thought: his enormous volume of guts.

While roaming around he usually carries a washtub full of clothes under his arm. No washing machine can be found anywhere in the prison, so the prisoners are forced to wash their clothes in plastic washtubs. Random concrete areas beside the bathrooms, like small pools, are appropriated for laundry. The prisoners wash their clothes in the midst of chaos and commotion and they hang them out to dry on the metal railings. Once a week every person in the prison can get hold of some laundry powder, if they wait in line to collect it.

When The Cow finishes his breakfast, he departs from the end of one of the halls with his washtub and his famous towel. He starts scraping his slippers along the floor in the direction of the bathrooms. He walks as if he is a watchman for some premises where sleep has been suddenly disrupted by a sound, forcing him to open the door. A morning scowl increases the wrinkles on his sunburnt face. He walks as if someone has just forced him out of the showers. When he gets close to the bathrooms he pauses for a moment – looking around in all directions. He checks in on the first bathroom available – usually it is the filthiest. Like a blind mouse sniffing out every corner he checks each bathroom. He starts swearing and roars out loud. Once he realises that everyone is aware of his presence, and after a suitable bathroom becomes vacant, he enters.

Is his delay in choosing bathrooms the result of the busy queues? Or because he wants to find the cleanest bathroom? No. I'm certain that for The Cow it makes no difference where he rinses his body. For him, only one thing is important. He wants everyone to pay attention to the fact that he wants to take a shower. He wants everyone to experience the inconvenience he causes. He wants everyone to know he is there. He seems to construct his sense of self through disturbing others.

He disappears into one of the cubicles for some time. The sound of objections and protests from others who want to use the bathroom increases. He exits with a very different look on his face. Every now and then he creates a new style with his thin beard and moustache. You see, someone like him never has to go without basic supplies like razors, which are rare here. Even the washtub he carries all the time is a luxury item because only he and a few others have been able to withstand the long queue to obtain them. When he opens the bathroom door, he erupts with laughter. The people bashing on the door just moments ago now encounter an individual with a fascinating appearance, emerging like he is stepping on to the stage of some ludicrous theatre. They respond by bursting with hilarity. For a few moments they comment on The Cow's new look in the most vulgar ways possible, greeting him with amusement. Every person tries to create the funniest account of his latest appearance and share it with the others.

Most of the time The Cow makes new designs out of his moustache. Sometimes his long, thin moustache resembles that of a feral city cat that has just lifted its head out of a sack of charcoal. His pointy and slick moustache spreads over his flat, round face; it is a hilarious combination. His life is full of minor activities of this kind, not to forget his defining role: leader of the queue.

—

Who knows, maybe The Cow has the best methods for enduring the prison as the rest of us try to get by on near starvation. Living within the pointless cycle of three courses: breakfast, lunch and dinner. These periods of the day are interlinked with humiliation. In its own way, breakfast is the most problematic meal because the time between dinner and breakfast is so long, so long that the stomach contracts.

Every night the smell of starvation circulates from one end of the prison to the other. When I say the smell of starvation, I'm not making things up. I believe starvation has a smell. A smell that is wedded to our instincts at the deepest level. It makes human beings act like wolves in the wild. When human beings are starving they are completely capable of sinking their horse-like teeth into the belly of one of their own, devouring with the fervour of an animal.

Breakfast, more than any other meal, is a twisted game. On many occasions there is practically nothing available to eat; nothing can be found. A few officers sit on chairs. After they tick off our numbers, they direct us to a vast array of empty trays and chefs fitted out like professionals. When we reach them, we realise nothing is provided, nothing to eat. The trays are empty, licked clean. When a prisoner gestures to his hungry stomach in anger and yells out that he is hungry, he receives the following polite answer: 'Unfortunately, breakfast has run out.' When that prisoner, now in a rage, screams at the top of his voice asking the reason why the chefs are standing in their positions, he just receives another polite answer smack in his furious face: 'Unfortunately, we have been ordered to stand in these positions for another hour. I apologise, we are fulfilling the duty assigned to us. We have no idea.'

This situation only affects the individuals in the second half of the queue and those few poor, miserable guys right at the end. A disconcerting thought plagues the mind of the prisoner: no doubt The Cow and his friends have devoured all the breakfast. The prisoner walks away bearing that feeling of resentment within himself.

At times breakfast consists of a piece of bread and peanut butter. When these two things combine, when the prisoner spreads the peanut butter on the bread and then swallows it, the food blocks the throat. The prisoner becomes like a hungry chook trying to eat pieces of dry dough. When the oil from the peanut butter mixes with bits of bread and saliva, it sticks just like glue. To swallow a morsel requires a number of attempts.

At times the cooks express a small amount of generosity and pour half a glass of milk for every prisoner. The cook is so stingy and calculated and careful not to exceed the halfway line when pouring the milk into the small plastic cups that he is like a woman from the village extracting milk from a cow. He pours out some milk, lifts the cup, takes a really close look at it, and, if he concludes that the amount he has poured is below the level that The Kyriarchal System has determined as exactly right, then he will add a few extra drops. The cooks have become so skilful that they usually fill exactly half the cup in one go. If it so happens that a cook miscalculates and the milk exceeds half a cup, he puts the cup of milk aside and prepares another with more precision.

I don't understand why he doesn't have plans for the cup of milk that contains a little extra. For instance, why not empty the extra milk into another cup or container? There is a stupidity in this practice, and by the end of breakfast the few cups of milk that are filled a little over halfway accumulate at the side of the counter. At the end of the shift the cook throws out all the spoiled milk. The precision exercised by the cook when throwing out the milk also has a particular logic. An officer stands beside him, whose duty is to be an extra set of eyes to ensure that the cook has not issued any cups of milk that are over half full. It is perplexing. The officers fulfil this duty with such concentration that one is left thinking that the milk must be medicinal or chemical – that is the extent of the care they take.

But then our understanding of this scenario suddenly collapses. On rare occasions the generosity of the cooks peaks. On these occasions they pour a full cup of milk for each prisoner. I mean, exactly double the usual amount. Occasionally, they pour only a quarter of a cup of milk. In all these cases the cook completes the task with precision, careful not to pour one drop more or less than the limit prescribed. As he watches this duty carried out, the prisoner is reassured that this white substance is actually milk because it is poured in one run. He is sure because if some artificial substance has been fused with it – or if it isn't milk at all – then why would they pour a full cup this time?

One cannot forget about this issue; that is, is the cup filled with milk or is it half milk and half drugs? Or, conversely, is it possible that all the cups are full of just milk: the full cups, the half-full cups, and the quarter-full cups? Or could none of them possibly contain milk at all? What does this mean? Whether they pour a full cup, or whether they pour half a cup, or whether they pour a quarter of a cup, one consideration prevails. That is the precision and care exercised by the cook, and the officer always on hand to ensure the cook completes his duty in every respect.

It completely baffles the prisoner how this total control is not practised with other drinks such as fruit juice. Serving of other drinks is regular and routine, so much so that when they give the prisoners fruit juice it is always a full cup. The cook performs this without thinking, without paying attention to what he is doing. Like a person going about their day-to-day business at home, like he is preparing a glass of fruit juice for his partner on a pleasant spring morning.

Another difference is worth noting. Often they serve warm fruit juice, but occasionally it is cold. This is really significant for the prisoners because there is no water-cooling machine available in the prison, so on hot days they are forced to drink lukewarm water all day. When the fruit juice is served cold, a prisoner expresses joy and looks at his cup over and over again. Then, with calm and care, to multiply the pleasure, in a few successive gulps the prisoner quenches his thirst. The chill of the fruit juice becomes ingrained in the prisoner's memory; its significance remains even while he has access only to lukewarm water. The dream of sipping cold water grows stronger, greater.

A recipe for torment: long nights of starvation, hungry

stomachs, empty guts, and the multifaceted, twisted interaction with the cooks as they serve milk, fruit juice and the various foods. Even the most shrewd prisoners are incapable of unravelling these entanglements. It is impossible to find a prisoner who has not struggled to unriddle the complexities of the queuing system and the food situation to which it leads. I dare say that the mind of every prisoner is caught up with these perplexities.

At times a particularly clever prisoner might decipher a kind of order in the system. For instance, he will say to himself, 'Very good, on Sunday these guys serve us a full cup of milk, then every weekday they serve half a cup, and Saturday a quarter of a cup. The following week they serve a full cup on Monday and Tuesday instead of Sunday, half a cup on Wednesday to Saturday, and a quarter on Sunday.' Or he'll reach some convoluted formula for the serving of fruit juice. In uncovering this, according to this switched-on prisoner, a marvellous truth is disclosed.

Under the illusion that he has worked it out, he will even try to prove to all his friends that he has decoded the system. Then all of a sudden his calculations are debunked: he enters the dining area and stands opposite the breakfast – the likes of which he has never even eaten when free. Various kinds of fruit juice, milk, pistachios, mushrooms, butter, jam, honey, baked beans. All designed beautifully. And a few other things. But also that peanut butter.

Hopelessness arises when the prisoner realises that his discovery about the order of things is wrong. He continues trying to unlock the logic of the system, looking for solutions in his surroundings. This induces perpetual questioning. He searches for the answers to the questions that plague his mind, searches for them in the eyes of the cooks, searches for them in the eyes of the officers. Maybe there are differences in the personalities of the head chefs. Maybe some officers are less brutal.

The schedule for the people working in the prison is based on rotation. The officers and cooks work two-week shifts and then leave the island to be replaced by a fresh group. No-one works more than two weeks at a time. The exception is when the system falls into crisis. Then they have to work a few days extra. In these situations the prisoners analyse many of the prison regulations and think that the rules might change with the transition of teams.

In relation to breakfast and other meals, some think that Team 1, or the head chef for Team 1, fills the cups a little more than others. Or provides a little extra fruit juice. Or that the quality of his food is better. Or that the officers from Team 1 are not as harsh in implementing the rules of the prison. This perspective doesn't develop without good reason. The differences are real. Team 1 officers *are* less brutal. But as soon as this perspective is consolidated in the minds of the prisoners, suddenly, to everyone's surprise, the officers in Team 2 transform their mode of engagement and become friendlier. In turn, Team 1 becomes more brutish.

In sum, a twisted system governs the prison, a deranged logic that confines the mind of the prisoner, an extremely oppressive form of governance that the prisoner internalises, a system that leaves the prisoner simply trying to cope.

Trying to understand the conditions of micro-control and macro-control /
Trying to understand the perpetual flux of everything /
Trying to avoid tipping over the edge /
Trying to avoid tipping into insanity.

———

Every prisoner is convinced that they or their group are *the* critical theorists of the systemic foundation, the chief analysts of the system's architecture. But the greatest difficulty is that no-one can be held accountable, no-one can be forced up against the wall and questioned, no-one can be interrogated by asking them, 'You bastard, what is the philosophy behind these rules and regulations? Why, according to what logic, did you create these rules and regulations? Who are you?'

No person who is a part of the system can ever provide an answer – neither the officers nor the other employees working in the prison. All they can say is, 'I'm sorry, I'm just following orders'. In reality, those who are apparently part of the system also have no idea what is going on. They just enter the prison for two weeks, doggedly carry out the rules and regulations, then leave the island.

The system can be summed up in one way: first, a condition of dependency is established, then that dependency is framed in the context of micro-control and macro-control govern-mentality – even though the interconnections vary. Eating is a necessity and prisoners have no choice but to hustle to meet this basic need. And this is the point, this is the tactic used to keep them in captivity. Like being caught in a spider's web, the harder you struggle, the more entangled you become.

Starvation has two objectives: to implement a variety of control mechanisms on the minds of prisoners, and to make the prisoners enmeshed and complicit in the system. The prisoner's stomach leads him to know the system. And after reacting with resistance, and going through draining, drawn-out phases of action in solidarity with others . . . nothing.

It leads nowhere /

Nothing /

No answers to his futile questions /

Nowhere /

Nowhere except the threshold of insanity.

He suffers through a form of oppression, the origins of which are hidden from him. Isn't it better to be just like The Cow and The Mules, to refrain from rebelling, to cooperate with the system? Yes. Maybe. This might be the simplest and easiest method. This method may reduce the suffering; it may mean there is less to endure. And this is exactly what the system is based on and is designed to accomplish.

To tame /

To produce fragments of metal /

A production line /

A factory /

We have become a replica of caged baby chickens /

The prison has become a replica of a chicken coop /

Modern /

Industrial.

The Kyriarchal System presents the prisoner with the blueprint. That's right. And that blueprint is manifested in The Cow. In simpler terms: whoever wants to endure less suffering must live like The Cow. Eat. Sleep. Don't come up with any questions.

You can't understand the system. Even the officers are ignorant. You shouldn't rebel. Just submit to the power of the rules and regulations. According to our basic needs:

- Every prisoner needs to eat.
- Every prisoner who smokes needs cigarettes.
- Every prisoner needs access to the phone sometimes.
- Every prisoner might fall ill and require medicine.

I imagine the intertwining rooms in the area behind the prison. The administrative quarters with employees wearing uniforms or formal clothes, sitting behind their desks, typing away regularly, writing daily reports – reports about the events within the prison. There are other employees, as well. Employees with large dossiers under their arms. They walk back and forth between the offices and halls. The regular sound of business shoes . . . tick, tick.

The longer the time in prison, the greater and more elaborate my imaginary office scene becomes. The rooms multiply to such an extent that I imagine a multi-level building behind the prison.

The top floor of this building is surely occupied by old men and women with white hair. They sit behind a slick, oval conference table. Formal meetings behind closed doors. Yes, these stylish old women, these stylish old men, they need to be confronted. Right in the middle of an official meeting, as they draw up plans for new rules and regulations, they must be confronted by suddenly opening the door and bashing down on the oval conference table. Right at that moment it is necessary to cry out, 'You bastards, you've been caught out! Where's your boss?' But, as usual, the big boss is nowhere to be found.

Whatever the question, whoever you ask within the prison, the answer is the same: 'The Boss has given orders.' Whenever a stubborn prisoner makes inquiries and finds The Boss of that individual who has said 'The Boss has given orders' and then confronts that person, that person also responds with 'The Boss has given orders'. It is just a pointless effort. All the rules, all the

211

regulations, and all the questions about those rules and regulations are all referred back to one person: The Boss. It is astonishing how The Boss also responds with 'The Boss has given orders'. A long chain ascending through the hierarchy.

The bureaucratic ranks are determined by relationships of power. Every boss is subordinate to another boss. And the superior boss is also subordinate to another boss. If one investigated this chain it would possibly lead to thousands of other bosses. All of them repeating the one thing: 'The Boss has given orders.'

As time drags on in the prison, the oppression inflicted by The Boss becomes more destructive, more violent. In a way, the notion of The Boss in our imagination becomes paler and paler, so much so that later on I don't even feel he is in that tall multistorey building behind the prison.

Perhaps The Boss has accompanied other bosses off the island to inhabit a larger building /

Off to a distant city /

Off to a distant land /

Off to a place beyond the ocean /

A place with thousands upon thousands of tall buildings /

A place right next to the parliament /

A place with women and men decked out even more stylishly /

All gathered around an oval conference table for a meeting /

There are certainly other wise old women and other wise old men in attendance /

Also sitting around the oval conference table /

A table with a red finish.

The system is now simpler. The officers write reports in notebooks. At the end of the day they are all transferred to the multistorey building behind the prison. Many extremely hardworking employees type up the notes. Finally they are summarised and formalised into an official dossier and delivered to the office for the bosses. Necessary decisions are made there and sent upstairs to the next floor. Other employees are deployed there, working on the dossiers. Subsequently, the whole dossier is summarised into a smaller dossier. Again, it is sent to the office for the bosses on that floor. Important decisions are made there, and then the dossier is transferred upstairs to the next floor. Once again, on the new floor similar activities are carried out . . . and then on again to the next floor up. And then again from there up to the next floor.

Just like that, the dossier garners an array of official approvals and multiple signatures from the bosses. With these it moves up higher and higher until it finally reaches the top floor and is placed on an oval conference table. When the dossier reaches the building in the remote city designated for the bosses of Manus, it arrives signed and sealed. Many employees there receive the dossier with anticipation. And so the dossier undergoes the same process through the multiple floors within this new building for the bosses. It is elevated higher and higher till it reaches the oval conference table of the boss of bosses. It is delivered directly to those stylish old women and stylish old men, the ones with the scent of perfume and cologne – delivered to those who are always resolute.

There are possibly other bosses there too. I don't know . . . maybe. Maybe old women and old men who are also wiser and more stylish. Maybe they hold meetings in another building. Perhaps thousands upon thousands of bosses are involved in imposing each

213

rule and regulation. No doubt the opposite process is also possible: the most boss-like of all bosses passes the orders down through the floors, over to Manus and finally, The Boss descends into the belly of the prison. In this case, instead of the dossiers decreasing in size – summarised into smaller and smaller dossiers – this time a minor decision increases in size – grows larger and larger – as it is delivered downward. This process continues until the decision reaches the prison. Along the way it becomes so convoluted that now it is impossible for any prisoner to understand it.

The rules and regulations are derived from an unknown source or developed using some esoteric rationale, and they always just hurl down on top of the prison, weighing down on the prisoner's psyche. There is no alternative. It is a priority that these rules and regulations are implemented precisely – and so with all his feelings of hopelessness, all a prisoner can do is simply smash his fist against a container wall, just bash against it hard, bash his fist against it in rage.

—

Based on mysterious logic, new rules and regulations are imposed every week for the cigarette queue – unfathomable, like the situation in the dining area and the other queues, driving everyone insane. The cigarette queue is arranged such that it coincides with the malaria-treatment queue. A few local women push a trolley stacked with boxes containing dozens of packets of cigarettes in the direction of the little office. As they walk they emanate conceit. They are the centre of attention, and they are also certain that they are carrying a valuable product, like a crew that drives the vehicle to transfer cash between banks. There is good reason for the prisoners to stare with enthusiasm at the boxes on the trolley right throughout that short trip, a distance of a few metres, from the gate to the small office. Good reason to listen to the song played out by the women's footsteps. Good reason for the longing. It must be so surreal for the women to sense the prisoners' captivation with them.

The trolley enters the small office through the back gate . . . clang, clang. The queue is bursting with tension. Then from behind the window of the small office, the women hand out one or two packets of cigarettes to each individual. They record each prisoner's number in a large logbook.

The small office is titled 'Shopping'. It would be better if it were called 'Tobacconist'. Every prisoner has a weekly twenty-five-point quota with which he can purchase three packets of smokes. Whatever he doesn't use for buying cigarettes he can, in theory, use for buying other things, such as lollies, biscuits, or a pen and notebook. But these items exist only on paper. Only cigarettes are delivered on the trolley. The prisoner can buy nothing but cigarettes. It isn't possible to save points. Every Monday, each prisoner's account is wiped. Even if someone doesn't purchase anything all, his remaining points are erased, and the next twenty-five points registered.

Even though he doesn't smoke, it is bizarre how The Cow is always the first in line again. An amazing sight. Maybe The Cow has discovered the best approach to life. He knows how valuable the smokes are, how desperate the inmates are to have them. The Cow queues and collects them so that he can use them for personal gain.

The cigarette queue has its own complexities. In the beginning, they sell loose smokes on the hour once every three days. Then every two days. Then after that every day. And on every one of these days, the time for distributing cigarettes fluctuates. So much so that sometimes the designated timeframe changes within an hour, sometimes within two hours, or within one-and-a-half hours. It isn't always the case, say, that this occurs from two o'clock to three o'clock, or from two to four. Sometimes it so happens that the small office opens at, let's say, nine or ten in the morning and everything is sold out by noon – then nothing goes on after midday. In the first week, the small office posts something on the window informing prisoners whether or not cigarettes are available that day. The notice also announces when to approach the counter of the small office.

It isn't as if one can spend all twenty-five points in one go. If one could, then it would be necessary to wait in line only once a week. Considering the circumstances in the prison, this could only be a good thing. But this issue can't escape the omnipresent gaze of the prison's Kyriarchal System. The rules and regulations dictate otherwise: 'Every individual request receives only two packets of cigarettes.' This means that every prisoner has to endure the torture of the queue twice a week at the very least.

The availability of smokes in the prison is like a gift that the system graciously bestows on the prisoners. First impressions are of amazement: Why are they giving prisoners cigarettes? How can a system grant the prisoner smokes when it is committed to capturing his range of basic needs and holding them captive, confining those basic needs within its own cage of violence? For instance, why doesn't the system enforce a rule from the very first day: 'Smoking is Prohibited'? How can it be that soccer balls are prohibited? But cigarettes are always available. As months go by it is clear to everyone that cigarettes are the lifeblood of the prison. No. It's more accurate to say they are the pulse of the prisoner. Whenever the system feels it is necessary, it tightens the arteries.

The system is so intelligent and experienced that it uses cigarettes as a tool when it wants to resolve a crisis. It can always use this tool against the prisoners. Or it uses it to drive recalcitrant prisoners to surrender their cause, give up their resistance to the rules and regulations. On Sundays when the smokers are bustling around, these prisoners are slowly but surely morphing into beggars. A cultural stratum of beggary forms in the prison, a subaltern group within the system. A new social chasm forms; new social divisions take shape. Prisoners who smoke become dependent on prisoners who do not.

The Cow and his friends have an excellent understanding of the spirit of the prison. They stuff their mattresses and pillows with packets of cigarettes; all the while, the smokers become increasingly addicted, beg more, and become weaker. The non-smoking prisoners aren't thinking of the consequences when they generously pass on cigarettes to their smoking friends. Social etiquette in the prison is being conditioned by smokes.

Another issue is the extent to which the Papus are crazy about cigarettes. This is their Achilles heel. One can win over their kind hearts by offering them a single cigarette. The cunning prisoner knows this and manipulates it. When a Papu sees a cigarette, joy sparkles in his eyes. He'll take it and smoke the whole thing, enjoying it over in a remote corner of the prison. For the Papus, generally, the act of creating smoke is like something sacred. This pertains to women and men, young and old. It is almost impossible to offer a Papu a smoke and have them decline it. It would be even more unlikely to hear them say they have quit. The Papu loves to smoke.

—

The queue for the phone is possibly the best place to make use of cigarettes because here the Papus are assigned more authority.

But once every few days an Australian officer – usually the most serious one – takes the identity cards off the Papus and enforces the rules, maintaining order himself. It's impossible to imagine the prison without the pandemonium of the telephone queues. These queues are definitely the most tumultuous. These queues attract more people than any other queue because they form in the telephone room area where the prison population from the three separate sections of Manus congregate.

The telephone room is a large room with seven or eight phones, but several are always broken. The room is right alongside the fences in the right-hand corner of the western wing of Fox Prison. This is where the employees have lopped the trees and are putting the containers in place, the ones brought on trucks. Morning to noon is designated for prisoners from Fox. The prisoners wait in line from early morning in front of the watchman's kiosk. Then, after the officer reads out the numbers, groups of a few people enter the telephone room. They launch in on the phones like hungry lions. They aren't aware which phones are busted. The attack has to be fierce; the prisoner only has time to test his phone quickly. If it is broken, he has to find another.

On many occasions two savvy prisoners realise their phones are broken right at the same time and at once set on the phone in the corner. One grabs the handset, one grabs the base. Then a tough struggle ensues, and the telephone might split in half, or the one who is less powerful might withdraw from the conflict. Like a wild creature that relinquishes its prey, he retreats to the corner and kicks and punches the wall. Some occasions end with sparks flying and fights starting. There are always a few heavy-built officers standing there ready to use violence to separate the two. Out of a group of seven or eight individuals, just a few find functioning telephones. Demoralised, with nerves on edge and nothing to show for his efforts, he returns to the prison. He accepts defeat, or begins to queue again. A wasted day.

The whole thing can be described like this: two officers stand at the front of the line, one of them completely vigilant and watching over the numbers as they pass the gate, another calling out the order of numbers at short intervals and matching the image on the identity cards with the person entering. Then the two officers behind the gate open the lock. After the group enters the telephone room the officers lock the gate again. The role of the officer standing there is to keep locking and unlocking the same gate the whole time he is on duty. Imagine after a day at work the partner of that same officer asking him something like, 'Sweetheart, what did you get up to today?' If he is at all honest he would answer, 'Darling, today from morning till afternoon I unlocked and locked a gate dozens of times, and now I can finally be in your arms.'

The system discriminates between the prisons. Sunday is scheduled for Oscar, Monday for Delta, Tuesday for Fox. But, at the moment, the prisoners from Fox can also access the phones every day from morning till noon. They have so much more time than those in the other prisons. This program is not permanent – there are some weeks, for instance, when the prisoners in Fox can't use the phones at all. The rules and regulations change weekly. Sometimes at the beginning of the week all the numbers are recorded on perplexing schedules. And it is confirmed that, for instance, MEG45 can make a call on Thursday morning at ten past eleven. But this is not always practised. At the start of the following week the rules and regulations might become less formal. Whoever stands in line earlier might get to call.

There are times when the telephone queue starts at nine o'clock in the morning. Sometimes at eight. And other times at ten. And telephone time expires maybe at midday. Sometimes at one o'clock. And other times at two. For weeks these rules and regulations seem not to change, but when the prisoners get used to them new rules and regulations suddenly emerge. More distortions within an incomprehensible system; a system that engulfs one's consciousness deep inside it. The system fragments and disorients the prisoner to such an extent that he is alienated from his sense of self.

Prisoners from Oscar and Delta are transported to the telephone room in a small bus. The bus trip is under the control of three or four officers who position themselves on the front and back seats like a blockade. Imagine such a scene with prisoners queuing up in Oscar and Delta – one body after another. Imagine the competition as they try to claim the closest seat to the bus door, a struggle that lasts all the way to the telephone room. The competition inside the bus is to get a seat as close to the door as possible to guarantee a quick exit and get to that functioning phone.

No doubt the people who built the bus never imagined a short trip of this nature – the designers never thought that the bus they drew plans for would be used for a roughly twenty-metre trip. The bus has to travel on the dirt road outside the prison. It seems there is no choice but to circle the prison. More than anything else, using the bus for this short trip escalates the security tactics governing the prison. The Kyriarchal System can't fathom or trust that the prisoners can walk a short distance with an escort. The objective of the system is possibly to ensure that the prisoners never set foot on land that isn't a part of the prison – not even for a moment.

It is clear and simple. Oscar Prison and Delta Prison continue on their way inside the bus. The bus is an organism growing outward, an extension of the prison. Or it is an outgrowth of the prison that gravitates to the telephone room, and when the prisoner finishes his call the bus recoils back down the same path. During this short period the prisoners can't contain the joy of having been outside the prison for some minutes. They wave over at the prisoners in Fox who watch from behind the fences; they wave over from behind the closed windows in the bus. At times they sing songs at the top of their voices. Like schoolboys returning home for the weekend from boarding school. Or like fans cheering for the victory of their team.

So extremely serious, so restrictive – the officers are unbelievably strict when implementing the rules and regulations pertaining to phone calls.

It isn't as though it is impossible to believe /

It is just extremely hard to believe /

It is painful to be in a situation where it is difficult to believe so many things /

When an individual is in a situation in which it is difficult to believe that so many things are a certain way /

. . . That situation becomes the cause of suffering.

9

—

Father's Day / The Magnificent Mango Tree and The Gentle Giant

A grandfather, a father, a months-old child /
A day for fathers, a day for all fathers /
It's always Father's Day here /
That's why there are no fathers here /
Fathers don't exist within The Kyriarchal System.

I see a young man with bruises on his body, and I become curious about how his struggle to use the phone has led to this harm.

This man is a father – the father of a months-old son.

For the whole time he is in prison he identified as The Father: his whole understanding of manhood seems influenced by the notion of fatherhood. On one occasion, a Sunday, The Father wants to talk to his own father, The Grandfather, who is old and ill. The Grandfather has sent his friends a message and they pass it on to the son: his father wants to speak to him.

This isn't a simple message. The Grandfather has sent the

message under exceptional circumstances, from one hemisphere to another, to the hemisphere where we reside, to the hemisphere that contains our island location.

The Grandfather conveys that he is in his last days.

This is a message of farewell, the message of a father who acknowledges the coming of death. The son, The Father Of The Months-Old Child, feels at that moment what it means to be a son; the grandeur of fatherhood momentarily relinquishes space for the emotions of a son. Yes. The Father Of The Months-Old Child receives the message and immediately hastens to the telephone queue.

First, his friend with the thick moustache, who more than likely is father to one or more kids himself, notifies those in the queue that this man's father is ill and that the situation is critical. They are told that he needs to speak to his father right then. This is done respectfully, the announcement is whispered down to the front of the line. It is not a matter for everyone to know; most people don't appreciate their family matters made public. A few individuals at the front of the queue shake their heads in commiseration – commiseration with a touch of pity – but they aren't prepared to surrender their place to him.

In these situations, everyone shows sympathy; sympathy is expressed as a collective emotion. Now those at the front of the line agree to let him use the phone. The first step is achieved. It seems that The Man With The Thick Moustache negotiates with a Papu, but the Papu shakes his head in the direction of the Australian officers. The Papu states that he doesn't have the power to disregard the rules and regulations when there is a moral dilemma. Everyone knows that the Australian officer has the last word. When The Man With The Thick Moustache struggles to explain everything to the Australian officer in broken English, the officer answers, 'I'm sorry, but that would be a violation of the rules, it's not possible, unfortunately.'

The Man With The Thick Moustache explains again, this time using different words to evoke some mercy in the heart of the officer. He even goes a step further and announces in a loud voice, '. . . but this man's father is a sick old man who is about to die . . . maybe he has already died.' It is clear The Man With The Thick Moustache isn't concerned that his friend might be distressed by hearing someone say that his father might actually be dead right now. The Man With The Thick Moustache is determined to break the rules using any means possible to help his friend enter the telephone room. However, the Australian officer just keeps saying, 'I understand how you feel, but unfortunately this would be a violation of the rules. I'm sorry.'

It is as though all the efforts of The Man With The Thick Moustache have only one outcome, that the sentence 'I understand how you feel' is uttered again and again. But these words don't mean that he can break the rules. The Man With The Thick Moustache, however, tries even harder to convince the officer to break the rules by appealing to his sense of morality and sympathy. He tries more extravagant forms of appeal. Even the Australian officer's family situation gets caught up in the mix. Something like: 'You might be a father yourself and then you certainly would understand the relationship between a father and son very well. Or at least if you're not a father you're a son, and so you have a father, or you had a father before.'

Now the son – The Father Of The Months-Old Child – steps in and tries to convince the guard. With tears welling in his eyes, he appeals even more strongly than The Man With The Thick Moustache. The frenzy at the beginning of the queue draws the attention of all those waiting in line. Everyone has found out what the situation is about. But the Australian officer is so very decisive in announcing that he can't break the rules. After some minutes the son – The Father Of The Months-Old Child – and The Man With The Thick Moustache manage to attract public support for their cause. Almost everyone in the queue rallies behind them. The ruckus of their protest pressures the officer to break the rules. The Papu is powerless to have any impact and just looks on; it is obvious that if it were up to him he would have broken the rules without hesitation, or if the Australian officer hadn't been there he would've broken the rules in exchange for a single smoke.

The pressure on the officer increases to such an extent that he eventually steps back and announces to everyone that it is better to speak with The Boss. The officer gets on his walkie-talkie to inform The Boss that tensions are high in the queue and that one person wants to speak to his sick father. He waits for The Boss to determine the outcome. Everyone is quiet during these moments and in an atmosphere of hopelessness they try to make out the voice of The Boss from behind the walkie-talkie. When the conversation is over, and the officer is empowered by his boss, the officer announces with great confidence and decisiveness, 'I'm sorry but it's not possible.'

This creates chaos in the queue, chaos in everyone's behaviour. Immediately, many of those who have been deeply involved in the situation anticipate a call to action from The Man With The Thick Moustache, a man who has felt a deeper sense of responsibility. But this time the language he uses is a mix of things: a language for shouting down, a language of fury, a language of resistance, a language of violence. The Man With The Thick Moustache raises his voice and announces:

'Where's The Boss?

'We want to see The Boss.

'This man must be permitted to make a call immediately.'

One or two individuals hold up their identity cards to indicate that they are prepared to give up their places to the son – that is, The Father Of The Months-Old Child.

The queue has gone into such convulsion that other Fox prisoners approach the queue and stand in front of the gate. Many of them just stand there from a distance not knowing what is going on. Straight away the officer gets on the walkie-talkie to The Boss again, creating calm. Within minutes The Boss arrives. But he comes with an escort of ten or twelve heavily built officers. Upon seeing The Boss and the entourage of men, the action changes course. This time The Man With The Thick Moustache tries to convince The Boss by complaining about the officer who wouldn't allow the phone call, trying to persuade him by appealing to his sense of moral responsibility. Whatever basic reasoning both he and the others deliver this time, using precise and logical discourse to explain, simply rebounds off the hefty biceps of those ten or twelve officers.

In the prison, the power of biceps can determine the result of many things in many situations. The Boss has complete faith in the biceps of the men in his team and therefore announces with decisiveness and respect, 'I'm sorry, these are the rules and it's not possible, unfortunately.'

The decisiveness of The Boss is so striking that the prisoners are taken aback, including The Man With The Thick Moustache and the son – The Father Of The Months-Old Child.

The prisoners conclude that it is better not to interfere, and just look on impartially. The Man With The Thick Moustache and The Father Of The Months-Old Child continue trying to appeal to morality and explain the situation in different ways. The Boss becomes more defensive. It is clear that the words of

The Man With The Thick Moustache have made an impact on him – skilful, practised rhetoric detailing the love and affection of fatherhood. The Boss's only flexibility in the matter, however, is to put his hand on the son's shoulder – on the shoulder of The Father Of The Months-Old Child. With his hand on his shoulder The Boss says, 'I'm sorry, it's not in my hands. The Boss has given orders. It's just not possible.'

The Boss absolves himself of any blame.

The Man With The Thick Moustache accepts the dismissal and just holds his friend's hand, comforting him, saying, 'No worries. You know what these bastards are like. I'm sure nothing has happened to your father. Three days from now you'll be able to call according to your place in the schedule.' They leave that place.

—

Three days later. Wednesday. The sky is cloudy. A crowd has gathered outside the gate. Many have pushed themselves right up against the fences. And many have also pushed themselves between the joints in the wall separating the telephone room from the outside area. They peer outside. The prisoners have begun to gather in an irregular way – something unusual is taking place. A few prisoners swear loudly; it isn't clear who they are. A few people bash the fence with their fists. But most of the prisoners aren't doing anything in particular and just look on.

Four officers positioned behind the fences have The Father Of The Months-Old Child to the ground. One individual who seems stronger than the rest is twisting The Father's arm. Using one swift technique, he cuffs both his hands. Another individual presses on the prisoner's back with both knees. And another officer gathers up his bare and dusty legs, legs with many small wounds all over them. Others grab his head so he can't move, lock his head that is covered in blood. Six or seven other officers also stand there, just watching their colleagues. And over on the other side, three or four officers try to distance the people who are watching the situation from the other side of the fences.

The Father Of The Months-Old Child musters up all the strength he can, concentrates all his energy so his voice can be heard, and from what seems to be a crushed throat he cries out, 'You bastards, let me go. You bastards, you've killed my father. You've killed my father. Let me go. Let me go.'

But The Boss has become even more brutish than the rest. He is one of those people whose eyes fill up with bruised and swollen capillaries when he gets angry – eyes red with anger. As he removes his walkie-talkie he screams at the officers to enforce their powers. Defusing a situation with such intensity is unauthorised.

Humans are so bizarre. It is unbelievable that this could be the same man who just a few days ago tried to resolve the situation calmly. He even put his hand on the prisoner's shoulder with care and consolation, the same person he has now pinned down under the weight of many bodies. I don't know. Perhaps he feels more dominant on this day.

A few minutes later The Father Of The Months-Old Child is forced into submission.

No more swearing /
A short faint cry /
Silence.

The officers are certain that he has stopped resisting, or maybe he just doesn't have any more power to absorb further damage, or inflict any damage on the officers. Whatever the case, he is like a limp corpse, thrown into the back of a vehicle that looks like a Jeep . . . transported to the solitary confinement cell called Chauka.

His crime?

'This prisoner disrupted the telephone room and smashed the phones against the wall.'

No, actually it is more like this:

'This man, this father, The Father Of The Months-Old Child, has lost his own father.'

Throughout the whole ordeal, however, The Man With The Thick Moustache doesn't say a thing. He stands alone behind the fences just watching on. When the incident is over he returns to his room, a room beside the fences, set up near the ocean. His appearance arouses curiosity: he is silent and looks ambiguous.

Over all, The Kyriarchal System of the prison constructs landscapes the likes of which the prisoners have possibly never encountered in their entire lives. In this scenario, for instance, what could The Man With The Thick Moustache possibly have done? His internal dialogues perhaps led to certitude and maybe he asked, 'Haven't I fulfilled my responsibilities towards the friendship?' He probably considered many possibilities.

Disrupted and fragmented thoughts /

Thoughts that intended the best outcome for his friend /

Just think what would have occurred if his friend had taken a few steps back and stayed put firmly along the fences but shouted with a formidable voice like an angry ram /

Or think what would have happened if his friend had acquired one of the blue-handled razors from somewhere and bloodied himself /

What would have happened? /

Or imagine if he didn't engage in any of these approaches and just ploughed his nails into his face like a woman whose baby has caught fire /

Imagine if he just died /

Imagine if he just screamed /

Imagine if he swore at the top of his voice /

What would have happened? /

Imagine if he tried every method possible to unify the crowd in solidarity /

Imagine if he motivated the crowd into collective action, into breaking down the fences /

What would have happened? /

Imagine if he hadn't used any of these aggressive tactics at all /

Imagine if he had approached things peacefully /

Imagine if he had spoken through the gaps separating the walls /

Imagine if he had spoken through the gaps in the fences /

Imagine if he had spoken respectfully to the officers and particularly The Boss, the same individual who just a few days ago expressed care and kindness /

Imagine if he had asked these same people to forgive him and let him go /

Imagine if he had focused on the love and affection between father and son /

Could this have led to a better result?

Perhaps the son – The Father Of The Months-Old Child – would have preferred that his friends held back a bit, held back from swearing, held back and stayed calm, held back while he was being crushed under the weight of the officers' biceps and knees.

No. No.

None of these reactions would've helped. They all would've diminished him even further. Aggressive measures end up nowhere except solitary confinement in Chauka. And peaceful means did nothing for him or his friends.

In the context of all this, how should we interpret the meaning of their friendship?

Out of all the options available to him, The Man With The Thick Moustache reaches this conclusion: stay silent, accept that his friend has been degraded, accept that he has been forced into submission, accept that all he can do is bear witness. Just like his friend, he has to remain silent and allow the thinking organism that is the prison system to operate, and allow those brainless officers to carry out their orders. They have the necessary and sufficient knowledge of how to extinguish controversy.

—

There are so many times the prisoner is forced to straddle the border between human and animal. One has to decide whether to uphold human values or live life like The Cow. In most cases the human is reduced to an animal in order to survive. However, not the kind of animal that is totally dependent on its instincts and acts according to its predetermined condition. Rather, an animal with intelligence and will, a human being. There's a clear distinction between an innocent goat that sleeps without a care in the world and a vicious human with twisted, intermingled guts who violently hunts down anything and everything for survival – even preys on its own species. Cynical, but it's the truth. When a person is hungry they rush anything that smells like food. And if there's competition, they attack with even more ferocity.

Sometimes, at night, a kind-hearted officer enters the prison and comes by with beautifully coloured cakes. He creates a scene that could be interpreted as a barnyard. The officer leaves the watchman's kiosk just for a moment and enters the prison. Everyone is hyper-alert to anything with the slightest scent of food. The officer puts the box on his shoulder and then strolls over to the farthest corner of the prison, just calmly strolls over, taking his time – we are about to witness a special function of The Kyriarchal System in operation. A few officers inside the kiosk stare at the officer with the box on his shoulder. As the officer walks over in a straight line, dozens of prisoners start moving rapidly in the direction he is heading; they shoot out from various places in the prison. The greed and longing in the eyes and actions of every prisoner is like a flock of sheep that have just seen a sack in the hands of their shepherd. In their madness they have one eye on the shepherd and another eye on the smooth stone surface where the shepherd plans to distribute handfuls of salt and minerals. The prison has become like a sheep pen. On cold winter days when there is nothing around to eat, the shepherd throws some barley or alfalfa in the corner of the pen so the sheep don't suffer from hunger. The sheep are grateful for the kind gesture and they flock in the direction of the shepherd. But humans are a lot more clever than that. The prisoners differ from the sheep in one particular way: they don't rush the officer – or the shepherd – not directly, not like the sheep. They move in the direction that he is moving.

There is some basic and understandable competition. Whoever arrives sooner has a better chance of gulping down one or a few pieces of cake; small pieces but so delicious. When the prisoners arrive at their destination, all of a sudden the officer becomes just like a shepherd who reaches his hand into the sack of salt and minerals or alfalfa; the officer pulls out the cake portions one by one. But he is sure that he doesn't need to divide the quantity, since as soon as he reveals the cakes they are devoured right off the cardboard.

The method of distributing the cake doesn't involve awareness of who gets how many pieces. As soon as the box is open, dozens of hands extend right in front of the officer. The officer has no choice but to lift the box and hold it above his head and shoulders. Sometimes the force of the crowd is so great that the officer loses balance and almost falls over. To stay up, he has no choice but to throw the box metres away with all its contents inside. The consequences are obvious. The bodies of all of those hands suddenly change direction. They swarm towards the box and all the pieces of cake that have scattered all over the ground. During these moments the prisoners are transformed into something way beyond sheep – maybe more like a group of predatory wolves, hungry wolves in the middle of winter, transformed into starving wolves pouncing on their prey with no mercy.

The Cow is a fascinating man.

In these particular instances there is no way that he will be deprived. Perhaps he isn't the first one to arrive at the scene, but it is impossible to imagine that by the end of the whole thing he won't be left holding one or two pieces of cake. But I never go towards the officer to get any cake. On no occasion do I ever take even a step in the direction of the mayhem. It's not that I'm an extremely proud person. It's not even that I want to maintain my humanity when faced with the option of behaving like a sheep. No. I swear, it is nothing like that. There is a particular reason for making my proud decision, a decision made during moments when my appetite governs my soul.

What influences my decision is the feeling of weakness that takes hold of me. My body is faint; I am just like a hungry fox. I imagine this particular feeling to be evidence of maintaining a basic sense of what it is to be human. From the very first moment when the officer begins his kind gesture, I know I am an animal that has already lost the game. For this reason I always watch the spectacle from a distance. I simply watch the gorging of all those beautiful, delicious cakes.

There are a few times when it just so happens that I am standing beside the kiosk when the officer emerges suddenly out of nowhere and passes by me with his box. An exceptional moment, one that perhaps someone like The Cow dreams of. I am one of the first on the scene, which means that I have a higher chance of success. But again an enormous sense of weakness comes over me, so I just look over at the prisoners with regret, watch as they emerge out of this corner and that corner, watch the speed with which they zoom in on that zone. I don't see myself as having the capability to compete with The Cow and his friends. It is difficult for me to even contemplate the possibility of snatching up a piece of cake ahead of someone like The Cow.

—

Corridor M is on the other side of the prison. It is close to the fences opposite the ocean. It has become known as Little Kurdistan. Here a different form of competition over food has developed.

Kurdish prisoners live in the rows of rooms alongside these fences. They have brought their repressed political aspirations with them into the prison and adorned one of the rooms with the tricolour flag: white, red, blue, with the image of the sun painted brightly on it. It is interesting how even though they have been deprived of even a single pen, on one morning they awake to find the Kurdish flag emblazoned on the door. Something akin to a miracle. Maybe an officer of Kurdish heritage has drawn it there. But regardless of who has put it there, the existence of the flag means that this small region is no longer identified by a number.

Right there, right by the fences, a mango tree with the most magnificent trunk grows straight up. This tree challenges the prison fences. Its long branches reach out in the direction of the prison, reach inside the prison, reach over onto the roof of the corridor, and reach down for the rooms. It reaches out in a way that it can't be seen from inside the corridor; one can only see it from a distance and when near the toilets. The smooth exterior of the trunk and the thick branches of the mango tree are so extraordinary that practically no-one could climb it without a great deal of difficulty.

Mango, such a juicy yellow fruit, nestled within the tree's wide leaves – this tropical tree flaunts its mangoes. When one experiences the sight of such a tree, joy takes hold, joy from a tree overflowing with goodness, joy from the abundance of its blessings. Perhaps it's the same glorious feeling a man experiences when his wife is pregnant. Without a doubt, the feeling that transfixes the hungry prisoners is something that transcends the experience of simply gazing on its beauty. It is beyond the pleasures associated with sight.

This tree is undergoing a passage of growth that does not pose a threat – and so there is no reason to cut it down. A tranquillity emanates out of its very essence. It is a symbol of the majesty of nature, a grand power that reaches through to the depths of the prison.

As night falls, its presence can be felt even more, because once every few minutes a piece of its fruit falls onto the roof of the corridor, with the sound of a solid object banging against metal walls. And it seems that the fruit tumbles over a few times on the roof and then falls down by the container walls. There are a number of stages:

First, out of the darkness, a bird arrives to choose the ripest fruit hidden between the leaves /

Next, trapped in silence, the bird starts to eat /

At once, the weight of the eaten fruit shifts /

It loses equilibrium /

The fruit is left dangling after a peck of the beak /

And so it drops down onto the roof /

It rolls over and falls again, this time onto the grimy dirt floor /

Finally, the hungry prisoner follows the sound of the fall /

Follows it to the place where the fruit lies /

Finds it among the piles of dirt and dried leaves.

The prisoner cannot be completely certain that the fruit is just moments away after he hears the sound of its first drop. In most cases there won't be a second drop onto the ground. The project is aborted on the first drop – the fruit will remain on the roof forever. Out of maybe three or four fruit droppings, only one will roll enough to reach the edge of the roof and so drop a second time. Still, if it drops a second time – I mean, if the fruit drops to the ground – it isn't yet certain that the prisoner is guaranteed fruit. You see, on most occasions the fruit falls behind the containers or it disappears into the darkness – it is really hard for the prisoner to find it among the withered leaves. Even if he finds the spot, he has to rummage around on the ground for minutes to retrieve it.

The prisoner isn't a creature driven by instinct, passively sitting in a corner somewhere waiting to jump whenever fruit drops. He has to use his intellect. From the time of the first drop – the fruit falling on the corridor roof – till the second fall – the fruit falling from the corridor onto the ground – he has to fine-tune his ears with perfect precision so that he can estimate accurately where the fruit has landed.

Even the slightest distraction means that he may never find the fruit. Some of the fruits that fall to the ground are halved. Some only have a few holes. Others are so crushed they are inedible.

Up in the treetop a competition is taking place between the birds and the bats. However, the bats are few, and most of the fruit that finds its way onto the ground is due to the birds. The tropical bats are as big as pigeons. The colossal bats eat fruit in a way that horrifies the spectator. It is easy to imagine the battle between the birds and the bats as completely one-sided. With one short screech the bat scares the bird so badly that it escapes in search of another tree.

There are periods when the prisoner's attention lapses and he stops listening. Then he can't tell the exact place where the fruit has landed. After hunting around for a while in the dark, he returns to the corridor empty handed. But this time he concentrates in earnest as he sits there in anticipation. Nature has determined the destiny of these pieces of fruit. In the morning, the prisoner sees that there is almost nothing left of each fruit except for the large pip. There they are under the containers, pips released from their skins, the flesh carried off by crabs with the help of little red Manusian ants.

The crabs are experts; they drag every mango from under the containers, carry away without hesitation every one that drops. They can hold their own in competition with the prisoners. From what we witness, the crab's eyesight is keener than the prisoner's hearing. When a prisoner approaches, the crabs usually hang back, stay away regardless of their claws. I think the crabs exercise a special kind of intelligence – at least in these instances.

This terrain is marked as Kurdistan. Whoever knows the Kurds understands very well the level of respect they have for one another. But the respect embedded in their culture begins to wane as hunger takes its toll, day after day. Slowly but surely starvation lowers their flag from the pole.

The Kurdish prisoners promote themselves as the sole proprietors of the mango tree. In the first days there were times when the prisoners would loiter there in hope of grabbing some fruit. But the Kurdish prisoners stared condescendingly. They threw kicks at anyone who came over and wouldn't let them even look at the fruit, let alone allow them the pleasure of waiting there in anticipation. They blocked out any competition for eating fruit. They preferred the competition to remain within their small community rather than permitting others to the tiny table. They had no tolerance for anyone who wanted to enjoy the offerings of the mango tree.

These days aren't like the early days. Not like the days when the first to get to the fruit would divide and share it. Now, the prisoner finds the fruit and devours it right there in the dark. When he returns to the corridor, there is nothing left for him to offer his friends, and he performs no gesture of courtesy towards the others.

So as time passes, hatred grows among the prisoners in that area. Reza is the most powerful and tallest man in the prison and engages in a way that is completely different from the rest. Throughout the prison are many men who try to maintain their dignity. But the gentleness in Reza's behaviour is much greater than you might see in others. In some particularly kind and forgiving people, there is also a strain of self-centredness, which gives them fortitude to tolerate life, to see its sophistication, to see it with balance. But Reza is different. His generosity amazes those around him. All the Kurds, and then everyone else in the prison, know him as The Gentle Giant. Although, sometime later, we drop the adjective 'Gentle', as it makes his name too long. We just call him The Giant.

Perhaps for those in his intimate circle, 'gentle' has more emotional significance. But for most of the prisoners who see him in the queue for food, see him in line for the toilets, see him in various regions of the prison, he probably appears more like The Giant than The Gentle Giant anyway. In fact, when this nickname was first created it was the result of jokes. You see, for those who lived around the neighbourhood of the mango tree, it was hard to believe that a giant like Reza could also be gentle.

In contrast to many others, when The Giant gets hold of some fruit he offers it to others without any expectations, a gesture of courtesy in the manner of a child, with all the emotion that colours the world of children. And this is the behaviour that the other side reflect on, realising that they themselves are completely incapable of such an act. This is the way that we create The Other. When people don't have the capacity to comprehend noble behaviour they become haunted with despair and confusion. They feel insecure. Then they suppress this using anything at their disposal.

The Kurdish prisoners form a kind of unspoken fraternity; they prefer to keep the mango tree to themselves. No-one else is granted a share. They make it a requirement that anyone who finds fruit has to gobble it up with joy, without dividing it and sharing it with the rest. The Gentle Giant challenges this way of thinking with his childlike generosity. He confronts them with a different way of being, he offers them new horizons, access to a better reality.

On one night of hunger, a young man passes by the prisoners who sit in front of the rooms in the container that makes up Corridor M – that is, Little Kurdistan. The gazes fixed on his steps carry a certain weight. It seems as though he wants to do something out of the ordinary. It is written all over the prisoners' faces: he shouldn't be prowling around here at that time of night. He doesn't have the right to explore the mango tree. But still we aren't sure why he has journeyed here.

As The Cunning Young Man is walking along, he arrives behind the containers and the district where most of the mangoes have dropped. At once, the sound of a falling mango resonates as it hits the roof of the corridor. Then it drops right at the foot of The Cunning Young Man. Apparently, this is a gift from the tree right into the hands of The Cunning Young Man. Perhaps, with this grant, the tree wants to test the humanity of the prisoners. It seems The Cunning Young Man doesn't have a good under-standing of what is going through the minds of those in that area: they are all curious about this foreigner. Basically, he shouldn't be standing there picking up the fruit from the ground with delight.

The Cunning Young Man stands there, just looking up at the tree, stands there with a smile on his face. The tree looks more glorious than ever. By the way he is craning his neck up towards the tree, just gazing at it, one can see he is in enraptured by this unexpected gift from the heavens. And his smile is one of gratitude. The prisoners look around at each other. In a flash they come to an agreement. They look deep into each other's eyes and understand – he has no right to take fruit for himself. They have to attack. Two or three individuals hunch together. But only one of them, the joker of the group, moves in to rough up

The young man, to face off with him like a bandit. The Joker is like a schoolboy with a devilish grin. Without saying a word he signals to The Cunning Young Man with his hand: 'Give me the fruit.' The Cunning Young Man looks extremely frightened, shakes his head, and prepares to toss the fruit over to The Joker.

Right at this moment The Giant appears beside them. He stares down The Joker and then wraps the fingers of The Cunning Young Man around the fruit. He says that the fruit belongs to him. The Joker and the others don't make another move and keep completely silent; they have been struck by the phenomenon of The Giant and simply stare. As soon as a sense of security comes over The Cunning Young Man and he realises he is protected by the powerful muscles of The Giant, he is freed of the fear that gripped him moments ago and he smiles. He holds the fruit tight between his fingers and quickly leaves the scene.

That night /

The Cow /

The Man With The Thick Moustache /

The Father Of The Months-Old Child /

Maysam The Whore /

The Cunning Young Man /

The Joker /

And The Gentle Giant go to bed /

Go to bed as they usually do /

Go to bed with hungry stomachs /

Go to their sweat-drenched beds /

The crabs . . . /

The ants . . . /

The bats . . . /

The birds . . . /

And the officers . . . /

They all remain awake /

And the breeze rustles the leaves of that magnificent mango tree /

The sound of the waves drifts in /

The sound of the ocean reaches in /

That sound creeps in from behind the jungle.

—

In the western section of Fox Prison the labourers are busily working. Dozens of large white containers have been stacked on top of each other. A multi-level edifice full of hallways has been erected. The jungle has disappeared from sight, and additional fences have been implanted. What is this thing they have built? Ready-made homes for the army? Maybe.

Rumour spreads through the prison that lawyers have been sent back from the main airport to the place from which they came.

During these days the first group of refugees are manoeuvred into permanent places /

A settlement on the island /

And after a few weeks a second group is settled /

And then a third group is settled /

And then a fourth /

And finally every one of these groups is settled /

The Chauka bird releases a perpetual cry as it perches on top of the tallest coconut tree /

The Chauka is singing /

What can be interpreted from deep within its voice? /

Sunsets are always melancholic.

10

—

Chanting of Crickets, Ceremonies of Cruelty /
A Mythic Topography of Manus Prison

The human being is born enduring affliction /

The human being lives while enduring affliction /

The human being dies by enduring affliction /

The human being realises affliction /

The human being is cognisant of whatever pertains to affliction /

Lamentation /

Crying out /

Wailing /

Weeping /

The human being experiences all of these things /

The human being has deep knowledge of all of these things.

That night. The one night that I'm talking about is the night when
I am having convulsions as a result of toothache. I bash my head

a number of times against the metal structure containing the bathrooms.

I hear a faint moaning sound.

The intensity and fear resonating in the sound completely stop me in my tracks. It is the sound of painful moaning. It is the sound of a man that seems to be convulsing in pain. These particular kinds of sounds make one's hair stand on end.

The sound of the deepest kind of affliction /

The sound of hopelessness. A nightmare about the nights. A nightmare about loneliness /

The sound of moaning inside the cauldron of the dark night /

The sound of moaning floating over the ocean /

The sound of moaning wading through the jungle that lies beyond the fences /

The sound of moaning drags itself along in combination with other sounds /

The sound of moaning, like a poisonous arrow from the archer's bow /

The sound of moaning, a sound without rebound against the darkness of night /

The sound of moaning, then it disappears out into the universe.

The prison has fallen into a heavy silence; the prison has fallen into heavy sleep. Only the sound of crickets; they hollow out the depths of silence even further. The very great weight of the silence has infused the moaning with a destructive power.

My god, prison is so horrific. Prison is so oppressive. Prison is so merciless.

The moaning could even be the sound of clouds tearing

apart – this is the way it feels to me. Exactly like the intensity of wrath and power manifested by thunder and lightning strikes in springtime. Perhaps deep wounds and scars struck down from the clouds and heavens with higher voltage than thunder and lightning. The coconut trees, however, offer their hair up to the zephyr. They quiver; they are also frightened.

A Papu rests his back against one of the containers, his cap on his lap, twirling a stick in his mouth. I think he is at the peak of getting high off betel nut; his mind is free and he closes his eyes without a care for anything going on around him. This experience is a mix of slumber, wakefulness and a drug-induced state; however, it is a special moment of liberation unique to the Papus. The Papu pays no attention whatsoever to the moaning that spirals out through the atmosphere. He has completely dedicated his mind and body to his betel nut intoxication.

And so the moaning continues. But on every occasion it hides deep within the heart of the dark sky with another kind of shudder and force. Every instance of moaning, more than anything, evokes the eerie sublimity of the jungle, the ocean, and the prison.

My toothache begins to settle. Perhaps when the forces of two forms of affliction, from two separate origins, collide, one has to succumb due to the impact and resistance. Maybe something like this has occurred for me. My toothache is directly connected to interweaving nerves deep within the core of my gums. And my affliction is facing off with the affliction of another just a few metres away – behind the fences – it sounds like hopelessness – the sound comes from a place of profound hopelessness – my toothache is forced to withdraw. Maybe we share the same feeling of affliction; one and the same substance: the affliction at the root of the moaning, the affliction down there in the depths of my soul.

The Papu, however, remains indifferent to this – flying high there in his own realm. He twirls that small stick in his mouth. The moaning coincides with weeping; a peculiar mood distributes itself all over the terror-stricken landscape. In a landscape of this nature one is left with no more than two options: either to rely on the indifferent Papu and not give it any more thought, or follow the sound and discover its source. Knowledge can always set one free. So I must confess that I am mainly looking for a way to reach up high; that's right, to climb over the fences or the container walls.

As I approach the source of the moaning I become more confident that I have guessed correctly. Everything points in the direction of the solitary confinement cell called the Green Zone. There behind the fences. Right by the telephone room. That's where the Green Zone is.

I can't scale the fences. However, it isn't like it's impossible to climb over. It is easy to do with some effort; even someone with the skinniest muscles could get over. But scaling the fences rattles them as well. It produces a sound that can only resemble that made by thieves who try to climb barriers in order to get into people's homes. A few Papus and Australian officers sit along the fences a great distance away. If the fences are rattled they will certainly become suspicious of the shaking followed by the sound it creates. There would only be one result. I would be hauled over to the solitary confinement cell and join the one who is moaning. Scaling the fences isn't an option.

I recall a time during my childhood when I was a skilful thief capable of anything. I remember the days when I used to run and jump over our neighbours' enclosed gardens with a quick one-two move; I leapt like a cat, pulling myself over the wall of the enclosed gardens. There I sat on the branches of walnut trees

248

like a monkey. Kilometres away from our home, there among the orchards of Kurdish chestnut oak trees, I searched for pigeon nests. By now I am sure that anyone who could climb the coarse trunks of chestnut oak trees without a hitch could also climb the hardest and most slippery obstacles with ease. It's no joking matter – I'm a child of the mountains. No different to a cat.

The Papu is so high that he has drifted out over the sea – I know that kind of feeling really well. Nothing is going to ruin his mood and sensation, not even if thunder and lightning erupt from the skies. Maybe I'm overstating it, but I think that if this were to occur the Papu might open his eyes, and gather himself up, his arms, legs, together with the cap resting on his lap; then for some moments he would stop twirling the small stick inside his mouth. I have no doubt that once the thunder and lightning had passed he would be lifted back up to being high again.

This is particular to the Papus. Liberated. Free. Happy. And I have forgotten my toothache now that I am in the mood and state of mind of being a cat. Actually, the huge leap I want to perform requires that I forget about my toothache. Yes. The mind can sometimes also consciously control one's physical pain. In three moves I quickly manage to get myself onto the roof of the corridor. First of all, I jump half a metre off the ground and position myself on the metal pole that functions as the base of the corridor. It is still twilight and focusing my eyes I make another move; with the concentration of a hunter pursuing prey, I peruse the roof of the corridor. Applying this move means that I have selected the best place for gripping my hands, and then I leap half a metre and hang off the edge of the roof. Imagine carefully. Exactly like a monkey that dangles off the branch of a tall tree. The only difference between a monkey and me could be that I am hanging off with the support of two hands, whereas it's usually the case that monkeys look ahead while hanging from one hand. By hanging from one hand they exhibit their control of the tree, the branch, and gravity. Even playful monkeys do that in some instances just for fun. They play and fool around. In any case, a human being like me hanging by two hands is enough to feel like a monkey, identifying with the monkey more than any other animal.

My hands are locked really firmly. Now is the time to prove to myself the extent to which I can embody a monkey. To do this I launch out using all my muscles and, without releasing my hands from the roof, toss myself over the edge. The outcome of all this is sitting up there on top of the roof, feeling a sense of achievement by completing the ascent, and subsequently, a great feeling of success.

I am there now – sitting there in the dark – on the roof – near the mango tree – it is a small dream of mine to reach that tree. The Papu is no longer in eyeshot for me. Even the officers are out of sight; the ones I saw in front of the gate when I was down below.

My god, it is remarkably dark behind the prison. Certainly the darkness expands way beyond the limits of my imagination; in fact, the ocean and the jungle evaporate into nothingness. I can't tell on which tree the crickets have nested, or in which area they reside, but the whole atmosphere is captivated by their sound. The crickets . . . the darkness . . . the silence . . . the awe . . . that is the entirety of the whole scene.

It might seem contradictory but the crickets even pause for a moment from their chanting so that I can absorb the magnitude of the silence. The sound of the crickets and the sound of silence: a contradiction. It is awe-inspiring. Tell me someone who can hear a cricket in a noisy environment? The chanting of the crickets is the harmony to the melody of silence. Silence refines its identity by virtue of the sound of the crickets, and vice versa.

The moaning has stopped.

From over here one can see the Green Zone; I mean, one can see it from on top of the corridor roof. A solitary confinement cell that until now I have only heard about. Terrifying.

A lamp with a worn-out yellow light faintly shines onto the surroundings. With its help one can see two containers opposite each other. In place of glass, wooden planks cover the windows. The rooms are matchboxes with a single open door. And a single ceiling fan spins monotonously around while giving the impression that it is about to stop spinning at any moment. The spinning fan makes one's own head spin. The spinning blades of the fan seem weary. A group of mosquitoes that seem to be from the same genus as butterflies spin around in front of the yellow lamp creating a transparent cloud. My eyes finally acclimatise to the darkness.

The Green Zone also has a yard of three or four metres with two coconut trees growing right at the end, right near the fences. The coconut trees seem scary and have an air of reverence about them. Their trunks are black and they seem taller than the coconut trees inside the prison. It is necessary to turn one's head up to the sky, all the way up, in order to witness their full height. However, when standing there it isn't clear exactly where the head of the coconut trees is capped; it appears that most of the trees' tops have merged with the clouds. The coconut leaves and the fruit have mixed in with the black clouds and the black sky.

I can also see an extremely small kiosk beside the fences. It looks like the frame of an unfamiliar animal. The kiosk is also dark. And a Papu is hiding away and smoking some Brus[15]. Like

---

15 Brus is a local dark-brown tobacco, extremely strong and intoxicating, and abundant in the jungles of Manus. The Papus place the dry leaves in newspaper and smoke it.

the Papu twirling the stick in his mouth, this Papu leans his back against a coconut tree and takes puffs of Brus, behaving in the same customary way.

For a moment I think I see his eyes, identify his eyes, although everything is dark and I can't make out his face. His nose and mouth are indistinguishable, so seeing his eyes seems impossible. I must confess that from where I am sitting it isn't at all clear if the smoker is a Papu; therefore, it is also impossible that I can make out he is smoking Brus from that distance. Is it really a Papu? I don't know. Is he smoking Brus? I don't know that either. Does the human mind also deceive so much so that it overrides the function of the eyes and nose? Yes. Faith in the absurd.

In any case, I conclude that the smoker is a Papu. I even take it a step further and conclude that the Papu is of old-age, smoking Brus like old folk. The moaning, however, stopped a while ago. I think that during my first effort to reach the roof someone has zipped up his mouth. Silence everywhere.

This particular ceiling fan is the only thing indifferent to its surroundings – it spins . . . just rattling . . . hanging loosely. Beside it a family of moths are conducting a ceremony of ecstasy – they whirl around the yellow lamp. For a moment I forget why and how I came to be on top of the roof. It is a period during which I am an emancipated being; emancipated from the prison; emancipated from the prison system. I even feel proud of myself since I am the only human and the only prisoner who has come this close to the mango tree – I have come this close to the unconquerable mango tree. So now here I am, even my nose rubs up against its broad leaves. So here I am, I have made it up here, up into the ether, up on top of the prison, witnessing the spectacle, witnessing the jungle and the ocean, observing as I evaporate into the darkness.

Even the crickets have fallen silent. They understand perfectly well that another animal now occupies the domain of the cricket; an animal with different skin; an animal with different blood; an animal with different smelling breath. It seems that the harmony between the total landscape and all of the elements within have realised that this animal is incongruous with the whole. And for this reason they now perform silence; they discontinue their exuberance. Only the Papu remains there, in his own realm. Even in a deluge he still wouldn't be concerned with the outside world.

My eyes have adjusted to the dark and have acquired relative proficiency in perceiving the landscape, sensing the muted external world. The only problem is that I have to keep still since the roof of the corridor is constructed from a layer of thin metal and the slightest move would cause a lot of noise and disrupt the tranquil setting.

I admit that the thing I am most afraid of is that I will be wrestled to the ground and dragged and pulled across to the Green Zone or other solitary confinement cells in the prison like they did to The Father Of The Months-Old Child. Especially since I have an overwhelming tendency to imagine myself in the same situation as the man who is moaning, the man whose moaning has dragged me here, the man whose presence compels me. Who knows, this could be me, diminished to moaning, on some future night; it could be me just left there wailing.

Perhaps another would end up on this side of the prison looking for me as I moaned, end up right here as he tried to locate me. He would end up on the roof of this corridor, right by the broad leaves of this mango tree, and position himself here together with the crickets that have declared themselves to be the shahs of this empire.

I shouldn't move, I should just take pleasure from the tempo-
rary freedom I have. In any case, I am here for whatever reason – no
doubt, reasons that defy any logic I can apply. What difference
does it make at all what drew me here. What is important is the
feeling of beautiful freedom. I have forgotten my toothache – what
a relief. Every now and then a pain shoots through the inside of my
gums. But the feeling of freedom is so powerful that the pain just
darts past, stops straight after, and then disappears.

Crickets are such extraordinary creatures. As soon as I
enter the space, they all fall silent in sync with each other. It
is as though they are a group of musicians collaborating at the
peak of their composition, and then with one signal from the
conductor of the orchestra, they all stop playing and just stand
up. And now that they are completely sure that this new animal
that has disrupted their period of tranquillity is no threat they
resume their chanting. However, this time it is different; on this
occasion they return to the earlier rhythm after a number of
successive stages. First, one of them that I feel must be more
of an elder cricket uses his extremely loud voice – louder than
the usual sound of all the other crickets combined – to start a
very different song. The song becomes a steady monotone. Then
others join in at different intervals. The result is evident. A choir
in perfect harmony.

The silence and peacefulness of the night has become
twofold – the night has become a paradox. The terror is now
more formidable; the sky now darker; the coconut trees now more
deranged. The sound of trembling branches and clashing leaves
are amplified and can be heard with full clarity. Even the sound of
the ocean's waves pounds the body of the island with more fury
and fuses with the sounds of the night. I still say this, everything
is held together by the mysterious sound of the crickets.

This creature is engaged in an inseparable friendship with the night /
This creature knows full well the language of the night /
This creature has full knowledge about the dark /
This creature has a full understanding of terror.

So I have become completely fixed in this place. I have become part of the landscape. All the elements of the landscape there accept that this green-eyed or blue-eyed creature lying down on the roof of the corridor is a constituent of the domain. This refreshing sensation of calm and the grand feeling of a new sense of self makes me want to stay here longer. I don't even think about returning to prison.

Every time I'm in these situations I desire a cigarette. A bad habit. Or maybe it's good. I don't know. But I've always welcomed this addiction, this desire to smoke. Every now and then I forget my smokes – like this very night. I look up above, up at the dark sky, it makes no difference whether I brought my smokes or not. I can't smoke in any case for the simple reason that we don't have lighters in the prison. Perhaps if I had my cigarettes with me my desire would have been heightened and I would have had to descend from the corridor roof to light one. So then I would've disturbed the Papu, the Papu twirling the stick in his mouth.

Forgetting about smoking means that I stay longer; it means that I listen more to the sound of the crickets, that I listen more to the sound of the ocean, that I listen more to the sound of the night, listen more to the sound of the coconut trees; it means that I let the sounds reverberate in my eardrums. Little by little I forget about the moaning and wailing coming from the Green Zone, the sound that drew me here in the first place. It doesn't make any difference at all. I don't have the capability to change anything.

I am nothing but an incompetent thief. A creature that only knows how to climb up onto the roof.

Does one have to formulate a logical reason for every action? My god, the human mind can be so deceptive. I am left here breathing under the awe and majesty of the night. This night the heavens are insane . . . but they are quiet. The clouds have acquired a thick layer of darkness. I can only really feel the stars in the furthest reaches of the dark, feel them as they keep expressing themselves, feel them till they disappear.

For a second, I turn my body completely towards the Green Zone, my right hand holds me up like a pillar, my head is positioned a reasonable distance from the hard corridor roof. This is another of my habits. Unconsciously, my body parts move; they make decisions of their own outside my control, with no role played by my mind, and they are indifferent to my feelings. These are decisions made by my bones – not my brain. During these periods my careless body parts disobey me and figure out how to move on their own. I don't put any pressure on my mind to order them to get back to their original places. I don't show any resistance when my body turns onto its right side. Exactly onto my right side, my arm like a pillar, and then rests my head exactly on the palm of my hand, aligning the muscles along the side of my body, and my arm, all in unison.

My eyes also undergo an unusual feeling, a unique experience, in contrast to my other body parts as suddenly the images before them become strange.

There must be good reason why I just jumped on the roof within a few short movements like a cat. No doubt, while I am up here my body seems to operate independently of my mind, and perhaps my idle mind is processing why I am even up here in the first place.

And so I am here, lying down in this particular way. At this moment I want to express how everything is reduced to the crickets. But no. I am here too.

Maybe it is something pertaining to the peacefulness of the night /

Maybe it is something pertaining to the indifference of the Papus towards the events all around them /

Maybe it is something pertaining to the soothing nature of the mango tree /

Whatever it is it probably involves all these reasons.

Maybe there is also a form of interaction taking shape, a connection between something internal and profound in my unconscious and the totality of the landscape. An unconscious potential full of unattainable and distant images.

Thoughts full of the smell of gunpowder and war, full of love and chestnuts, full of wheat, full of pigeons, full of partridges, thoughts full of mountains. More than anything else, thoughts of peaceful nightfall and the deep fear evoked by this tranquil reflection; a thought that takes me away, somewhere way back in the day, back to a faraway homeland.

Truth be told, I am a child of war. Yes, I was born during the war. Under the thunder of warplanes. Alongside tanks. In the face of bombs. Breathing gunpowder. Among dead bodies. Inside silent cemeteries. These were the days when war was a part of our everyday lives and ran like blood through our identity. A meaningless war; a pointless war. Absurd. A war with ridiculous objectives. Like all wars throughout history. A war that devastated our families and sizzled and incinerated all of our vivid, green and bounteous homeland.

I am a child of war. I don't mean to say I've been sacrificed. I never ever want to be labelled with this word. That war has taken its sacrifices . . . and continues to make sacrifice.

Sacrificing out of the blazing fires of war /

Sacrificing out of the desolate ashes of war /

On the threshold of life and death /

Smiles enamoured with staying alive; mothers wailing and soaked in blood /

A region full of storehouses of affliction. Suffering and starvation /

I have to say it. Hear me as I cry out: I am a child of war /

A child of an inferno. A child of ashes. A child of the chestnut oaks of Kurdistan /

I'm insane, I am. Where is this place? /

Why has the night become so terrifying? And why can't I fall asleep? /

Let me say something; let me surrender myself to the realm of the imagination and amnesia.

Where have I come from?

From the land of rivers, the land of waterfalls, the land of ancient chants, the land of mountains.

Better to say I've come down from the summits. I've breathed in the ether up there. I've laughed up there. I've unleashed my hair to the wind up there. Out of a small village that stood in the middle of a forest of old chestnut oaks.

In the past, we were weary from the war. The war elephants from the neighbouring lands had decided to wage battle for many years inside our vibrant and luscious plantation. Their heavy legs and bulging bellies rampaged; every place was crushed underneath them. That war wasn't our war. That violence wasn't our violence. The theatre of war wasn't our production. War was uninvited. A calamity from the heavens just like a famine. Just like an earthquake.

My mother always sighed and would say: 'My boy, you came into this world in a time we called the flee and flight years.' This phrase was commonplace during those miserable years. A time when people would run to the mountains from fear of the warplanes. Everything they had and could carry they took with them. They found asylum within chestnut oak forests.

Do the Kurds have any friends other than the mountains?

Horrified mothers . . . mothers wrapped their children within the instincts of motherhood and escaped to the mountains. Young girls were searching for their dreams within the hearts of men rounded up into groups – so many groups – and being led down a road to the front lines of war. Groups – so many groups – returned as corpses. Again, it is those same chestnuts that became the solace for buried dreams.

Those chestnuts were proud /

Those chestnuts joined in mourning /

Those chestnuts from those mountains /

Only those chestnuts know how beautiful the dreams of maidens /

Dreams resting on the rocky slopes /

Dreams dying there between the deep valleys, dying young /

There alongside the coarse tree trunks /

A short life ending inside dark forests /

The flee and flight days /

Days of terror /

Days of darkness /

Days of affliction.

Every one of them headed for the mountains using all the power in their legs.

Overcoming so much, they found asylum on the cliffs and within the dark caves. Under the roofs of abandoned village homes, abandoned but still with a vestige of home life. Similar to a candle burning but unlikely to last the night. Old men with long clay pipes. Men of old age . . . sacrificed . . . sacrificed as the more able fled . . . sacrificed as the young men fled. They remained there through the nights and recollected, remained there with their memories until they died of hunger and thirst, remained there till the end. The older and weaker among them wasted away. Whoever couldn't reach the mountains had to die. These were the rules, this is how things played out during those times, this is what was expected.

The law of nature, however merciless. Out of the ravaging belly of nature emerged both a human being and a destructive warmonger. Everything blended into the colour black and into a mood of bitterness. Dreams . . . hopes . . . fertility . . . smiles . . . beauty . . . all decimated.

These were the rules of war. The period was ruled by the dynasty of terror and death. No-one, no-one at all, was spared. Fathers against sons, sons against fathers. All because of fear, and because of the neighing of that one horse, because of the horse that manifested death. Everything had been painted like a nightmare. And in the last days . . . love.

Animosities reached climax and teeth gnashed from extreme hate. Old wounds were opened and blades of battle tapped into the cesspool of history, the history of hate, and disseminated its loathing, spread across what once were fields of goodwill; our vivid, green and bounteous homeland. A putrid smell came over the whole place. Enemy also didn't recognise enemy. On one side, corps with steely determination whose objective was to fight in the name of religion. On the other side, corps who also fought in the name of religion. On one side, Iraqi Ba'athists[16] would empty their rounds. On the other side, Iranian zealots would open fire. In the middle were our homes – our homes left desolate. Two grand war elephants – administering nothing but hurt.

The Peshmerga[17] also battled from within the mountains. Their very name represented defence of homeland and dignity. It was a war with no end, like all the other wars of history. A war with roots in earlier wars. And those wars had roots in other wars. A chain of wars born out of the nether regions of history. And so it was a seed of resentment that blossomed after centuries with the colour of blood once again.

It was these very mountains that witnessed the spectacle /

It was these ancient chestnut oaks that lamented.

I was born in the cauldron of this war. An abominable nativity that stank of cow dung. And so all the beings in existence joined forces; they conspired, and finally, their collective will hurled me into this world. Like an arrow released from the archer's

---

16 Ba'athism: the Arab nationalist ideology promoted under Saddam Hussein.
17 The Peshmerga are Kurdish military forces and freedom fighters; a guerilla organisation during the Iran-Iraq war fighting against armies from both countries.

bow and submerged into a chamber of afflictions. Suffering and revulsion. Arranged into a harmony of obscenities and configurations of pain. War. An abandoned village. Elderly men with long clay pipes. And then one filthy stable. The whole scene was complete. Just like a theatre imitating life, featuring the stench of fresh manure.

So what difference does it make whether a human being is born into such a world, to be born beside cows and within an abandoned village? /

So what difference does it make whether a human being is born into an environment like paradise, somewhere graced with the fragrance of prosperity?

Was that stable selectively designated to quarantine the excrement exuded by a newborn baby? To confine the filth of an infant who had just entered the world, a war-stricken newborn? Now here's a simple aphorism for you: 'A house must always be kept clean.' Really, how ridiculous. How absurd. In fact, it's even insulting. How is it possible that a vulnerable newborn, and the even more vulnerable mother, could be bearers of filth? Bringing filth into this world? What filth? Was there even one unsoiled site left anywhere? All the alleys, all the villages, all the cities . . . all of them overflowing with shit. All the buildings. All the orchards. All the gardens. All the farms. All the minarets. All of them left defiled. So what's this nonsense about the necessity of bringing a newborn into the world inside a barn designated for cows? And among stacks of manure for that matter. My thoughts run on. I'm certain that at the moment when I cried out for the first time all the cows were shocked and they just swayed their heads.

It's a remarkable event when a cow realises that something special is taking place around it and something unique is coming into existence. When a cow sways its head within a war-ravaged city it's possible that the war-ravaged people interpret it as something awe-inspiring and rich with philosophy.

My mother used to tell me the following: 'When you were struggling to throw yourself into the human realm, when you were throwing your final kicks at the wall of my womb with your tiny legs, I drifted away, unaware of what was going on . . . and lost consciousness.' Now I know what you're thinking: the passage was tight and my head was big! That I had a mischievous character right from the time I was born? No, no. So go the thoughts of those who reside in a position of privilege, those who benefit from the caesarean scalpel as a scientific advance. My mother was starving.

I was born in a time of war. A war that plummeted down from above. And even the one-day-old child's psychological schema and mental state were traumatised . . . like shrapnel within critical parts of the body . . . imprinted . . . forever. However, childhood is even more vigorous than war. As I express these words it feels like the calm after the war, when everything has morphed, everything has mutated exactly to the same degree.

Childhood constitutes our very first battle; childhood is a mythical tale, a complete epic. People are all born naked, born tiny, completely bare, exposed; one is always on a journey. A childhood that replicates death, forever intertwined with death, and always in perpetual flux.

But I write my reflections as though I were an observer, an observer with a view from above, enabling me to cut through my experiences like a knife, cut through with aggression, with a tongue like a sword, cutting deep within oneself, cutting deep within, like those moments after waking from a nightmare, a nightmare depicting an arid and freezing night, a nightmare depicting life itself.

My earliest childhood memories are of warplanes ruthlessly raiding the skies. Warplanes splitting the sky over a village nestled within forests of chestnut oak trees; my earliest childhood memories are of the fear that ran deep within our bones. Dear god, when the sirens screamed, when the planes thundered, when tanks roared, the women became the most avid spectators. On many occasions I imagined people lying dead there on the mark of destruction left by one-hundred-tonne bombs dropped on homes, on top of the dwellings that represented the birthplace of those same people. The waste, the smoke, the dust, the smog, the shockwaves, the heat, the multi-coloured sparks . . . the volume of it all . . . all penetrating the inner sanctum of the mind. However, this was considered to be the most painless and most gracious form of death. Even for me, it seems to be the most peaceful way to die, a scenario where one is totally annihilated in an instant.

It is quite possible that I received the impressions and hurt that arose from the war through my mother. The women perceived the war as a kind of deluge or typhoon. A struggle for survival – they survived right throughout the war. Out of everything that I can remember about the war, I can't recall the presence of even one man. Only children and women could be seen.

I am a child of war /

War is like a myth or an attack by a giant /

War is one of quadruplets: war is born with destitution, poverty and terror /

Life always means much more than war, much more than destitution, much more than deprivation /

Life for me always emerges from within desolation /

Life for me always emerges out of the beauties hidden within
desolation. And the bloodiness of desolation is laid bare for all to see /

Life is exposed like an open book, exposed just like the silky smooth legs
of a woman, like her long neck, like her hair, hair that is the colour of
red wine /

Life is like an accident; destiny just carries on like a beat; the light
of the world appears like a miracle, like an explosion that eventually
cooled down.

I am disintegrated and dismembered, my decrepit past fragmented
and scattered, no longer integral, unable to become whole once
again. The total collection of scenes turns like pages of a short story,
churned through with the speed of light. In Eastern societies, it
seems to me, something limits people; the mind matures a bit
late; the mind realises its potential a bit late. And often the people
are unaware of what it truly means to know such realisations and
emancipations. Growth and development of a lifetime takes place
by perpetually traversing from the foundations of family life to
our times with friends . . . from friends to other friends . . . from
our city to another city . . . to another love . . . and to another
life . . . and to another death.

I must confess that I don't know who I am and what I will
become. I have interpreted my whole past over and over again.
Parts of my past have been unlocked as a result of the death of
my loved ones. And, in addition, other parts are frozen; they have
become fixed in my mind. As I grow older, the images form into
coherent islands, but they never lose that sense of fragmentation
and dislocation. Life is full of islands; islands that all appear to be
completely foreign lands in comparison to each other.

And school – a structure that always confined me. What

I learned there were practices of escape. Necessary practices of escape, signifying practices. Practices of escape that reform real-life encounters into fantastic scenes and incidents, reformulate reality in the most brilliant of ways.

Escape due to the appearance of a watchdog, attacking the back door of exuberant garden enclosures /

Escape so I could perform the role of thief /

And enter enclosed apricot orchards of a bad-tempered old man whose only weapon is his cane /

Escape so I could take eggs from a dizzy and love-struck turkey; then I would get lost in those golden wheat fields, fields that were the purview of the village /

Escape from school /

Escape so that I could evade the farmer's clutches within the orchards /

The seasons; the long winter slumbers.

Escape and standing firm are two irreconcilable positions, two uncompromising positions. The virtue of each one is reflected in how the individual manifests their capacities, how the individual displays volition, through tenacity, through a rebellious spirit.

I have fallen in love a few times. Love. Possibly the most unresolved issue of my life. The love between two people. Resonating with the harmony of the most ancient chants, surging like the refreshing water of mineral springs, exhilarating like visions stimulated by the omnipresence of the bluest skies. Encounters with love, encounters numbering a few, each time a special someone, each time a special encounter.

In love to the point of death /

In love to the point of tears /

In love to the point when the stomach dissents and refuses to digest /

One particular form of attraction /

One particular ecology of allure /

One particular strategy of escape /

The richest truths bundled together by two people.

Love, like that felt for an *ašāyer*[18] girl, the crown of her clan; love, a longing for an ašāyer girl, a longing for the majestic maiden of her kinfolk; love, the desire for an ašāyer girl on seasonal nomadic migration; love for an ašāyer girl atop a mare with scarlet mane; love for an ašāyer girl transmigrating on a mare in raptures.

I fell in love up on a hill where I was entranced by the fragrance of prickly artichokes /

I fell in love on a spring day /

I fell in love together with the scent of chamomile flowers /

I fell in love as I sat on a throne made of stone from the mountains /

I fell in love as I drowned in my hopes and dreams /

I fell in love as I sank into the anxieties of youth /

I fell in love as I directed my gaze towards the horizon /

---

18 *Ašāyer* (ashayer) are pastoral semi-nomadic clans that move with the seasons between two main sites identified for fresh pastures: *qeshlāq* (rural settlement in lower valleys for winter grazing) and *yailāq* (highland rural settlement for summer grazing). Most ašāyer have now become urbanised but tribes still exist that preserve communal pride by maintaining practices of seasonal semi-nomadic movement and traditional lifestyles and cultures.

267

I fell in love as the horizon carried away the dignified glories of the migrating tribe – the tribe that was also carrying away their daughter /

I fell in love as the tribe drifted past, wayfarers travelling through as I remained there in the midst of a village tucked away within forests of chestnuts /

I fell in love as they journeyed away, slowly, step-by-step, towards a lost destination.

Now I am past thirty years of age I look back at my behaviour and emotions – now I can't find any way to turn back, no way to recover that previous state. However, I retain the embers of those feelings – to hold on to this distant moment is one of the biggest achievements of all my days of searching.

—

The sound of a cat is profoundly esoteric, an unfathomable sound, a deeply mysterious sound, a sound that makes one's hair stand on end. A faint miaow comes from behind the Green Zone. Cats always suggest something of the occult. Especially when these mysteries appear during twilight, they cause a strange fear. Terror is evoked even if one were sitting at home and one's own pet cat threw the kitchen into chaos in the darkness of the night, just kicking at the dishes. So just think what it's like if the colour and look of the cat are alien and the sound it makes is more like a wail than a mew.

It is clear to me that an incomprehensible dynamic has come into existence: the darkness of the night, the eyes of the cat, the chanting of crickets, the whirling of the moths and, finally, the voice of the cat. An uncanny dynamic that registers in one's unconscious that something of grave significance is imminent, an occurrence right there in the immediate surroundings. Animals are always a step ahead of human beings due to the way they draw on their intuitions. The unfamiliar neighing of horses, the different forms of prowling conducted by dogs, the restless aura of the sounds of pigs, the poorly timed song of roosters . . . each and every one of them could be omens for a dreadful occurrence about to take place.

In these moments I try to draw on my poor knowledge to interpret the sound of the cat. I curl up my arms and legs with all my physical and mental powers in preparation. The cat eventually appears, out from beside the room, the one with the door that is visible from my standpoint. It approaches with a steady rhythm. Its manner of walking is more like when cats try to traverse a whole stretch without losing a second. I read what is in its cat-mind and it only wants to pass from the area. Therefore I also feel that its little legs exhibit a sense of escape.

When we reach the threshold separating the brightness produced by the light from the yellow-coloured lamp and the darkness of night, the cat disappears with one great leap. From a distance I can't tell what colour it is, but the image of something black is engraved in my mind regardless of the colour of its fur. In its final leap across the border of dark and light, the cat bumps into a few tables and chairs, shattering the silence of the scene.

Suddenly, within a few seconds, bodies that look like ghosts exit the rooms. One person escapes in the direction of the dark with startling speed, and a few other heavy-set individuals enter the scene. The first man to escape cries out a number of times making an ear-splitting sound. Moments later he stands next to the Papu leaning his back on the coconut tree. Immediately those few heavily built men – who I quickly make out to be Australian officers – aim their flashlights in the direction of the face of the man who escaped. Clearly, he is one of the prisoners. The officers are three in total; in fact, four guards with the addition of the Papu who just moments ago was resting against the coconut tree. The reason I don't really see the Papu as a real officer and consider him as just a kind of extra person is because Papus are basically stripped of any kind of autonomy or power in the prison. They are only there because the system is obliged to accept them as part of its agreement.

The prisoner is now under the flashlights; they shine directly onto his face and entire body and he is easily identifiable. A mostly naked man who is only wearing underwear. One can tell that he has just been wearing clothes but for some unknown reason has taken them off. Possibly others have stripped him. Based on my first impressions I notice the following and am left aghast: he is extremely skinny, so much so that his ribs protrude; he is tall with a face like a bare skull; he has two large hollows under his cheeks. His abnormal emaciation is the reason his arms and legs look so long. His eyes . . . no, I can't tell anything about his eyes because the colour and size aren't clear to me . . . but I can feel what they are like. Both eyes look terrified, it is clear by the way they sink into cavernous holes within his skull.

The prisoner has his back to the kiosk; he stares straight into the blinding flashlights. He is puffing and panting. The sound of his breathing extends out to me, joins us, joins the crickets and me, congregates with the crickets that are now silent. His stance is that of a warrior encircled by the enemy.

Until just moments ago the Papu has been floating up in the clouds, leaning against the coconut tree; now he arrives to join the officers. He too shines his flashlight directly into the weary face of the prisoner. Actually, as soon as he gets involved, the Papu walks to the spot where the officers stand, walks in order to be alongside them, walks to wait behind them as if in a queue. The eyes of the prisoner and the flashlights stare each other down. For some moments they stay there, facing off. As the officers direct the blaze of the flashlights straight ahead they habitually take one or two steps forward.

The prisoner doesn't move. He just curls his fists. Like an animal ready for an attack, he bends over, ready to pounce. He clenches his teeth in rage, his lips unveiling his teeth. The prisoner takes the form of a dog that has buckled under a similar kind of frightening force, emitting obscure growls. But the weak sounds of the prisoner in turn empower the officers to take a step forward. And the beams of the flashlights seem to target the prisoner's face and eyes with a greater collective aggression. Perhaps this is part of their previous agreement, to direct this particular brightness from the flashlights right into his pupils and throw him into dizziness. Or they want to briefly disorient his mind with the ultimate intention of bombarding him.

An unexpected roar . . . suddenly . . . unconsciously . . . the prisoner reacts by crying out with fury. The officers are forced to retreat. They give up the terrain they advanced earlier.

The prisoner cries out with such ferocity that it's hard to fathom; such a small human voice box, only powered by lungs, only supported by select body parts and organs . . . how can this human project such a booming sound? He releases that yell only once. But no doubt the bellowing sound I'm describing here has reached Delta Prison and Oscar Prison. No doubt, at this time of night, there are people awake in those other prisons who hear this sudden inscrutable noise; they experience it and just glance over at each other. Then they focus their listening powers but aren't able to make any sense of it; then they just redirect their eyes back to the space they were gazing into before.

The prisoner is not content with delivering this one and only cry. Like someone who engages in combat sports he raises his right leg up as high as it can possibly go, then bashes it down against the ground. He subsequently cries out again, saying: 'You bastards, you bastards, you sons of bitches.' Until then I haven't seen anyone with that kind of flexibility in their legs, someone who can raise their leg that high. He actually lifts his leg higher than his own head. The power and force of his leg when it hits the ground is like a real whip and it is enough to make the officers cower together in a bunch; they withdraw not one but a few steps and lose control of their flashlights for some moments. I'm certain that if they were fewer in number they might even piss their pants. Maybe they do piss their pants – it is just that I can't tell from where I am. Looking down from my position I am sure I haven't urinated; I don't feel any hot liquid sliding along down my legs. I am shocked, but I am sure about this one thing.

The officers are in a panic. One of them immediately switches on his walkie-talkie and mutters into it gruffly. Clearly, they are disoriented and all over the place.

This prisoner is incredible, what an extraordinary being. He is unbelievable. Looking at his ribs just moments ago I felt a strange sense of pity and revulsion, but now I am stunned by the frighteningly formidable being that has emerged. And those eyes. I feel I am looking into the eyes of a leopard.

The Papu is the most placid individual there. He is still just holding his flashlight and pointing it in the direction of the prisoner. But he is holding it with cool and calm, holding it without much effort. He is basically a cool, calm and chilled-out personality, which explains why he is standing there like that, so very indifferent. He is no way near as frightened as those others standing right next to him – his colleagues who are really quite petrified. More than anything else it seems that he is pointing

272

his flashlight towards the prisoner because he wants to check out his skinny muscles one more time. The way he is waving his flashlight resembles an investigator and it is obvious that he is scanning the prisoner's arms, legs, ribs, neck and biceps. Without a doubt his Papu state of mind is searching to answer the question: what the hell is this phenomenon? And he is wondering about the source of this man's power, wondering which muscles, wondering about the nature of those muscles.

Humans are like this, after all. Even in unexpected situations they become gripped by wonder, gripped by the fascination provoked. However, the unpredictable is also fearful. In this particular situation I think it is very natural to be afraid.

The officer who is speaking into the walkie-talkie has completely removed himself from the scene. All along, the prisoner is curling his fists, just staring down the officers. I'm sure that this time he has the inner strength and ability to set everyone running with just one more yell; that is, scare off the officers and the one nonchalant Papu.

All of a sudden a group of men appears on the scene; they enter from right there where the officer has disappeared to communicate by walkie-talkie. They are a few groups consisting of a few individuals who emerge from the rooms and head straight for the prisoner and the few officers surrounding him. Each one of them has a fully built, broad physique. The officer holding the walkie-talkie links up with them by following behind. He manages the situation with precision. He has called in the Strike Force. This is the same group that badly abused and debased The Father Of The Months-Old Child.

I've always had a special talent with numbers. I have multiplied the few groups of four individuals and calculated twenty. With the addition of two more the number comes to twenty-two.

Two others are already there from before, so that comes to twenty-four. The Papu and the officer with the walkie-talkie: all in all twenty-six individuals. Rhinos up against a leopard. This is how I imagine all the men in that colosseum. Yes. That's right, twenty-six Rhinos and one lone leopard. The Rhinos – basically I mean the officers. No, it's much better to say Rhinos because I think it's a more fitting name. I mean, at least for the setting on this very night, this particular name is essential. Yes.

Each and every one of the Rhinos is wearing black gloves. These gloves are full of little metal spikes around the hand-wraps. Like boxing gloves or something like that. I'm certain that this information about the gloves and the little metal bits attached to them is not obvious from this distance; it is something that I have already heard about through others who have experienced the vengeance of those gloves. However, it is later proven to me beyond a doubt that they aren't ordinary gloves.

Their way of doing things is always like this; I'm talking about the Strike Force. They get involved in any situation that requires a beat down or, as in most cases, pinning someone to the ground. Prior to getting involved in any of these incidents they put on their gloves. Putting on the gloves is in itself a warning. It is a warning that means the stage is set for battle in every respect, so the prisoner just jumps quickly towards a coconut tree and wraps himself around it. A strange thing to do. His biceps completely hug the trunk and he turns his head in the direction of the Rhinos. It could be seen to be a love affair between the two; I mean, between the coconut tree and the prisoner. The combination of his biceps and even his thighs wrapping around, and the enthusiasm with which he is embracing the coconut tree, reinforces the impression of a love affair.

When the prisoner places himself in this position the Rhinos rush him; they don't just take one step forward, rather they run over in his direction. They rush him in a way that makes it easy to trap him in a small net, like the ones that hunters use. They aim to trap the prisoner and completely trample him under their Rhino-like arms and legs; or, from their perspective, they aim to carry out the operation with success.

Without hesitation the prisoner kisses the coconut tree trunk – looking on from a greater distance, the tree's branches look like they are lovingly caressing the gentle breeze. The prisoner's kiss on the body of the coconut tree attributes a particular kind of splendour to the branches and fruit, it also awards a touch of beauty to the subtle breeze that is drifting past, the breeze that whisks between them. After sharing a kiss he separates from the body of the tree. He faces the Rhinos. He clenches his fingers but lets one finger free. It is like a dictator giving a command:

'Listen up, everyone listen up. I am a prophet.'

Upon uttering these words he suddenly switches from his initial domineering stance to the personality of a dignified prophet orating a proclamation to his disciples. This time he uses a more soothing tone, he extends the declamation of his words, he proceeds to blazon:

'I am a prophet. I will be here until I direct everyone onto the path of righteousness. My companions, my beloved disciples who have always accompanied me, my disciples who I know will always stay by my side . . . today is the day of vengeance. Today is the day of revenge against those who have replaced virtue with injustice. Today is the day of revenge against those who just last night killed my wife and took away my child as a spoil of war.'

The Rhino holding the walkie-talkie, however, continues communicating something through his device. And the other Rhinos are in a very different emotional and mental state from when they first got here, and they just stare at the prisoner, just stare at him with a few shining their flashlights on him to witness the event.

The prisoner continues:

'We are all human beings. Humans caring for other humans. This is the righteous path. And this is the affliction of humankind. Humans caring for humans. Humans against incarceration. Not humans antagonising humans. And not even humans against this very coconut tree. This coconut tree is also a human being. This coconut tree is my beloved. Is it not the case that the wicked among us killed my wife? However, this coconut tree tonight ascends into the abyss of the starless heavens, this coconut tree embodies the soul of my wife. Yes. My companions. *Humans caring for humans. And not humans antagonising humans.* Today, my disciples, today is the day of vengeance. I therefore, in the tradition of Moses; I therefore, in the tradition of Jesus; I therefore, in the tradition of a prophet for this age; I therefore, on this day, on this very spot, beside this very coconut tree, and beside my beloved, reveal to each and every one of you this proverb: *humans caring for humans, and not humans antagonising humans.* I welcome you to acknowledge this.'

One of the Rhinos tries to open a dialogue with him with these words: 'What are you asking for, to put on your clothes like a good little boy and go to bed and rest up?'

The Prophet responds as his mood transforms once again: 'Hey Papu, did you know that you are the most esteemed person on this island?'

It is clear that his thought processes pertaining to the study of geography and place are still functioning well. It is also clear that he understands very well the cultural identity of those he is confronted with; this utterance means that he has a symbiotic relationship with the world of ordinary people and the very land he stands upon.

He continues:

'I know that you are the most esteemed person on this island. And I also know the kind of smell emitted by those very boots that you are wearing. I know that they stink like shit and filth. But it makes no difference. What is important is the proverb: humans caring for humans, and not humans antagonising humans. You are a good man but I have received a revelation telling me that one day demonic dignitaries will order you to kill me. Do not fear. I am not saying that you killed my wife. However, right here, right beside this coconut tree that embodies my beloved, right here I accuse you of one day attacking me, one day you will be deceived, you will eat the demonic fruit, and then attack me.'

As soon as he completes this declamation he embraces the tree again and administers a series of kisses. He then returns to his initial position and bellows:

'Accept this, accept that this tree is my guardian. This tree is my saviour. I want to absorb into its trunk. Me. Me.'

He performs this word 'me' again with remarkable power and command.

It is obvious that the Papu is petrified. This prophecy of murder must be frightening. However, at the same time, there is also a sentiment of mercy and kindness towards The Prophet in the Papu's behaviour because he is flattered from being addressed as 'the most esteemed person on this island'. The Papu moves his arms in a way that seems as if he wants both to hug The Prophet and to cuff him. As this is playing out he addresses the prisoner a number of times in a faint voice: 'Brother, Brother, move away from the tree. Come here. Go back to your room.'

The Prophet doesn't allow him to speak any more and shouts back at him: 'Did you kill my wife? Yeah, did you kill my wife?' He goes into attack mode and advances in the direction of the

Papu who stands at a reasonable distance from him. And it is here, as he is in mid-air, that the Rhinos smother him, pinning him to the ground within a few seconds, restraining his hands behind his back. Their method is swift and violent; The Prophet is a piece of meat crushed beneath the weight of arms and legs. Two overpowering hands grip his head; their fists are full of his short hair and his neck. He is pinned.

Putting him in this position crushes his face into the ground, a surface that is so hard and rough that I can't even imagine. Every part of his body is completely under the control of those powerful hoofs and one of the Rhinos plants his knee in the dip of his back, putting pressure on it. As things develop, The Prophet can't move an inch. All this crushing restraint and violence is possibly more about the whip-like manoeuvre of his leg at the very beginning of this fiasco. In any case, this is just some excuse that the Rhinos come up with. The principle being: force must be met with force. In reality, the extent of the violence administered on the body of The Prophet is equivalent to the power that he took from them.

The objective of this whole undertaking is to annihilate him, and I think they achieve their purpose to the best of their ability. Just moments earlier he was The Prophet, now he is simply crushed.

As The Prophet's face is forced into the ground he cries out in a loud voice. He calls out for his mother a number of times; he does this without ever mentioning the name of any woman. He is only crying out: 'Mother, mother.' But as he tries to utter 'mother' his words are cut off, and he can only say half the word. You see, part of his mouth and lips are flat against the ground. Right there on the ground his words are extinguished.

The Rhino who has his knee down on The Prophet's back has a bizarre determination to increase the pressure. The Prophet tries to express words that directly represent the pain inflicted on his body. He utters unfinished and broken words such as: 'My arms, my neck, my back.'

From what I can tell, the Papu now experiences an outpouring of emotion, he now expresses mercy and pity, and the fear he experienced at the beginning of this encounter has dissipated. He opens his arms in a way that indicates he wants to free The Prophet from the hoofs of the Rhinos. But he knows better than anyone else that he is powerless to interfere in any meaningful way, or say aloud anything that might release him. He remains helpless and anxious, knowing that he can't really do a thing.

The Rhino who is continually talking on his walkie-talkie throughout these events continues to communicate behind the centre of the action, without expressing any emotion towards what is taking place. Perhaps he is in the process of reporting to his superiors, giving the impression that everything is being managed well and being defused. By now The Prophet's hands have been cuffed and one or two Rhinos are holding his legs. Most of the Rhinos have let him go and the gloves come off.

The Prophet moans. A kind of moaning that resembles the moaning that drew me to the roof of the corridor.

Moaning that doesn't involve words or meaning /

Moaning, perhaps wailing as well /

And perhaps also weeping /

And perhaps all of them together /

Crying out. Moaning. Wailing. Crying.

For some moments The Prophet lies there feeling relieved, lies there free of it all. His ribcage is flat against the ground. His head and neck are twisted so that only half his face is exposed. He is probably foaming from the mouth, but that isn't clear from a distance.

A single Rhino is squatting down, the rest have dispersed. Moments later another group enters the scene. People wearing white come from the direction of the clinic. Like all doctors and nurses they carry bags. In all societies with organised practices this group is usually described in the following ways: 'Mobilised Medical Team' or 'Emergency Medical Crew'. And sometimes the phrase requires something additional, something along the lines of 'Mobilised Medical Team that attends immediately to incidents for assisting an injured person or injured people'. The term 'immediately' is a necessary addition here; usually the one who announces this tries to emphasise this word. In any case, the identity of these groups is tied up with the concept of time. It's important. It's necessary. It's interesting that all of them, on all occasions, attend to the injured person or people in a way that looks like they're in a hurry or a panic. In this particular instance, this kind of professional conduct is administered without error. A group of a few individuals. With medical bags. Wearing white apparel. Moving in haste. You never see them without one or a few women among them. As if the presence of women is part of the essentials.

When they arrive to attend to The Prophet, the Rhinos have completely withdrawn. Yes. In the minds of the Rhinos it is certain that when the mobilised medical team enter the space they have to retreat and declare the operation a success. That woman. By that I mean one of the women nurses. Or one of the women doctors. Or one of the women psychologists . . . That is, just one woman of this kind. One woman kneeling over the crippled body. This body that has been crushed under knees. The body of The Prophet.

At once, the medical team begin conducting the examination. A woman in white garb, under a powerfully bright light, touches the dip in his back. His body jolts a little. His body moves as if he feels a sting. This time the woman touches his ribs and again the body of The Prophet jolts. More than a jolt, it's a sudden leap. Then the fingers of the woman touch his neck and head. Again, The Prophet jolts. It is as if the sensation of the gloves shatter and raze his body. Are these gloves really so extremely rough and sharp? But anyway, the problem isn't the difficult texture of the gloves and the metal instruments that have been used. That isn't important. What is important is the body of The Prophet which jolts with every touch. Better to say, he leaps out of his skin.

During all the tests one of the men dressed in white switches on his flashlight. They have also given themselves the right to use their equipment in whatever way they see fit, to use their flashlights however they want. It is necessary for their role. The woman in white apparel touches approximately every part of The Prophet's body and afterward she bends, hunched over a bit more, and says something to him.

It isn't clear what she whispers in his ear. But whatever it is, it seems to work. Without any further debate she asks one of the men in white apparel to open a bottle of water and then gives The Prophet some pills. The Prophet's head and jaw seem more like those of a goat receiving pills from its shepherd. He swallows the pills without using his hands. By applying some minor pressure the woman presses his mouth open and pours in a handful of pills. The water helps wash down the pills.

The Prophet is incapacitated. The Prophet is passive; he has been disgraced. The Prophet has been forced into submission. Exactly like a goat or another similar animal. It is like watching a sheep and a shepherd; this is the imagery that comes to mind.

Once he gulps down the pills, the woman opens her case; it is one of those cases that all doctors carry with them; the ones that open from both sides; the ones filled with containers of pills, the accessories required for dressing wounds, and ointment for sterilisation. The Prophet remains languishing on the ground. Clearly, the Rhinos don't feel it is safe enough to free his hands and allow him to sit up or at least turn over. In a few quick moves the woman applies dressing to The Prophet's back. Now it is obvious that his back is stained with blood. All these steps are completed with concision and precision and once they are done the woman runs her fingers through The Prophet's hair with tenderness. Her actions are like those of an older person trying to console a child. The group of nurses seem satisfied that they have fulfilled their tasks. A number of them smile; smiles directed at the Rhinos – and then they exit.

Now The Prophet is all by himself. The Rhinos have decreased in number. Some of them leave the scene as they escort the nurses away. Throughout this encounter The Prophet's breast remains flat against the ground. His neck is skewed. His legs are numb and lifeless. The only difference in his situation is that some dressing has been applied to the dip in his back and to his shoulder, and that there are no Rhinos hugging his legs tight in a tackling position. He is like a war casualty whose body has been tossed aside, discarded on the outskirts of the battlefield. The Rhinos are standing a few metres away from him and his motionless body. None of them feel the need any longer to direct the beams of their flashlights towards him.

—

Nightfall. The night has finally taken over. The grandeur of the night, the magnificence that makes the night what it is, has finally taken hold.

Silence once again. Silence creeps in under the skin of the night. Slowly but surely the earlier paradoxical silence dominates the landscape. The sound of the rustling branches of the coconut trees and the whisking of the serene breeze between the leaves amplifies and tempts the ears. And the waves of the ocean are manic; they thrash the body of the island as their madness intensifies.

The darkness of the heavens further imposes itself on the senses. It seems as though the clouds decide to function as stairs descending to earth. Or maybe the earth has extended stairs up to the clouds and the darkness of the heavens is fleeing up even higher. The fragrance of the sky and the clouds captivate the environment.

My arm. My back. My ribs. And, consequently, my head begins spinning again. Up on the roof of the corridor, where the slightest move makes a clatter, this action would cause an uproar. Again, this occurs without the approval of my blank mind. What I mean is that once again my mind is under the orders of my insubordinate and recalcitrant body. Although, we can't read this behaviour as a revolt against orders, since no demands at all issue from the domain of the mind. Let me modify what I am saying, it's actually like this: I rest exactly onto my body parts as they persuade my lethargic mind; my mind drifts into sleep so my mutinous body parts dictate the terms. Now my arms function like pillows under my head and I just look up at the sky. By doing this I detach myself from the stage with its characters of The Prophet and The Rhinos.

Only some branches of the mango tree are visible from this spot, in addition to a section of the sky – though the icons in the sky are completely indistinguishable. The sky doesn't resemble sky in any way whatsoever. No stars in sight. No clouds floating around. No colour but black. Again, the silence of the night. Yet again the auditorium around me that has transformed into something like a festival of crickets.

This time it is just like the initial encounter; that very same elder cricket starts singing. His voice halts periodically. Then after some moments the monotone chanting erupts again; the sound that is the essence of the cricket performance. Other crickets join in and swell the sound. The splendour of the night multiplies.

A river re-emerges from the caverns of history, a river full of bends and turns, a river that maps the earth in a way that writes its own destiny, a river that mirrors a history inextricably encrusted and embedded with chestnuts. Upon the zenith one can see the river with ease; it is possible to see the slithering, looping snake that emerges from deep inside the faraway mountain ranges. Those faraway mountain ranges are decorated with a milky colour. Over and beyond those mountain ranges appear other mountain ranges. And over and beyond those mountain ranges, there are other mountain ranges. And it continues, reflecting a chain of mountain ranges, mountains the colour of milk, mountains becoming milkier in colour, mountains becoming more translucent.

The river surges through the mountain ranges until it arrives at the ranges that cradle the summit, the peak on which I fell in love. We shared company with the scent of prickly artichokes and fresh soil. I sojourned there, under a lone chestnut oak tree that crowned the zenith. My dog accompanied me there. Just moments ago, perhaps, it has left me to hunt rabbits. But I sense its presence.

Down below is scattered with chestnut oak forests /
Down below is flourishing with forests of wild figs /

Down below is the village I became accustomed to in every way /

Until I left it . . . only to return again /

Oh the joy, running ahead through the panorama of youth /

Through the smell of springtime /

Through the thousands upon thousands of chamomile flowers /

The season is spring, the season of youthful anticipation, the season that unleashes the smell of fresh grass /

In flight ahead atop the zenith and towards the mountainside /

Traversing over the hills /

Treading on fresh mushrooms /

Travelling past a nest of partridges /

Traipsing past a nest of sand pheasants /

Trekking past a nest of sparrows /

Touring past a nest of nightingales /

Rushing towards the river.

Jumping across thrones of stone; in fact, flying over fortresses of stone. The sensation of the rushing wind, firing past, sliding off my head, the wind blustering alongside the temples on either side of my crown. Sprinting. Racing towards the roaring river. Running towards the fields full of reeds. Dashing towards the angst of love.

She is there. The woman is named Jezhwan[19]; the maiden has sojourned there at that place. She is there, in all her majesty, daughter of a noble, nomadic people. Her skirt is adorned with

---

19 Jezhwan is a Kurdish name for women and a Kurdish word used to describe an arranged meeting place for a couple in love. The term is untranslatable in Persian and English.

thousands of golden coins and golden spangles; thousands of flowers decorate the sash hugging her waist; and two crimson flowers lie on top of the curves of her breasts. Doves fly over the river and head for the forest of that one dream.

There I am, standing by the edge of the river, there on the citadels of stone, poised with my body laid bare . . . naked . . . cold. In the distance I can see Jezhwan saddled upon her mare. She is proud, she is dignified, she is noble. Jezhwan is on her way, trotting on her mare. Her hair is the colour of red wine . . . her hair surrenders to the dictates of the wind. The pleat in her skirt dances to the rhythm of the wind. All the flowers on the sash encircling her waist, all the coins and spangles decorating her skirt, all carry away, all swirl through the wind. The skies transform into a bouquet of flowers and thousands of butterflies possess the atmosphere. Jezhwan can sense my longing. Jezhwan can read my heart. She is approaching, she is smiling. She is shedding her clothes, she is revealing her body, soon . . . both of our bodies will stand naked together. Her glowing calves dip into the cold water, her waist submerges into the cold water, she disappears within the waves of the river. From that spot, from atop the throne of stone, I witness the river as it breathes, it is telling me about the smell of her perfume.

A feeling of concern comes over me /

I cup my hand and drink . . . it delivers her fragrance /

My concern won't leave me /

I inhale the smell of the air /

Again, the feeling of concern /

I gaze over at the mountains that encircle me /

Once again, my concern /

I remain fixated on the rampaging river /

And I remain concerned.

And in the end, my Jezhwan appears, draped only in her red hair. She is regal. She is a mermaid. She is as free as anyone could be. Her eyes are closed. Her eyes reflect freedom. Her eyes are ethereal.

I always have tremendous faith in waves and rivers. Now, at this last stage, I jump down from the palace of stone and, just moments after, I am holding Jezhwan in my arms. Just like I imagined, she is ethereal. Just as I thought, she is free. Just as I pictured, she is beautiful. Her smile blossoms into a kiss, I taste walnut.

Dreams represent life /

Dreams are life itself /

Dreams are poetry /

Moaning. Suffering. Weeping . . . And love /

What a fluid stream of consciousness, what a disturbed state of consciousness /

What a pointless flight back into the past /

And what a dreadful mood for encountering life /

A dreadful mood for engaging with love /

A dreadful mood for interacting with a person /

And all throughout, the stars remain hidden /

I can't see them but I can tell they are there, sunk deep within the heavens /

Is it possible to imagine a sky without stars?

—

I hear the sound of moaning. I hear the sound of a cat. I hear someone uttering 'Mother, Mother'. I roll over and face the Green Zone. My eyes have to adjust again. The cat has returned. It is passing through in the same manner as before, just stepping through as though it were agitated. With a short leap the cat merges with the dark and is out of sight.

The Prophet isn't in the same spot anymore. I think a few of them have dragged him over beside the wall. And that's where they leave him, that's where he lies. However, this time his position is completely opposite and he faces the sky. Two officers are there, sitting on chairs and just glancing over at the wounded body of The Prophet. The officers look as though they are sitting around a bonfire and trying to keep warm. One of them uses a short, thin stick to beat The Prophet every now and then. He looks over at his colleague and they say stuff to each other. Then they just laugh. They beat that bonfire, they beat The Prophet, poking a stick into the swollen parts of his body, just poking the fire. The Prophet's body doesn't react to any of the strikes. However, there are times he responds with a muffled moan after receiving a slight budge.

The Papu is also present. But he is a few metres away, sitting on a chair. He just stares ahead looking unconcerned.

During this time the atmosphere changes and becomes even more ghastly. A figure resembling a phantom dressed in a white hospital uniform emerges from one of the rooms. Straight after, two officers follow. The phantom carries himself like a sleep-walker. Stepping slowly, stepping carefully, he walks along. And all the officers do is watch him, without any contact; they keep him under surveillance. I see him, I recognise him under the dull light of the yellow lamps: it is Grizzly.

Just the previous day they found him under one of the containers, passed out after self-harming, cutting his own body.

According to the prisoners he is a madman. From the moment that he landed on the island he has spoken to no-one. If he does utter something, no-one can make sense of it. His trademark antic is that he likes to strip naked and piss in front of everyone in the corridors. This night it becomes obvious at once why he has left his room. He is headed straight in the direction of the coconut tree. He pulls down his pants and takes a piss; he pisses for a long time, pisses for an unusually long time. It is clear that he has been in bed with a full bladder and has woken delirious with sleep. Once he is done he slowly and carefully walks back to his room as before.

Through this whole scenario, two officers just watch – two officers who have been sitting silent beside the body of The Prophet, sitting next to the Papu as well. The crickets continue their ruckus.

The waves continue to smash the body of the island, the soundwaves extending over to us. And the coconut trees tremble. Dawn is creeping up. I am hungry. I have completely forgotten my toothache. It is time to return. In a flash, without glancing at the officers, I shift into action and jump down. The fences have a metal covering and when I jump down my communication with the Green Zone ceases completely. The prison is silent. Only The Gentle Giant is sitting in front of one of the rooms. He just smiles. Moments later I lie down on my bed, next to the fan, next to my roommates sleeping there in front of me. The stench of breath wafts over. The stench of sweat. The stench of bad breath, rotten human breath. The stench of foul human sweat.

—

A group of lawyers from the Department of Immigration enter the prison on a hot day. A group of young and beautiful women wearing fitted suits. They are sweating; their breasts and asses are striking. It is a wonderful sight. The presence of these attractive women in the prison is stunning. Many of the prisoners mistake them for lawyers who will organise and arrange files for their release. However, the officers announce that they are lawyers from the Department of Immigration and they will immediately submit cases for claiming asylum.

The dilemma is this: submit a case for refugee status and settle on the island forever, or fill out a voluntary deportation form. The lawyers don't engage in discussion; the lawyers just smile. The scent of sweat. The scent of a woman's breath. The scent of the city. The scent of freedom. The scent of life. All together this fragrance permeates the prison, swirls throughout the interstices of the prison.

The presence of the women lawyers represents an enormous shift. Upon seeing the women the prisoners overflow with joy; they become happy just like young boys. They grin; there is even rapturous laughter. But at the same time they are anxious. They are restless, they are distressed. Ultimately, they are frightened. Everyone knows that a convoluted process awaits them. These women are unusual women. Clearly, their beauty is cause for suspicion. However, a lack of trust takes over, it takes over the emotions . . . but that isn't any reason to stop laughing.

The western wing of Fox Prison now hosts a building with steel fences set up around it as perimeters. Who is that place built for? A prison, a prison white with steel. That place is another prison in and of itself. They have cut down the trees for this simple reason: to build another prison. A prison has evolved there in that space.

In the following days, or maybe it is in the following weeks, maybe in the following months, a group of prisoners incarcerated in Fox Prison are transferred to the new prison. Now this jail is called Mike Prison. It needs some time; I mean, it needs sufficient time before the space can fully cultivate an identity, before it can absorb a prison identity, absorb the stench of the bad breath and sweat of the prisoners. The space eventually morphs into a prison. The prison takes the colour white; the floor of the prison is white; the fences are white.

Between one day and a few days, on days with hot afternoons, the prisoners transfer their belongings there; most of these prisoners know each other. Familiar faces, familiar personal effects, familiar things carried over in trolley hand luggage. A foam mattress, a small foam pillow, a plastic bedsheet, and nothing more, nothing at all.

While he is being transferred to the new prison, Maysam The Whore is singing. He sings. He laughs. He dances. The Cow pays tribute to his gluttonous desires as he exits Fox Prison for good, gestures towards his greedy tendencies as he anticipates the new prison. As he leaves, The Cow has one hand on his stomach as the other hand pulls his trolley bag along. I don't wish to exaggerate but as he glances over at Fox Prison for the last time his stare is fixed on the dining area. He is a savvy and resourceful individual; you see, on the days leading up to this time he has been announcing to his friends loud and clear that the dining area in Mike is decked out in white and beautifully set up. And when a dining area is clean white and stunning no doubt the food is the same; not white and beautiful, but rich, well-cooked, abundant and luxurious.

The Gentle Giant also leaves; he has bestowed his kindness upon most of the other prisoners during his time there, and then leaves. He hugs all the prisoners in Fox, rounds them up in his big embrace, and then leaves. As he departs, as he is about to leave this prison for good, as he is about to exit this prison gate, he shouts out: 'My mates, I hope I get to hug all of you again, one day soon in a land of freedom.' He proclaims this statement to everyone with an air of certainty.

Their friends follow right behind these guys. Fox Prison isn't the same anymore. It is quiet. It seems gloomy. This night, and the nights that follow, the Chauka bird continues to sing that song. Its calling heralds terror. Its calling expresses apprehension, an anxiety for what is ahead. Its calling makes one's hair stand on end.

Chauka fears the prison /
Sunsets are frightening /
Sunsets deliver the scent of death /
Chauka sings the song of impending death.

11

—

The Flowers Resembling Chamomile /
Infection: Manus Prison Syndrome

On rainy days the island has a different colour and fragrance /

When the rain pours down there is no sign of mosquitoes /

*When it rains, one doesn't feel the heat that drenches bodies
in sweat /*

The Flowers Resembling Chamomile /

Dancing incessantly /

Breathing heavily /

Gasping as though in love with the cool ocean breeze /

I love those flowers /

A zeal for resistance /

*A tremendous will for life bursting out from the coils and curves of
the stems /*

Bodies stretching out to reveal themselves for all to witness.

Sitting on a piece of coconut tree, stripped and tossed aside. Sitting on that piece of wood on a starless night, beside the fences, opposite the beach, behind the water tanks. The natural environment is fresh and vibrant with petrichor after a sunset shower. Long white flowers that look like chamomile have grown all around the strip of wood, as if someone with particular finesse has scattered seeds along the sides of that bit of tree. A few of the flowers have risen in a phenomenal way from under the broken part of the tree; with a gorgeous twisting manoeuvre they have raised their heads towards the heavens. I feel that there is a special connection between the flowers and the spirit of this coconut tree which has died young. The corpse of the young coconut tree has been chopped down by a merciless saw. It will last out there for years until it rots away, until it deteriorates bit by bit and is absorbed back into the dirt from which it was born.

There are other flowers too, a little further away on the other side, near the sewerage drain. The drain protects the flowers because the prisoners are afraid of its filth. No-one dares get close. The area around the drain is so rich in dirt and nutrients that the flowers there grow taller and more vibrant. Those grounds are full of flowers that sense the presence of humans. If a human hand approaches their broad, swirling petals, the flowers freeze up and withdraw. For this reason they are named the 'sulky' flowers. Whenever I reach out my hand to touch them they frown and retreat into themselves. Moments later they slowly and carefully open their petals. I annoy them again. And again they go back to that same insular position, keeping to themselves. I have never seen this species before. When I sing, I feel that they are cognisant that something significant is affecting the world of being. I sense this because they move slowly and delicately and raise their heads.

The Manusian ecosystem, characterised by all this diversity . . . is now in twilight. In contrast to the scorching sun, the Manusian moon is the most benevolent element in the natural environment. When the moon is full it practises colour-blending on the layers of thick cloud like a watercolour painter.

An assembly of sorcerous colours /

Yellow, orange and red /

Talismans . . . /

Offerings . . . /

Gifts from each night.

Every time the Manusian moon appears, it is adorned with another rare and differently coloured halo. These auras are a spectacular gift, combining in the equatorial sky with a sea of eternal clouds.

It is the quietest place in Fox Prison – there by The Flowers Resembling Chamomile. A place where I can be alone for hours – away from the breathing of other people, the smell of other people. Away from the commotion, the ruckus, the tumult. In a relentless prison, even the most talkative and boisterous prisoners feel the need to seek isolation, to search for a quiet, removed place.

At best, no-one will speak to me. Yet whenever I try to isolate myself, I find myself accompanied by a few people prowling in the vicinity. Or they put their feet up on the fences in the same space as me. I always expect the presence of a few prisoners or G4S officers. It only takes one person to turn up and breathe in the area around me for it to be a nuisance.

I am glad that the prisoners don't crowd around the far-off sections and remote corners of the prison, that they don't feel the need to disrupt the relative tranquillity of this space. More importantly, they won't be coming to trample on The Flowers Resembling Chamomile. The damp area near the filthy pipes is the only location protected from people's aimless wanderings. It is not fit for strolling around.

During the first days in prison there were flowers all around the fences and beside the grimy pipes of the kitchen. When the vegetation was wet, it felt as if the jungle had entered the prison. Within only a few weeks, the vegetation and the flowers were annihilated under the footsteps of men. With the disappearance of each flower or piece of vegetation, the prison appeared more barbaric and more brutal. This transformation did not appear to cause even the slightest concern for those walking through the place.

——

During the nights I spend with The Flowers Resembling Chamomile, a smiling youth named Hamid, would visit the abandoned place. His smile was a permanent feature. Perhaps he wasn't smiling at all. Perhaps the smile was only a sketch transplanted on to his face due to some life event or series of events.

His smile is silent /

It emerges as a quiver, then blossoms /

His smile envelops his face /

His smile is a silent smile /

Possibly an anxious smile /

A quivering smile /

Equally beautiful /

His smile is an influential smile /

A smile in tandem with the ripples on his face /

A smile in league with his white teeth.

It's hard to discern a genuine smile on the face of this kind of person, though Hamid's smile never suggests inauthenticity. What is important is the smile itself, a smile that says, 'take heed, take heed of me, this is me, this is me adorned with my jubilee of smiles'. The Smiling Youth is like that – an eternal smile on his chubby face – thick lips – exuberant eyebrows – powerful muscles and bone structure. He even smiles at the flowers. And in some instances he smiles at the fences, and at his flip-flops as they perch up on the rigid fence. He is quiet and solitary. When he enters the secluded area of the flowers, he steps with caution. I think that he takes care that his feet do not destroy The Flowers Resembling Chamomile. The calm of each step makes it seem that he knows these flowers. He really does know them. Sometimes he jokes around with them. He strokes the flower heads and the flowers sulk as usual, and this amuses him, his joy like a child's.

Other prisoners, once in a while, become curious and roam this serene spot for no particular reason. Most never show their faces again after one visit. They wander around, striding through without consideration. They leave landscapes full of The Flowers Resembling Chamomile with broken necks and crushed petals ... oblivious ... in their own world. They just walk through without a care. They keep yapping away, disrupting the flowers, throwing the place into disarray. Then they drift away, like a herd of sheep.

But just like the nights that I experience here in this particular spot, just like the ocean behind the fences, just like The Flowers

Resembling Chamomile, The Smiling Youth is happy, The Smiling Youth is at peace, The Smiling Youth encounters moments of the sublime.

The Smiling Youth and I rarely talk. Two black stones, cold, solitary, out in the expanse of the desert, under the weight of the heavens and all the entities nested within it. Our only interactions occur here, in this place, in this cosy spot. I think there are times when each of us come here alone and then sense each other's presence. When we make our way back in different directions we morph into cold, lone shadows. A complete split – we don't even exchange a hello or a gesture.

I know The Smiling Youth moves back and forth from Tunnel P, from among the rusty fans, among the insects, among the sweaty, naked bodies. Yet seeing him beside The Flowers Resembling Chamomile always affects me. It feels resplendent and graceful. It is rare for an incarcerated person to feel this way for his brother behind bars. Prison imposes a form of ruthlessness and violence. A feeling comes over a person, one that pertains to violence, one that is essential to prison, and the prisoner has no choice but to hide his head inside his shell like a turtle and prepare himself for attack or pressure.

Defence against the fences /

Defence against the prison guards /

Defence against the other prisoners /

Until the death /

And the feeling of freedom /

Standing face to face with the awe of the boundless heavens /

The freedom of standing face to face with the stars /

The freedom of standing face to face with the immensity of the ocean /
The freedom of standing face to face with the splendour of the jungle /
The freedom of the dignified coconut trees.

Put simply, a prisoner doesn't have the capacity to feel sorry for the next inmate and incorporate that man's pain within his own. This is the reality of prison. But not for The Smiling Youth and me; things were slightly different. We have become indifferent to the mercilessness of prison. Due to the pain we both endure, we won't tolerate the slightest intrusion on solitude. Even though there are important reasons to develop and deepen our friendship, we prefer to maintain limits in our relationship. But these limits don't prevent amicable feelings connecting us. The silence of two men, it is that simple.

There are times in that cosy spot when I entertain some significant reflections, although they are both mentally and emotionally disturbing. Sometimes these imaginings, fantasies and dream states reflect reality and spur the body into motion, to exercise one's prerogative.

—

The prisoner constructs his identity against the concept of freedom. His imagination is always preoccupied with the world beyond the fences and in his mind he forms a picture of a world where people are free. At every moment his life is shaped by the notion of freedom. It's a basic equation: a cage or freedom.

In the darkest time of night, when the prison submerges into slumber, I discover an extraordinary enthusiasm for experiencing the world beyond the fences. The narrow gap between the fences and the ocean proudly showcases a jungle of crowded trees.

The sound of the jungle consists of the sounds of birds, insects, frogs and snakes. The jungle is made up of a whole range of trees, reptiles, insects, and even the gentle breeze gliding between the branches.

The jungle /
The fear of the jungle /
The love of the jungle /
The jungle is all these things.

The ocean is something else. When it descends into insanity its noise charges in through the fences; it is heard in even the furthest rooms. A prisoner lying alone on his bed is taken away into an imaginary realm by the haunting music of the waves. But when the sea is silent, its magnitude can be sensed in the smell of its breathing, the pungent smell of the ocean. To reach the ocean and its waves there is no choice but to wade through the darkness of the jungle. The fences aren't too high and the beams that connect the wires have enough room for feet to fit through and climb over.

Once again, a youth climbs the coarse trunk of the chestnut oak trees with his thin legs /
A young kid with his skinny legs searching for pigeon nests /
Once again, mountain ranges, rough slopes, enormous and smooth stone frontiers /
Once again, little feet stuck into narrow grooves within the cliffs /
The nervous tension associated with the space between life and death /
Once again, that glorious sensation of mountain climbing /

The fear of falling into the depths of the canyon of darkness and horror /
Once again, fighting to hang off the highest possible handle on those
tall, smooth mountain slopes.

In the middle of the night it drizzles with rain. For a short time the place is completely abandoned, not a human in sight. I gather the courage to throw myself into the world beyond the fences. With two or three quick leaps I am over the fence. Moments later I am in the dark and among the bushes. It is a form of mutiny, of rebellion, as I discover freedom, as I touch freedom.

Now here I am, a creature outside the prison walls, a creature on the other side of the prison enclosure. And I am now part of the jungle. I am the jungle, like the snakes, like the frogs, like the insects, like the birds. I am the jungle itself. In the darkness of the jungle, on the soft floor of the jungle, groping, fumbling, feeling my way towards the ocean. God knows how many trees and bushes I pull to my chest until I arrive at the waves. My feet touch frogs and crabs. It is a short distance, but full of marvel, full of delight, full of a fear of the dark and the fear of freedom. I am frightened of freedom. But I continue. Minutes later my feet feel the softness of sand. And the waves . . . how horrifying they are . . . how beautiful they seem.

When I reach the waves I look back for the first time. I turn around to see the prison. With all its agony, all its nightmares, the prison can hardly be made out through the layers of branches and leaves. Only a few flashes of light are visible. Under the weak light of the lamps, it looks like a forlorn village in the heart of a remote jungle. From the beach, I better comprehend the majesty of the small island, the magnificence of the lost island in the expanse of ocean, the island's thundering intensity. Yet, in contrast to the infinite greatness of the ocean, the island seems so humble. It looks like the end of the world.

Slowly I muster the courage to walk along the beach. I carry my flip-flops, surrendering my feet to the tides. What a delightful sensation it is when my soles sink into the tender sand. Emancipated from the flip-flops, my toes and the space between my toes feel the greatest freedom. I can't see my footprints in the sand, but I can imagine the footprints of a mortal man who has taken a long trek, the trek of freedom, the trek of mutiny.

When I have finished relieving myself, I sometimes disappear into the bushes for a long time. I peer over at the prison, piercing it with glistening eyes. An officer or a prisoner could be sitting by the fences. But a brief opportunity always emerges in which I can return to the prison.

During those nights when I go on the prison–jungle–ocean tour, The Smiling Youth will be scratching his feet as he places them up on the fences. On the surface, The Smiling Youth and I are indifferent to each other, but we pay attention to each other's behaviours. I feel that he is the only one who knows that I am climbing over the fences, although he will never let me know that. It is nothing out of the ordinary for him to see me hurriedly climbing over the fences. When he sees me, it is very likely that he is smiling. He just keeps scratching his wounds. His lower legs have become covered with infections. He leans his legs up on the fences and scratches his injuries, scratching the swollen bruises and open wounds.

On a few occasions I see him on the way to the clinic. I have heard that the mosquitoes have bitten him. He is in a terrible state. This phrase is common in the prison. The prisoners say: 'He's in a terrible state.' A dreadful feeling comes over them.

—

The health and medical service contracted for the prison is International Health and Medical Services or IHMS. A twisted and convoluted system that takes pleasure in observing sick human beings. When someone falls ill, the doctors and nurses have the perfect opportunity to unleash their power complexes. A prisoner is reduced to a useless piece of meat to be destroyed. Would The Kyriarchal System want it any other way? To see a defenceless piece of meat and then destroy it by subjecting it to a predetermined system, subjecting it to the system until swallowed up by it, subjecting it to the system until what is left is thrown away, back to the country or homeland from which the refugee fled.

The clinic is a few containers set up at the end of the prison, stuck up against Oscar. The site is filthy and the clinic makes a ridiculous attempt to look like a hospital. Warehoused in that site are tiny glass bottles of medicine and big glass bottles of medicine, thousands of boxes of pills and plastic tubes full of serum, equipment for applying serum, and more. But it is rare that any medicine other than paracetamol is prescribed. The medical staff torment the sick prisoners, feeding them pills until they throw their hands up in submission.

The clinic runs by a series of macro and micro rules and regulations, which serve as obstructions and diversions. When a person's report is submitted to the clinic, any bizarre thing could happen to them and anything at all is possible. Men and women decked out in white. Always smiling, but always examining the prisoner from head to toe with contemptuous eyes, always degrading the prisoner's dignity.

For instance, if a person has sharp pains in his heart, it is likely that the doctor will recommend, 'Son, drink a lot of water. Don't forget you need to drink a lot of water at all times.' Or, for example in the case of someone like The Smiling Youth, they may possibly connect blood serum transfusion tubes all over his body, and at times the nurse will administer injections and say with a serious look, 'My boy, lie down here and keep quiet until you become well and healthy. Don't worry about a thing. You'll be well and fine if you keep quiet.'

The system is designed in such a way that anyone who sets foot in the vicinity of the clinic containers is forced to return after a few days. This actually means returning a number of times. Ultimately, the patient feels that he will waste away if a day goes by without returning. An extreme form of dependence takes shape involving the sick prisoner, the IHMS system, paracetamol, and the smiles of the nurses. Day by day the long queues for paracetamol become longer and rowdier. They become an integral part of prisoners' everyday lives.

When a prisoner shows the first signs of falling ill, the first point of reference is his imprisoned mates. His friends show a special kind of concern – the feeling of brotherhood clear as they traverse the prison's hundred-metre distance in the direction of the officers' quarters. The officers in that little room take down the prisoner's number and then speak with their superiors using walkie-talkies. The response is usually immediate: 'Tell him to drink water.' His fellow prisoners respond, 'But he's sick! He's losing consciousness!' Or, 'He has a stabbing pain in his heart! He's dying!' The officers get back on the walkie-talkies, turn to the prisoner's mates and say, 'Drink water.'

With veins popping out of their necks and foreheads, the prisoner's friends take the hundred-metre path back again. They pick up the sick prisoner in their arms and carry him to the small office. At times, one of the well-built prisoners will put the sick prisoner on his shoulders and move forward towards the small office space, proud and taking pleasure in helping another. Other prisoners may also come and attend to him for the entire trip. The numbers of those there to care for him depend on how much the sick prisoner is loved. One thing is obvious . . . on display is the degree of moral excellence of a prisoner and his friends.

On many occasions the sick prisoner will lie down in front of the officers' quarters. He will do nothing but lie down, passive. Partly ill, partly playing possum. Through weary eyes he will watch the determination of his friends, watch them as he resigns from the situation. The officers generally try to announce in a friendly manner that it isn't their fault. They declare that the bosses have to give permission. Then the walkie-talkie conversations resume. Scenes like this usually end in violence. Prisoners come from all ends of the prison and it doesn't take long for a crowd to develop in front of the small room. Yelling. Swearing. Kicking against the fences. In the end, a few Papus arrive with a stretcher to transfer the ailing patient to the clinic.

It is a simple problem. It needs a simple solution. It is necessary to use all one's energy to initiate violence in order to transfer a sick person to the clinic. In fact, the system is designed in this way: 'If anyone is ill they or their friends must kick down the metal gate, swear out loud, bash their heads against the fences, until they're transferred to the clinic.' The Kyriarchal System of the prison has an appetite for spawning violence. Ultimately, for the prisoner's requests to get anywhere, the prison system incites the prisoner to employ violence.

When the sick prisoner is transferred, the crowd disperses. Only one or two of the sick man's friends remain sitting on the dirt in anticipation. However, it isn't as if sitting there represents anything like concern. No. This merely indicates a kind of moral obligation practised by imprisoned brothers.

Who knows? /

*Could that one sitting down over there suddenly become the one whose
head is laid out in the dirt? /*

Who knows? /

Maybe tomorrow, or maybe other tomorrows /

Or could he be the one who suffers a sharp pain in the heart? /

And could he then suddenly lose consciousness? /

Who knows?

The prisoners know the routine. The body has to be examined
four times over. Eight times at sundown for the sick patients who
have to take their sleeping pills or night-time tablets. Every sick
patient therefore has to have his body examined twelve times.
There is another queue for acquiring pills, going the opposite way.
And in the mornings there is another queue, making sixteen body
checks in total. Imagine a prisoner held in Delta Prison or Oscar
Prison who may want to use the telephone. Over there he will also
have his body security checked as he comes and goes.

A war waged with numbers /

A numbers war /

The frisking hands of the Papus /

The imposing stares of the Australian officers /

The prisoners trapped in a tunnel of tension /

A huge feature of everyday life for the prisoners /

Day to day . . . /

A monstrous part of life /

This is what life has become, after all . . . /
This is one model constructed for human life /
Killing time by leveraging the queue as a technology /
Killing time through manipulating and exploiting the body /
The body left vulnerable /
The body an object to be searched /
Examined by the hands of others /
The body susceptible to the gaze of others /
A program for pissing all over life.

—

The Smiling Youth is one of dozens of sick prisoners who have to endure such a system from morning till night. When a prisoner falls ill, it is as if his legs have been sucked into a maelstrom, drawing him down deep within it. No matter how he tries, the vortex just keeps pulling him under.

So it is clear exactly what I am up against. My teeth are causing me pain. However, I know myself too well. I have a peculiar tendency for drowning in that whirlpool . . . I am a being that IHMS could devour in just a few quick moves. I would never accept being discarded into the rubbish bin like scum. I would never allow them to throw me back to the land from which I fled. Yet I am a piece of meat that can be crushed with such brutality that I would fade into nothingness. I am scared. I am afraid of IHMS, frightened like a puppy of IHMS. This is the reason why I give up and allow myself to be operated on in the way a Papu does it.

It happens one night, right at the end of the night, when I am suffering from toothache. These Papus are extremely kind.

Two of them hold my arms. One shines the flashlight on my tooth. One of them lights his lighter, and another inserts a red-hot wire right into the hole in my bastard of a tooth. It blows my mind. It tears my gum. My eyes well with tears. I stop breathing, but it is good. The black cavity in my tooth is punished good and proper. And as I scream, the Papu places his hand on my head. He says nothing. But I can tell what he is thinking from the touch of his hand: 'Son, your pain will cease.' The hot wire does its job. A few traditional surgeries in the style of the Papus kill off all the nerves in my tooth. I know it. This I know all too well – if I had confronted the IHMS system my soul would have been engulfed in thousands of IHMS letters, reports and forms . . . and then annihilated.

—

At the end of every night, The Smiling Youth ends up in the company of The Flowers Resembling Chamomile – the place where he goes to scratch his bruises and wounds. Sometimes he scratches so intensely that he is embarrassed. He looks around and then scrapes his fingernails into the swollen and open wounds. I don't see what ends up happening to his skin, but it isn't hard to imagine. Flowing with dark blood, perhaps. And maybe emitting a load of pus. Possibly oozing a volume of pus smothered with dark blood. You can't see it; you can't fathom it; but on these occasions fingernails can no longer be controlled by the mind.

Doesn't he always have a smile on his face? /

A smile for the people /

A smile for the officers /

A smile for the prison /

A smile for the fences /

Yes /

He smiles for all of them /

I even think he smiles for the doctors and nurses /

The ones who also have smiles on their faces /

I'm sure that he even smiles at his wounds /

A smile for the blood /

A smile for the pus /

A smile for the pain in his bones /

A smile for the skin craving to be torn apart by razor-sharp fingernails /

He smiles for all these things.

—

It is as simple as this. IHMS makes the patients addicted to itself; it pulls them in. And then the sick person is caught up in hate and dependency – entangled. Recently, the prisoners queuing up for pills have started fighting. They are competing to behold the smiling nurses. They even run the distance between the main prison gate and the entrance gate of IHMS. This is dependency on the pills. This is dependency running through the blood of the prisoners – dependency is now a vital part of their biology.

When it is a prisoner's turn and he has undergone the last body check conducted by a Papu, the prisoner behaves like a thirsty horse that knows very well the location of a natural spring. Without thinking, the prisoners run like those horses. But not on every occasion. No.

Even the old men manage to compete against the younger men to swallow down the pills. Their thin muscles discover a fresh source of power, so much so that if it weren't for their white beards you could never tell that they were poorly or old.

The atmosphere inside the containers, inside those IHMS quarters, is always heavy. Maybe it is only me who feels like this, maybe just me with my preconceptions. It is a place I am determined to avoid. To me, the medical system feels like the blades of the fans in the prison – if some tangled hair from my head were to become stuck in there it would pull me in.

A proclivity for resistance against this system /
Trying not to let any part of my body get caught up in it /
Keeping my distance from those containers /
Keeping my distance from the smiles of those nurses.

Despite this conscious form of resistance, I still experience a yearning or desire for knowing. Sometimes it draws me in. Sometimes I even think that the nerves in my teeth are conscious and are producing pain, causing suffering.

When my toothache began I took an IHMS request form and wrote at the top: 'Hello prison boss, my tooth hurts. I would like to see the dentist. Please arrange a meeting for me with the dentist.'

Short /
Respectful /
But disrespectful /
What difference does it make to the system? /
What words could establish communication with it?

What is important from the perspective of The Kyriarchal System is that I endure affliction. Perhaps the system even smiled upon reading the words representing my anger. Even though the system is not human and can't smile, the bastard who reads the request letters could have laughed.

I knew all too well that there wasn't a dentist. And I knew that one week later I could introduce myself in a very respectful manner to the officer at the front of the IHMS gate as a way to advance through the bureaucratic process. In other words, the system would cordially invite me inside itself.

A futile act /
A futile process /
A pointless approach for meeting with the smiling nurses /
Nurses with futile smiles.

What I mean by 'respectful' is that there would no longer be any need to act violently   no longer any need, for instance, to bash my fists and kick in the officers' tiny quarters. My approach was clear, and when I arrived there one of the nurses would open a large logbook and write my name in the schedule. The names of hundreds of other individuals would have been registered there before me. After I would explain to the nurse that I was 'in a terrible state' they would transfer my name – sorry, they would transfer my number – from Schedule C to Schedule B. My number would never enter Schedule A, which is for people who are 'in a really, really terrible state'. The dentist scheduled to visit the prison the following month would be assigned to address the situation of those in Schedule A first. Then Schedule B. And, in the end, Schedule C. A psychological game.

The game looks like this: a professional and precise system in which one is registered in a mass of logbooks, a mass of numbers, a mass of figures.

You see, no dentist ever enters the prison. Yet the prisoners are fooled. They compete until they push each other aside, out of the way, so that they can reach Schedule A. Or by witnessing their number in Schedule B they at least feel they aren't so far behind the rest; they feel they still have a chance to see the dentist. Schedule A seems an unattainable dream. I have never met anyone who achieved registration in Schedule A, yet a whole list of numbers appears to have been registered there.

The IHMS system is even more convoluted for other sick people. A range of illnesses: bones, stomach, ear, throat, nasal passage, eyes. Each has its own schedule. The various kinds of doctors are perceived as messiahs, saviours, but none ever set foot on the island or in the prison. They are scheduled to come the next month. But they never arrive.

A person like The Smiling Youth fights to survive under these conditions. A person like The Smiling Youth struggles to breathe inside this system. Many others struggle for air inside this system, a system that grinds them down, grinds down their very bones.

I have become used to my toothaches. I even imagine that one morning I will sit on my bed like an old man who has lost all his teeth. I will sit there staring ahead, just sitting there, stupefied. Sometimes one kills boredom by picturing oneself in the worst possible scenario. Afterwards, slowly but surely, that harrowing feeling relinquishes into indifference. Engaging in these imaginings makes me feel vital.

—

In a situation plagued by blood, plagued by moaning, plagued by agony, in situations characterised by affliction, the slightest change or transformation can herald an enormous event. So just imagine when the Australian Minister for Immigration sets foot in the prison. Imagine the impact. The news sounds like a huge bomb. It explodes.

The coming and going of aeroplanes evokes fear. The prisoners develop a peculiar sensitivity, an acute sense for the sound of planes flying over, planes usually hidden by clouds. The hyper-awareness for the roaring sound of aircraft brings anxiety. The sound of a plane is ominous. It could mean menacing news. The plane could carry news like a sledgehammer about to smash the head of the prison. Or it could carry groups of imprisoned refugees, groups it is transporting from Christmas Island. That would mean longer queues, and double the bustling crowds. Or the planes could be taking groups of prisoners off the island, and that means deportation, sending them back to their countries of origin. So the sound of planes causes waves of hopelessness, waves of apprehension drifting through the prison.

The Immigration Minister traverses the short distance between Oscar Prison and Delta Prison, taking quick steps, not looking at the surroundings. He sits on a chair inside the container alongside Fox Prison. The officers gather five or six prisoners together, prisoners who don't even know where they are going, to listen to what the Minister has to say. The Minister points his finger like a dictator at these few individuals. He speaks in haste. He delivers his words with intentional force. He says, 'You have no chance at all, either you go back to your countries or you will remain on Manus Island forever.' He leaves in a hurry. This is the sum of the events of the day.

When the Minister leaves, a group of officials from the Department of Immigration enter the prison with a few interpreters wearing green. This is the standard approach when the government wants to emphasise an issue. They gather everyone in front of the dining area, where a staff member from the Department of Immigration will stand on a chair and read out loud from a document. The performance of this individual is designed to fool us. He sings a song created to trick us.

As we listen, our unconscious minds imagine him to be the most powerful person on this tropical island. He styles himself as the kind of individual who delivered the government's orders to the people once upon a time in the squares of old towns. He pushes his chest out in a ridiculous way. He sticks his ass out a little bit. He holds the top part of a piece of paper with one hand and the lower part with the other hand to keep it straight, as if the piece of paper is about to tear in half. Then he reads out the laws restricting life on the island, announcing them with a particular self-imposed eminence.

It gives him a feeling of power. It gives him a sense of dignity. It gives him something other than the wrinkles on his face, the grooves between his eyebrows, the way he holds his chest, the way he sticks out his ass. He acquires a fake form of power, an illusion of power created by performing these words, a direct result of these words. Maybe if a kid or someone better looking read that document they would also take on that kind of dignity or power.

He is like a male turkey and the interpreters are his turkey hens. The male turkey finishes his sentence and pauses. After every sentence, the interpreters respond loudly, conveying the information in a number of languages, transferring the words while in a state of bewilderment. It continues like this until all the sentences are read out.

The prison interpreters seem in some ways to be the most lost of all the people in the prison. They are totally alienated from their identities, from who they were; they seem confused about who they are and what they stand for. They have no agency. If I were really generous, I would say they are basically amplifiers with consciousness.

It astonishes me how vocation can influence character. However, in the case of the interpreters, this influence goes way beyond expectation. Their occupation positions them as subjects completely under control. They have totally surrendered their agency to The Kyriarchal System and have turned themselves over to the spokesperson. As a result, it is easy for me to write about them in this way: 'In Manus Prison an interpreter is a worthless human being. In Manus Prison an interpreter has no resolve. This is the case because they are completely forbidden to express any emotion.'

When a prisoner expresses resistance against their case manager, an official from the Department of Immigration or a nurse, the interpreter may feel helpless, but interpreters have no right to allow their faces to indicate even a little bit of sympathy. If they do, it means termination from work and being taken off the island. On many occasions I witnessed a prisoner speaking with one of the officials representing The Kyriarchal System and the official not ever acknowledging the humanity of the interpreter. Do people making a speech ever address the amplifier?

Once the staff members – no, once the turkeys – have left, anxious dread slowly and gradually encompasses the prison landscape like a flood. Uncertainty and stress have drowned the whole place. When the night falls, large groups run out from this corner of the prison and run out from that corner of the prison . . . they run to get to the bathrooms.

The sounds of moaning /

The sounds of walkie-talkies /

The panicked state of G4S guards /

The anxious state of prisoners /

Their deceptively anxious state /

The inaudible noises /

The sounds of the dumbfounded /

The sounds of terrified, futile attempts at escape /

The darkness of the night /

This is the total picture /

Someone has harmed themselves with a razor /

This is what has occurred /

It is all down to this one single incident.

The bloodied body of a young prisoner is carried in the arms of his friends and G4S guards towards the main gate of the prison. He is like a corpse being carried during a funeral procession. The concrete floor of the bathroom is covered in blood. He has slit his wrists with one of those blue-handled razors. He has cut into his veins.

Scenes like this play out in Manus Prison over and over again. Witnessing these kinds of violent scenes during the nights becomes normal. These situations engage all the prisoners in commotion. They fill the time. They are absurd. They emit the scent of blood.

I can say with assurance that upon seeing that blood-drenched body every prisoner undergoes a peculiar internal conflict. You see, these scenes give rise to a pulsating excitement. The prisoners express their moral sentiments out loud. They spit futile profanities at The Kyriarchal System. Their pointless swearing is even directed at their own fates. Their responses reveal an attraction to the thrills of a night of blood, a performance stained in blood, a theatre in which they all have a role. This lifeless body, these wrists with bloody incisions, a scene that captivates the attention and absorbs the emotions of all the prisoners . . . Are all these prisoners brave enough to strike their own bodies with sharp razors?

The scene is like a festival: a festival of blood, a festival of the dead. Witnessing scenes of blood is a catharsis that purifies the emotions and psyche. The scene is a mirror that reflects the prisoners, and they gaze into it. Not one individual has the courage to admit that he is in some way fascinated with this scene, not even to whisper it quietly to the person next to him. These are the wonders of the creature known as the human.

As night falls, all the senses become heightened, all the senses transform into those of a hunter, poised for action, in case a horrific incident takes place in one of the bathrooms. If blood is the primary substance and the source of all afflictions, it seems necessary that blood should splatter everywhere. It is enough for one person to bow under the dreadful circumstances of life, enough for the world to regress into the darkest darkness right before his eyes.

A razor with a blue handle /
He holds it in his hand /
He slides it along his exquisite skin /
Slides it along skin quivering with fear.

Self-harm has become established for some in the prison as a kind of cultural practice. When someone cuts themselves, it elicits a form of respect among the prisoners. However, the criterion for status pertains to the depth of the slit, the severity of the wound. The more terror inflicted, the greater the credibility. It is unwritten and cryptic – but it is real.

The faces of those who have self-harmed show peace, a profound peace akin to ecstasy, akin to euphoria. I base this observation on my rigorous investigation of faces, a detailed examination of the marks and wrinkles rippling across them. When a prisoner spills his blood, he appears to enter a state of ecstasy and euphoria for some minutes, an existential moment emitting the scent of death. The face, the face goes white like chalk.

Blood is an amazing element of nature: warm, crimson, and with a scent that induces horror. It's the colour of death. A wondrous craving for blood-spill, a wondrous yearning for self-harm; that's all there is to the tale.

—

The bloody incident is over. It is someone else's turn. Another prisoner, two bathrooms down, creates another bloody scenario much like the first. This time he tears into his own belly, a number of deep cuts into his hairy stomach. Narrow streams of blood cascade down his body, canals of blood flowing downward.

As always, a large group of prisoners climb over one another to see what is going on. The faster and more agile go to extreme lengths to see, close up, the body drowning in blood and sweat. When people start to disperse, some look around the inside of the bathroom. Blood is splattered all over the mouldy floor and walls, all over the fungus that spreads throughout the place. They inhale the smell. They whinge and whine under their breath, and then they leave. Those individuals know they can't see the whole incident play out because a group of local staff turn up with cleaning equipment. They clean up the clotting blood, directing it into the filthy drains.

When the blood blends with the water it becomes more interesting to look at, it seems. Rivers of blood flow from the hole at the end of the showers towards the ocean. And what about that blood! Human blood, the element of affliction. Some people wait in anticipation while the staff clean, waiting to follow the rivers of blood up to the fences that border the ocean.

After everything is over, in response to these incidents, I retreat to the space next to the strip of coconut tree, to the heavy emptiness of that spot, to the place with all the flowers. This night I have a particularly strong urge to free myself, to escape to the other side of the fences, to touch the plants, to feel the sand. But The Smiling Youth comes over.

Immediately, a few G4S guards pull up chairs and sit close by. I know well what these bastards are all about. When their numbers increase and one of them goes off to grab chairs they will sit for hours without getting up even once. They yap away, occasionally they bellow with laughter, spitting out hearty laughter for all to hear, laughing boisterously at utter nonsense. I am sure that there is no way I will be able to climb over the fences this night. So I just put my feet up against the fences . . . sitting there in silence.

I play with my toes. I smoke. It seems that my cigarette smoke is graced with a particular kind of intelligence. With each puff I exhale, the smoke goes up until it hits the wires of the fences. As it hits the fences it becomes invisible; it disappears. As the smoke passes out of the prison through the fences, it bunches up like clouds spreading in different directions. For the crabs, entering the prison seems an imperative mission. The older the crabs become, the further away from the ocean they venture. One of those mysteries.

The jungle seems broodingly darker than ever before /

But the crickets and frogs reign supreme /

This night the chanting of the crickets and frogs entrances the prison /

The prison has a spell on it /

The prison is possessed by the jungle /

The prison is absorbed into the jungle /

The prison is engulfed in a heavy mood /

The prison is terrified /

The elderly crab is gradually digging up the moist earth with its claws /

It is calmly excavating the soft dirt that lies beneath the fences /

The old crab digs until it penetrates the prison.

The Smiling Youth also sticks his feet up on the fences. Sitting with one's feet resting up on the fences is a common practice among practically all the prisoners. I know a prisoner who has his own special way of sticking his feet up while sitting on a chair. He sinks down deep in his chair, so much so that you can only see his head while his ass is somewhat suspended in mid-air. He balances there like that, determined to hang his feet from the highest point of the fence. If one were to look over at him from a distance, one would only see two long legs like two tall pillars connected to the fences.

I have my own particular way of sitting. I am more inclined to manoeuvre onto the back legs of the chair, to swing on it for fun. Most of the time I balance on two chair legs, sometimes even on one. This is just a form of play, the body in playful motion so that the mind can ruminate and focus on fragmented images. The body in jest while consciousness curates the mental objects for a parade, shattered thoughts marching in military procession.

The Smiling Youth always sits on his chair in the most standard way, like a manager at his office, except that he puts his feet up on the fences. On this night, however, it seems as if he is changing, as if he is crumbling. He sinks deep into the chair.

This night, we are clearly in each other's way, but we decide to tolerate each other. It seems that if one of us were to get up off our chair something bad may occur. Perhaps it is fear, or something like fear. But whatever it is, we have no choice but to tolerate this foreboding, to put up with the way things are. The two of us have to come to terms with whatever is causing the anguish. We are two individuals, two foreign individuals, two individuals trying to acclimatise to the scents of a foreign land – and this feeling of alienation, this encounter with what is foreign, is our shared experience.

This feeling comes to a crashing halt. There is an incident in another corner of the prison. The walkie-talkies of the G4S guards sound. They get up and run. When all the G4S guards run towards one location from all ends of the prison it means a red alert. And when the prisoners see the G4S guards running, they run behind them without hesitation and with no idea what they are doing. Within a few minutes, all this running ends up with a horde gathering at one particular point, a whole bunch of people crowding around.

The Smiling Youth and I also run. For a moment we look over at each other, we glance questioningly, and run. In front of the main gate of the prison The Smiling Youth disappears into the crowd. No doubt I have disappeared from his eyes too. I turn my back to the guards' booth. I am horror-stricken. I am amazed. I am watching the crowd. The crowd is horrified.

The blood pouring this night is like a flood or a natural disaster – the sight creates extraordinary anxiety. It is a young lad. He has sliced into the tenderness of his neck.

—

In these circumstances, someone always assumes a more responsible role. These kinds of people can be found everywhere inside a prison. These people go to any lengths to be in a ruckus, do whatever it takes to be involved in any incident. Little dictators with little minds, contained in a prison, with an enormous capacity for self-deception. This is the reality of prison. Self-appointed naive leaders who can easily gain a false sense of power simply by being acknowledged as a leader. Easily influenced, they become tools to resist The Kyriarchal System.

Taking on the role of a true leader involves courage. Real leadership involves guiding groups of people with fortitude. But consider this: the people also follow and support a weak leader if it serves their purposes, especially in prison. Courageous leaders require courageous men and women in order to create change. In our prison the prisoners keep their distance from those who express some boldness and bravery because that will mean that they will not have to exert courage themselves. Leadership and instruction also require a kind of idiocy – different kinds and degrees of idiot. This is all relative to their relationship with the community. It's stupid to think that one's life and liberation are tied up with the destiny and ambitions of another. Leaders can also have one-track minds, leaders can also be one-dimensional, they can also be simple-minded.

The only true leaders are those who embody a form of

prophethood. The quality of prophethood. Yes. This is a concept that makes a leader charismatic.

Prophethood means opening a new way forward /
Prophethood means initiating a new horizon /
Prophethood does these things by interlacing the poetic /
Prophethood does these things by infusing the emotive /
Prophethood is the emergence of an approach that creates love.

However, prophethood should not be equated with holiness. If that were the case then I could stand up right here from the chair that I'm sitting on . . . I could get up and stand on my chair, light a smoke, pull down my pants, and piss all over everything that is sacred in the universe.

—

As the figure of that youth who has self-harmed is carried outside in the arms of the officers, one self-appointed leader prepares an area to accommodate the body. He understands very well that this is a prime opportunity to elevate himself as a worthy leader. The whole time this middle-aged man has been in Fox Prison he has committed to one objective only: to promote himself to the status of a leader. His name is The Hero.

He has some of the characteristics of true leaders. Would I say he is kind? Yes, he is a kind man. He has a feeling of brother-hood towards the other prisoners. He is clearly a brave man, though his behaviour is extremely naive. This sometimes leads the other prisoners to manipulate him and take advantage of him. Whenever he enters any group someone will free up a chair for him, then they will proceed to mock him as though he were a cartoon character resembling a leader. But he remains courageous. If the other prisoners recognise his courage as something worthy of respect, he could pose a formidable challenge to The Kyriarchal System. Perhaps if he shows fear the prisoners would take him more seriously.

Every prisoner must look out for the prisoner standing next to him, no matter who that person is, no matter what social status, no matter what kind of personality. Even the stupidest prisoner tries to operate within the framework of this principle as much as he can. For The Hero, however, the most important thing is to challenge The Kyriarchal System of the prison. But the prisoners are afraid of him. They realise that he will create difficulties and problems for them. They avoid standing up to support him; they avoid getting behind him in action. In this sense they indirectly admit that he is courageous. He is a simple man, and the prisoners see this naivety as a pretext not to dismiss his courage but to leave his courage unrecognised. A kind of conscious dismissal.

This night, straight after the incident, The Hero gets up on a chair to give an address in the mode of a leader, to preach like those who spit fire in the town squares, speeches presented under the blindfold of revolutions, speeches for the enamoured masses. This night he gets up on a chair to ask everyone to disperse. Clearly, he takes pleasure in delivering his words. He is enjoying the way he has emerged in this moment, and he revels in it for a short time.

It is fine until he utters one phrase a number of times: 'disperse everyone'. One person standing in the darkness speaks up in a voice that sounds uncertain. He speaks up in a voice that sounds weak. He says, 'Ah man, just come down'. It is obvious that the speaker doesn't embody any particular kind of power. He doesn't see himself as empowered in comparison to the figure known as The Hero. He only really speaks up just to say something, to say anything. It is just some response, something he is keeping to himself. It isn't something that he wants to say out loud, to interject, to interrupt the speech of The Hero, not something for the whole crowd to hear. Yet that phrase is like a blow from a club, like a club bashing down on the leader standing on that chair, smashing the power he is wielding.

The Hero is silent for a moment. He doesn't expect anyone to have the guts to stand up against him, doesn't expect anyone to have the audacity to confront him. Furious, he hunts down the source of his humiliation. He is certain about where it came from; from where he stands he can identify the speaker faster than anyone else. The Hero is like a rhinoceros that only knows one way forward. Moments later, punches and kicks rain down, the only sound reverberating in that dim space, a place existing on the cusp of darkness and light.

In the minds of most prisoners The Hero doesn't symbolise virtue. They want to challenge him directly so they circle around him. However, some prisoners view him favourably; many of the younger guys get involved in the brawling in support of him.

The events of that night are limited to only a few punches and kicks, and even The Hero himself ends up resolving the issue peacefully. After all, isn't he a benevolent leader?

———

I don't see The Smiling Youth again that night /

I never again see him next to the fences /

I never again see him beside that strip of coconut tree trunk /

I never again see him enjoying the beauty of those flowers /

I never again see his smile /

I never again hear his laughter /

I never again see him scratching at his wounds in agitation /

The Smiling Youth is in the medical clinic, the one behind the prison /

The Smiling Youth is in the middle of a bunch of nurses, in amongst a cluster of doctors /

The Smiling Youth is caught up at the centre of their laughter, the laughs of a whole group of them /

Years later /

Or months later /

Or days later /

On a hot and sweltering day /

Chauka screams out from the highest point on the tallest coconut tree on the island /

The Smiling Youth is dead /

Just as the smile in the corner of his mouth begins to fade into an arid emptiness /

Hamid, the smiling youth, dies.

12

In Twilight / The Colours of War

In twilight /

I maintain the belief that the moon is out /

But perhaps the light from the lamps in the prison has created the illusion /

There is so much light flooding the space that we can see the gangs of men /

Masses of men standing on either side of the road next to the prison /

Bands of men holding long pieces of wood /

A path extends right through /

Right between the groups of men /

We have to traverse the passage /

Through the tunnel of people /

We have to escape from the prison /

Yes /

A collective escape with the assistance of the officers /

An escape under the orders of the prison wardens /

No running is involved in this escape /

A tightly controlled escape /

Orchestrated by the prison wardens.

On each side of the road is a long line of men. Two rows of men ready to rain down a bombardment of wooden implements on the backs and shoulders of anyone who deviated from the line.

We have been informed about the path. We had received the announcement. Everyone has to move in groups of five or six towards the grassed area or football pitch. But where is this yard?

It is an absurd question. The way there is obvious. One just has to travel over the road and between the men waiting with pieces of wood in hand. One has to move further and further away from the prison. This is the order.

However, right behind us, a war is taking place /

A real-life war is raging /

With all its munitions /

With all its yelling /

With all its moaning /

A war displaying a theatre of courage /

A war engulfed with terror /

Behind us, a war is taking place /

Or perhaps it is over /

Perhaps these are the sounds of the winners /

Breathing a sigh of victory.

The Australian officers are guiding prisoners in groups of five or six through the main prison gate towards the road. They just give orders, and the prisoners and Papus standing on either side of the path simply obey. The orders are: heads down, move straight ahead, remain silent. And for the Papus, their orders were: beat anyone who diverts from the path, remain silent, obey all orders. These orders are issued by a voice like a commander at war.

At the root of the orders and rules being blasted out are traces of the hierarchy of power. Without a doubt, this is an all-encompassing system of oppressive governmentality. This is clear from the way the Papus listen to everything the Australians dictate. The prisoners are nothing but a defeated and crushed division, nothing but captured soldiers, their bodies trembling with horror.

We are prisoners of war. As I begin to walk, all I can concentrate on is my shoulders – my shoulders made of all that hard bone, shoulders that I am sure will crumble under a blow from a piece of wood, shoulders which upon breaking would cause me to cry out, a bellow that would reverberate and ascend to the heavens.

My eyes are alert. I observe the whole situation that unfolds without ever turning to look at those bunches of men with wooden armoury. Yet my concern for my shoulders never lapses.

One cannot command each of one's eyes to observe two opposite directions; one cannot watch both sides of the road at the same time. I direct both my eyes to the left side of the road, and then I quickly direct both eyes to the right. It was as though I had four eyes.

Every now and then, the Papus deliver hard blows over a few waists and backsides. The prisoners afflicted had probably disobeyed orders. I hear the sound of the beatings. I hear my footsteps pounding, the sound of marching. I am unaware that my steps are in rhythm. I was unconsciously communicating with the Papus. The beat of my marching tells them that I am following orders, that I am submissive. One would be a fool to put one's life in unnecessary danger. The beatings make me lose focus and my mind becomes frantic with concern; concern for my legs, my waist, my bones.

Yet my eyes still function well, monitoring the situation. Eyes completely aware, completely attentive, completely astute.

As I proceed, my steps gain speed and I stumble a few times. I reach the end of the road sooner than I expected. It isn't really the end of the road, which continues out into the darkness. A few Australian officers request our numbers. The journey continues by turning left towards the football pitch.

It is wet. I notice this as I try to sit down after some hours. But many sit down regardless. A deafening ruckus floods the space. There are hundreds of individuals. Bodies intertwined in fear. Bodies fused together. Bodies like a herd of cattle under attack from wolves in winter.

The officers are herders with the duty of protecting their stock by raining down malevolent blows, administering their weapons of wood on the tails. Everyone had to gather together at one spot. Everyone had to accept that they had to stay there, in one place, together. In the distance we could hear screaming and yelling. We could hear the terrified sounds of a battlefield; the battlefield that was once a prison.

Over on the other side, on the road, vehicles that look like ambulances are driving off, fast. Maybe they are taking away the wounded. The destination is clear: a boat which functions as a dormitory for a group of officers. Or maybe the boat is for the bosses. The place has become a mobile hospital. A hospital on a boat. A hospital on the ocean.

Four prisons /

Four escapes /

Four prisons emptied out /

Four prisons out on the yard, out on the wet grass /

Four prisons out there in the field, soldiering alongside each other /

No /

I apologise /

Three prisons /

Three prisons, because the prisoners from Mike are elsewhere.

The focal point of the riot is Mike Prison. In the midst of the tumult, amongst the chaos of the crowd, sometimes one can decipher a phrase, some news of what is happening.

> *'I witnessed it myself. They beheaded him. Everyone saw it. It happened in front of the door. Two Papus and two Australian officers, they beheaded him right in front of the door. I'm sure he's dead.'*
>
> *'At least ten people have died in Mike.'*
>
> *'Yeah, basically the whole riot started in Mike. They've been at war with them for three days. The boys from our camp also broke down the fences. They went over to help them.'*
>
> *'Wooden clubs? What are you young blokes talking about? Didn't you hear the sound of gunshots? Obviously they had wooden clubs as well, but I'm talking about guns, and you're worrying about clubs?'*

These are the only exchanges between the prisoners. It is a landscape of insanity, a landscape of chaos. It is as if a spate of blindness had affected everyone. Our sense of smell has also been affected. No-one can recognise anyone else. We have no more than one identity – we are nothing more than prisoners.

Some people in the crowd are shedding tears. One of them is The Man With The Thick Moustache – he is sitting on the wet grass. His legs are shaking constantly, restless with anxiety. Another person is massaging his shoulders. And someone else is ordering another person to find a bottle of water, no matter what it takes. That person goes a few metres away and dumps the order onto someone else. In the end, all these other people reach a Papu who enters the crowd with a box of bottled water. The bottles of water disappear in no time. The people who had gathered there gulped them down without the bottles even touching their lips.

The Papu has no choice but to go back for more boxes of bottled water. This war has disrupted and severed all relationships; The Kyriarchal System dictates violence and antagonism. But now is a good opportunity for the Papus to reveal another side of who they are. It's clear that the prisoners resent them; what is even clearer is the fear that the prisoners have of them.

The Papus know the situation very well, and as they distribute the bottles of water they say, 'We're sorry, this is not our doing,' or 'It's not our fault. I wasn't involved in the attack,' or 'I didn't beat anyone. None of us beat anyone. It was all the work of the Australians.' The Papus are genuinely attempting reconciliation and feel deep regret that the situation has transpired in this way, under someone else's control. Under the total control of The Kyriarchal System.

But there is an important aspect of the Papus' culture – rituals are sincere and meaningful, there is a code of honour to be respected. One way to create friendship is through fighting and war. You fight as if to the death, and then, after the fight is over, a friendship emerges.

The subjugation and force of the system are too overbearing. Without a doubt, every Papu who said that the Australians gave them the orders or that they were innocent were in fact involved in the worst suppression and were guilty of the worst beatings. During the war, in this particular battle and under the weight of the system, it is difficult to distinguish between the face of gentle compassion and the face of violent aggression. The Papus are trying to restore their relationship with the prisoners. They engage in this act of reconciliation even though we can still hear yelling and moaning coming from the prison, even though it still pierced the atmosphere.

The weeping of The Man With The Thick Moustache is more like intense sobbing.

Just last night he was collecting rocks at the end of Corridor M in Fox Prison, to then throw them with force at the gate adjacent to the telephone room. He threw those rocks with hateful vengeance, with all the force his muscles could muster.

From where we are, it is clear what's happening in Mike Prison. It is the main battlefield. Two weeks of peaceful protest has culminated in a bloody war. It is so ridiculous to think that a group of prisoners on a remote island attempted a revolt by chanting slogans. As the sun set, the prisoners gathered in front of the gate and chanted against The Kyriarchal System, 'Freedom! Freedom!' They actually thought they were starting a revolution. But rather than challenge The Kyriarchal System or confront the bosses, the protest was more like a minor sneer at the grandeur of the ecosystem that encompassed the whole scene; the revolt was drowned out by the magnificence of nature.

An island /

A prison /

A jungle /

An ocean /

Squadrons of birds /

Casts of crabs /

Armies of frogs /

Orchestras of crickets /

Until then they had not encountered the breath of humans /

Political slogans /

Pristine nature /

Paradox /

A landscape of contradictions.

—

It took two weeks. Two weeks until the prisoners reached the conclusion that they should either remain silent and bow under the power of the prison, or challenge the system with a riot.

Violence expressed through the chanting of a pithy slogan /

Violence, rechannelled in questions by prisoners gnashing their teeth in rage and indignation /

'What is my crime?' /

'Why must I be in prison?' /

And other questions, more like demands /

'Won't you give me my boat so I can go back out onto the ocean?' /

'Won't you let me return to Indonesia?' /

And others, outright demands /

'Trial me in court.'

At sunset, the congregation at the gate was in a mood of terror. It was here that they realised the terror, came face to face with their fears, face to face with The Kyriarchal System. Their fear was now conscious, and the prisoners started to fall into a spiral of terror.

A few people appeared who chanted in unison, 'Freedom! Freedom!' This encouraged the others to band with them and join in. However, it seemed from the very beginning that fear had seeped in.

A shade of horror had coloured the movement /

Eyes become that shade of horror /

Faces painted in the colour /

War paint in that shade of horror /

Even the melody of the chanting took on that colour /

That same shade of horror /

The colours of war.

Maybe they did not believe it yet . . . did not believe that they could actually rebel against The Kyriarchal System.

The Hero was also there. As always, he was courageous. As always he exuded a special kind of enthusiasm, qualities only found in a person of his character.

From a distance of a few metres, others would look over at those who were more afraid. Others watched the protest unfold from dozens of metres away. And there were also those who hid in their rooms.

A spectrum of characters /

A spectrum of courage /

The splendid sensation of freedom /

The magnificent feeling of freedom /

In protest, a brand new identity, a remarkable identity, a phenomenal identity /

The prisoners sing out /

Their throats torn from the intensity /

The prisoners chant their slogan: 'Freedom! Freedom!' /

Revolt /

Rebellion /

Mutiny against reduction to numbers /

Slogans ringing out of Oscar Prison /

Slogans ringing out of Delta Prison /

Slogans ringing out of Mike Prison /

Call and response /

All calling out to each other /

All responding to each other /

A fabulous form of communication /

Orchestration of a fabulous form of symphony.

For the first time the prisoners could establish an emotional connection with the neighbouring prisons. However, at the same time, a kind of stupidity rippled through their emotions. The severity and power of the sounds became a competition. The prisoners in each prison wanted to prove just how extremely revolutionary they were.

Imagine that in adjoining prisons there exist a few people with certain personal peculiarities, like The Hero. For him what is important is that the sound ringing out of Fox Prison is more powerful and more awe-inspiring than the sounds from the other prisons. Sometimes he even incites other prisoners to make the sound heard throughout the island. Sometimes he shouts like a commander, 'Do you get it? Our voices must reach the entire island.' Under the influence of these actions, more prisoners join the protest. By the end of the week, the protest has transformed into an extraordinary alliance.

Now it was time for a performance of power. The Kyriarchal System with all its bosses had been challenged – and now it was deadly serious. The power of the rules and regulations had been weakened, the system can no longer enforce its oppression. This empowered the prisoners. It was phenomenal. It motivated them further. They chanted louder. They chanted with ferocity. By the time the protest reached its final days, prisoners were stomping on the ground, stomping with fury and indignation.

The sound from the men in Oscar seemed to echo out from another part of the island. The sound had such grandeur that it even made the body of The Hero tremble, so just imagine the effect on the prisoners still hiding in their rooms.

The sound ringing out from Oscar responded to the sound bellowing out from Delta. And the sound resonating from Fox even made the coconut trees quiver. This was the sound of power, the sound of an empowered prison population. It was as if the prison had morphed into one, a being without parts, a seamless life force. The sound that vibrated through the landscape was the sound of the entire prison compound at once.

The officers had run away. They were no longer a part of the prison. The place was a cage and inside it the prisoners rammed themselves against the fences. Everyone inhaled the ether of freedom. All the prisoners experienced the sensation of freedom.

During the final two nights before the escape, the prisoners of Fox Prison experienced a heightened sense of power, because the prison was the most centrally located. They were no longer simply chanting slogans; rather, they felt that they were the focal point, even the leaders, of the revolution. They chanted slogans at the main gate close to the front of Oscar Prison and Delta Prison, then they all clasped hands and approached the gate near Mike Prison.

Oh god, the glorious sounds of many furious men stomping their feet. The grandeur of those sounds can be extremely harrowing and thrilling.

The prisoners were on a raging high from all this power and energy. The Hero roared like a lion. A foolhardy leader infatuated with the situation, all his senses lost. He was terrified. But he proceeded as though he were brave. He was so captivated, so mesmerised, that he walked a few steps ahead of the community, tearing his throat apart with the noise he was making. He lost his voice completely. But even though he could no longer be heard, he became even more empowered. Like a wrestler preparing for combat, he beat his chest with his fists.

When the community arrived at the gate close to Mike Prison it seemed as though their energy was renewed. They continued chanting, 'Freedom! Freedom!', stomping, marching towards the prison gate. The sounds were a threat, a call to war.

—

After this had continued for a few nights, a chubby, middle-aged and foolhardy prisoner started kicking the surrounding fence.

With the first kick to the fences, war erupted /
War, with its great magnitude and enormity /
War, with all its violence and affliction /
War erupted with this simple act.

From a distance, looking down from above, Oscar Prison was visible. White plastic foldable chairs had flown through the air, launched onto the tops of the tents. Bed frames flew overhead. Light unidentifiable objects flew overhead. Dozens of pillows flew overhead. Finally, came the thunderous sound of hard metal up against the even harder metal of the fences.

This announced the beginning of the war, the start of the war in Oscar Prison. It was simultaneous with Fox Prison – the war there erupted at the same time, when the foolhardy man bashed the fence. The war erupted at the same time in Mike Prison and Delta Prison. It erupted on four sides.

Dozens of raging men followed the example of the foolhardy, chubby man. They were now attacking the gate. People collected whatever they could along the way and bashed the iron surface of the gate. A force conjured up from a very real substance and lived experience, up against hard metal. The plastic chairs were the first objects available for the men to pick up and smash against the gate. They smashed those chairs into pieces. A loathing of those chairs had grown deep in the souls of the prisoners. By smashing them up, they were ripping apart a piece of The Kyriarchy.

During the first onslaught, a short Lebanese lad we know as The Comedian, was able to find a way to climb to the top of the gate. By this time the gate had been bent down to some extent. In the middle of the tumult, The Comedian called out to the prisoners, encouraging them to go over the gate to the telephone room. The Comedian ripped out all the phones. He threw every single part of them out of the cubicles, even yanked out the cables from their sockets. He smashed the base of a phone on the concrete floor – smashed it down with extreme force. Then he picked it up, lifted it up from where it was a few metres away. With all his might, with all his power, he destroyed it against the metal surface of the containers.

The Comedian was a lovely kid, popular in Fox Prison. He sometimes taunted the officers while he waited in the queues, or he'd pull the most bizarre and hilarious faces. He would make himself the object of humour, getting the prisoners together and making them laugh. Now he was a force to be reckoned with, an arsenal of war. He was on the front line, raging masculinity, determined to bring down the prison gate.

He had developed such a skill for making others laugh that even as he was caught up in the violence on the battlefield he still found time to joke around with the telephones. Before he yanked out the cable of one of the phones, before he pulled it out of the cubicle and bashed it on the floor, he took the handset and held it up to his ear. With anger in his voice, he repeated, 'Hello! Hello!' Then he looked at the speaker grill on the handset, shrugged his shoulders, and then bashed that thing down on the ground.

The officers had all run away. They stood on the other side outside the prison, and on the dirt road behind the prison. They stood there, ready. The Papus also stood there. The walkie-talkies operated non-stop. Some of the officers ran around, from one end to the other, always on their walkie-talkies.

340

Slowly, gradually, a group of local people emerged on the dirt road outside the prison. An unimaginable alliance was forming: locals were uniting with the Australians. Those Australians, those bastards. Even in these circumstances they commanded the situation. They still ruled. We could determine what was going on from where we stood. We saw how they turned the Papus against the refugees. It was not long before the fence separating Fox Prison and Mike Prison was completely destroyed. Two prisons became one.

The Hero got himself there straight away. Behind him followed another group of prisoners from Fox Prison who combined with the explosively angry community in Mike Prison. The people on the road were arming themselves for war. The prison was totally in the control of the prisoners. Dozens of furious men had stationed themselves in the prison, soldiers positioned in their garrisons.

As this took shape, a downpour of rocks descended. It wasn't clear where they came from, but they rained down on the mass of prisoners on the battlefield. Without hesitation, the prisoners converted their war armour in response to the falling rocks. The attack from the sky became less intense due to lack of ammunition. Dozens of prisoners at the sidelines of the battlefield were preparing; dozens of prisoners were now within corridors breaking up the tiles. They delivered the broken pieces over to the dirt road to throw at the officers and the Papus. Over on the other side, however, Papus appeared with more power and more force. They launched bigger rocks at the prisoners with greater impact, wounding a number of individuals. But in the manic ferocity of war, it is difficult to pay attention to the injured. It is difficult to comprehend the extent to which they have been wounded.

The place was a cockfighting stadium. The only thing on the minds of the prisoners was to damage the organism that is The Kyriarchal System; to inflict a blow on those who had imprisoned them.

Still, the sound of the ruckus in Delta and Oscar reverberated through the atmosphere. It was the sound of an inferno – it was hell. Mike Prison struggled under a shower of rocks. But in these terrifying conditions, in this horrific arena of war, the prisoners felt free. The prison, and the power of the prison, felt small under their feet. It was humbled as they stomped on it. For the first time the prisoners did not feel oppressed by the fences. For the first time the rules and regulations meant nothing – the system of oppression had been erased. A bond of brotherhood emerged among the prisoners in this fierce movement, performed in the theatre of war for all to see.

This is an image of the glories of war. Under the weight of all the brutalities, a feeling of brotherhood reigned, a feeling the prisoners had for their fellow inmates. The feeling seemed incongruous, but it was real.

The prisoners gained total control over the prison /

They gained the upper hand /

They could now express delight in victory /

They could now look to each other and smile /

Smile at the rules and regulations /

At the oppressive system of governmentality /

It seemed that the war had suddenly ceased /

The rocks no longer flew overhead /

The prison was silent /

The atmosphere had entered a different phase /

The colours had transformed.

The Papus on the road disappeared from sight. The number of Australian officers reduced. The Comedian was laughing. The Comedian was smoking a cigarette as he leaned on a metal pole. The Comedian looked like an actor in a comedy film. Striking that pose, he simply looked over at the crowd.

The Hero felt more empowered than ever. He gazed at his surroundings in a way that proclaimed sovereignty over the region. He had elevated himself to the status of a conqueror. He smiled as though he were a commander in a revolution. He smiled as though he had reached the summit of victory. And he was right. His yelling and chanting at the top of his voice over many nights had mutilated his throat, but his cries of revolution had motivated the prisoners to riot against the rules and regulations, to riot against The Kyriarchal System.

War is such an extraordinary phenomenon /

Unpredictable /

It erupts unexpectedly /

It ceases unexpectedly /

There is a terrifying silence /

Like the calm before the storm /

Like the moment prior to death /

Even the prisoners found this silence peculiar /

Their blood still hot with excitement /

Their veins still rippling /

Their foreheads still streaming with boiling blood.

The silence did not last long. A team from the riot squad appeared at the prison gate. A team of about twelve individuals. They were like a contingent of iron men; individual iron units with their proud iron helmets; with iron body armour; holding shields in their hands. They were like animals off to hunt for prey. They linked arms, shields held up ready in front of them.

They took some steps forward /
Then they stopped.

Scattered rocks fell down on them like raindrops. The rocks clashed with the hard surface of the shields.

They stood there for a few minutes /
Then they moved forward a few steps again.

The Iron Men were now the focal point, the centre of attention for all those left staring. Objects of many types were hurled at them. Australian officers and Papus emerged again on the dirt road. They stared over at us. Everyone else simply stared at The Iron Men. The Iron Men were like robots that had been pre-programmed and were now being operated from afar, controlled from a centre removed from the prison. Perhaps it was on the dirt road, or perhaps it was in a small control station up in a tree, perhaps something like that.

Managing The Iron Men required a commander to take complete control, assess the number of prisoners and their locations and command The Iron Men accordingly.

The Iron Men stood strong /

Their legs seemed as strong as metal pylons /

They withstood the rocks /

The pummelling of random objects /

The fall of artillery on the chain of iron /

It seemed possible that at any moment the chain would break /

But they kept moving forward.

Perhaps half an hour elapsed until they invaded the centre of Mike Prison. Now they practically had the prisoners under siege.

The two groups were close to each other . . . so very close. So close that The Hero directed a whole tile at the force field surrounding the chain of iron. He threw the tile from only half a metre away. Not only did it not break a link in the chain, but The Iron Men progressed another two steps forward. The Hero's strike was so forceful that its sound amplified and echoed, it bolstered the sounds made by the other strikes and yelling. And the community of prisoners who witnessed the scene from Fox Prison instinctively encouraged The Hero's move with whistles and cheering. The Hero took new energy from the intensity of the encouragement. He moved back a few metres and searched for a harder missile.

This time The Hero obtained a metal pole. He approached The Iron Men. He bashed the force field of shields with supercharged power. Like frenzied bees, prisoners swarmed to form a battalion. It was not long before a few other individuals allied with The Hero to attempt to smash The Iron Men good and proper. The force of their strikes suddenly broke the chain apart. The Iron Men ran away with remarkable speed. They escaped so quickly that it was hard to believe they were the same people who earlier were taking only two steps every ten minutes.

As The Iron Men fled, the prisoners took a moment to bask in the glory of victory. They celebrated recapturing the prison with cheers and whistles. The Hero pursued The Iron Men all the way to the fences and launched the pole he was holding. His sense of victory was complete. He curled his fists and pounded his chest. He roared. His voice sounded nothing like that of a lion, more like a wild ass.

During all that time The Comedian remained in his same comedic pose. Then he suddenly ran in pursuit of The Iron Men, a run that looked like skipping. He ran and ran, and then as he returned to the community, he continued to run as if he were skipping. Finally, he requested a smoke from his audience.

The Comedian embodied an actor on stage /

The Comedian embodied a poet /

The Comedian, an actor in the theatre of war /

Victory had been achieved.

But then, after the victory, at the peak of elation, while enjoying the spoils of war . . . the generator suddenly shut off.

Darkness everywhere /

The Comedian . . . and his smirk /

The Hero . . . and his roar /

Dozens of prisoners . . . and their joyful celebration /

All lost in the cauldron of darkness /

The colours of darkness, and then the sound of gunshots /

The sound of gunshots . . . I mean, the sound of death /

The sound of death . . . the sound of war /

The sound of war . . . another battlefield /

Moments later . . . only the sound of moaning /

Only the sound of crying out /

The sound of solid objects clashing against the metal face of the prison /

The sound of tremendous missiles colliding with bone /

All these sounds came from Mike Prison and Fox Prison /

All these sounds penetrated the darkness /

Amidst all the noise /

Came a sound . . . a familiar sound /

A familiar sound from a forlorn point /

The sound pierced my ear like the wind /

It rested on my heart /

It was the sound of someone who uttered in Kurdish 'dālega!'[20] /

It was the sound of someone who cried 'Mother!'

———

In the deep darkness of the night, dozens of horrified shadows escaped. The prisoners from Fox Prison escaped out of the gate positioned along Mike Prison and moved towards the gate situated

20 *Dālega* is a Kurdish word; it is the word for mother in the Kurdish Feyli dialect. The Feyli Kurds live on the border between Iran and Iraq. A large number of Feyli Kurds remain stateless; they live in their respective society without any nationality. The Iranian and Iraqi governments do not recognise them as citizens even though they have been living on those lands for thousands of years and their heritage is connected with the Kurdish regions. According to Behrouz's articles, some of the refugees detained in the Manus Island prison camps are stateless Kurds.

near Oscar Prison. This occurred in minutes, accompanied by moaning and incoherent shouting. Soon a mass of horrified men gathered in front of the gate. The community was twisted and intertwined, and the men's hearing was heightened. They listened for the moaning, they listened for the faint cries coming from Mike Prison.

Some individuals were successful in fleeing from Mike Prison then. They managed to get over to Fox Prison. A few of the prisoners carried someone in their arms and rested him on the ground beside the gathering and in front of the gate.

Darkness everywhere.

It was hard to tell what had happened. But the whole community was mesmerised into silence for a few seconds, mesmerised by the words: 'He's been shot. Move aside. They've put a bullet in him.'

It was the sound of The Hero. He had escaped from Mike Prison and carried one of the injured prisoners over on his shoulders. His exuberance continued as he exercised his bravery. He revelled in having fled the main battlefield, in having moved away from the theatre of war.

The face of each prisoner was fired up, coloured by frenzy and terror. In one way, the noise was nothing more than a performance, totally pointless, without any purpose.

—

Who was the man who called for his mother? I only knew the Kurds well. The Kurdish mother-and-son relationship is different to the relationships of mothers and sons in other places and cultures. The tie between them is profound and complex. It is a relationship that is even hard for Kurds to understand, let alone non-Kurds.

When a son calls for his mother, a significant existential moment has transpired. This relationship is completely different to the relationship Kurdish mothers have with their daughters. It is incomprehensible even to me. But in the same way that I feel blood flowing through my veins, I feel a connection with my mother. In my view, this sensation establishes a profound connection between a Kurdish son and his mother, and this emotional connection exists whether one is aware of it or not. I am convinced this uncanny bond was affected by the elements of war. It is so incomprehensible, yet I know exactly why: no doubt, war left its mark on this relationship.

Who was it who called for his mother from this remote prison? /
Called for her from this island? /
Called for her from this jungle? /
Called for her on this night?

———

It was not long before the Australians showed their faces. They appeared in great number at the gate near Oscar Prison. Until then we had never seen so many Australians in the prison or even on the island. Maybe they are part of the dispatched Australian forces. Or maybe they are a contingent from forces operating in the background, working for the bosses – the bosses who worked in the multi-level buildings I imagined behind the prisons. One of the Australians requested silence in a voice like a war general. His voice cracked. Perhaps this was the same person guiding The Iron Men – guiding them and their shields from a control station – taking on another role.

'You must escape with us. Very quietly and calmly. Proceed along the path that we have instructed you to follow, and escape.

Be silent. Without even the smallest error, walk calmly, without diverting. Just keep walking. Remain completely silent.'

In these moments, with the sounds of shouting and moaning coming out of Mike Prison pounding through our ears, this offer to get away seemed too good to refuse. We had no choice but to escape.

Suddenly the gate opened. We embarked on a path that lead to the grassy area of the football pitch.

Now one can tell how terrified the prisoners were /

More terrified now than when they were under attack from the Papus /

More terrified now than when they were under attack from The Iron Men /

This is one of the colours of war /

The further away from it you are, the more terrified you become /

A kind of relinquishment of terror /

An acquisition of a new kind of terror /

This time at a distance from the battlefield.

Our backs are to the prison, but no sound comes from there. The landscape is calm, very calm. But a common mood penetrates the community, framing our short dialogues. We believe without a doubt a few people have been killed.

The coming and going of those vehicles resembling ambulances has ceased. Silence is everywhere.

For hours we sit on that patch of grass. We remain there until the officers order everyone back into the prison again. They shout with their loud voices.

Our emotions are haunted /

The prison a desolate cemetery /

As if not a single soul had passed through /

It is devoid of human scent /

The leaves from the coconut trees have drooped /

The stars have disappeared /

The moon is on the horizon, fading away into nothingness /

The ocean is dead /

The jungle is dead cold /

The sound of a whimpering child reached out from the trees /

Whimpering /

Wailing /

The corpses of the soldiers of war move through a grand military parade /

The guns have been retired /

But still /

Hot smoke wafts out of the barrels /

It whirls out /

Stretching out into the jungle /

It goes in search of the child who is lamenting /

The child is humanity /

Smoke spreads throughout the island /

There are men stationed there whose shoulders are covered in gunpowder and dust /

They have lost their shoes /

An old man is there, a long beard dropping to his knees /

He is smoking a pipe, his skinny body stuck up against a tree trunk /

Occasionally he laughs, occasionally he cries /

He laughs again, he cries again /

I see his yellow teeth, his mouth full of sludge /

An old man, his hair blowing in the wind /

Suddenly he looks like an angel /

He becomes younger /

His cheeks bright red, his teeth white /

The jungle a vibrant and luscious green /

The ocean benevolent and compassionate.

—

The gaze of those bastard officers scours the whole place. Their eyes are everywhere. The prison again swallows up hundreds of men, contains their heavy steps as they walk, constrains their sunken shoulders. The place is like a land of ghosts, an abandoned territory, a former battlefield. Once upon a time a war took place here.

The prisoners are docile sheep. They re-enter the prison as if they are mute and deaf. The officers also look weary. They are silent. They use only hand gestures to direct the prisoners along the trail. Perhaps the prisoners are so submissive and obedient that the officers have no reason to shout as they guide them back into prison.

But the bastards always have something to prove. When we re-enter the prison, rather than accompany the prisoners from Fox Prison to their rooms, they take us towards the large tent called Charlie.

Dozens of individuals laid out on the floor /

The ground covered in blood /

Men all over the place with crushed bodies /

Men all over the place with smashed bones /

Men all over the place with cracked faces /

Men all over the place with broken legs /

Men all over the place with fractured arms /

Faces mashed /

Lips split /

A youth whose face has been cut up /

As if they have ploughed his skin and blood is spewing out.

No-one except prisoners are in that space. We are to witness a scene that will ensure no-one will ever again risk even contemplating the possibility of challenging The Kyriarchal System.

Alongside the walls of the tent enclosure /

Bodies on top of bodies /

A mixture of blood /

Different blood flowing into each other /

One blood /

The sound of moaning /

A crescendo /

Different tones, different styles, different vocals /

A war ballad /

One bloodied mouth sings /

Another bloodied mouth follows.

As time passes, the more familiar the prisoners seem. In the corner of the tent is a fat man, his belly bloated. He lies there on the wooden floor of the tent enclosure. His arms are spread out next to him in opposite directions. He stares up at the ceiling. His breathing and his moaning have merged into one sound. I can't see his face under the coagulated blood; however, his broad, elongated almond-shaped eyes exposed his identity. It is The Cow. And his eyes are still hungry.

Over on the other side lies a young lad, his eyes in pain, calling for his mother. It is Maysam The Whore. All his cheerfulness, all his childish playfulness, all seem to have faded from his face forever. He is a different man now; crushed, terrified, annihilated.

The Father Of The Months-Old Child is also there, right there in the corner of the tent enclosure. He sits as far as possible from all the other men who are writhing in pain, trying their best to treat their wounds. He leans against the wall of the tent, his knees gathered up in his arms. His face rests on his biceps. His eyes are the most brilliant part of his face. His eyes seem about to erupt in resistance, on the verge of rebellion, but the revolt has been cut short. His eyes contain a quashed uprising.

These men are reunited, but they are strangers /
They are remote and forlorn islands /
They are alone.

———

Chauka is chanting. The melody wandered through /
Chauka is screaming /

Screaming /

Chanting /

Screaming and chanting fused in the voice of the bird /

Silence for a moment /

Chauka screams once more /

A harmony linked by screams /

A chain extending into the furthest depths of the jungle /

Down into its darkest cavern /

Screams reverberate from the throats of all the birds on Manus Island /

All of the birds on Manus are in symphony /

All reach their climax in the voice of the Chauka.

We can hear The Hero /

His voice echoes in the distance /

He is wailing /

His grief poured over the prison, pounded down on the prison /

Chauka falls silent /

We can only hear the voice of The Hero /

The entire tent descends into silence /

All the men inside become silent for a moment /

No-one is around him /

The Hero is alone /

Lamenting /

Wailing.

Chauka flies down from the summit of the tallest coconut tree in the prison to unite with The Hero /

Chauka laments /

The Hero laments /

The chant of a bird and the chant of a man /

Both chants blends into one /

This lament . . . of nature . . . this lamentation of nature /

This lament . . . of a human . . . this lamentation of the human being.

The message arrives.

They had killed Reza. They had killed The Gentle Giant.

The Manus Island Regional Processing Centre was declared illegal by Papua New Guinea in 2016 and closed in October 2017. This book was completed in the weeks following that closure, during which the author was arrested by the PNG paramilitary and then released without charge. The hundreds of men who were detained there at the time have been moved to other accommodation facilities on the island. At the time of printing, Behrouz Boochani remains on Manus. He does not know what will happen to him next.

No Friend but the Mountains: Translator's Reflections

There is an island isolated in a silent ocean where people are held prisoner. The people cannot experience the world beyond the island. They cannot see the immediate society outside the prison and they certainly do not learn about what takes place in other parts of the world. They only see each other and hear the stories they tell one another. This is their reality; they are frustrated by their isolation and incarceration, but they have also been taught to accept their predicament.

News somehow enters the prison about another island where the mind is free to know and create. The prisoners are given a sense of what life is like on the other island but they do not have the capacity or experience to understand fully. The people on the other island have special insight: they see things that the prisoners cannot, they create things that the prisoners cannot, and they certainly know things that the prisoners cannot. Some of the prisoners resent the people on the other island. Some simply do not understand the people there or try to undermine them. Some are indifferent to the other society. Some prisoners feel pity for them because they are confident that their own situation is changing for the better and will eventually provide greater freedoms.

The two islands are polar opposites. One island kills vision, creativity and knowledge – it imprisons thought. The other island fosters vision, creativity and knowledge – it is a land where the mind is free.

The first island is the settler-colonial state called Australia, and the prisoners are the settlers.

The second island contains Manus Prison, and knowledge resides there with the incarcerated refugees.

—

Behrouz: 'Can I please ask what your discipline is? . . . Mine is political science. I'm currently working on the issue of systematic torture. It would be great if more research could be done on the topic of Manus Prison . . . but I think that the realities of this place can be better exposed through the language of art and literature.

Over these last few days my situation hasn't been the best. I was removed from where I was held and it takes some time to get used to this new environment. I can't even listen to music. But I'll try to send you some of my previous work, my past articles. I have one article that I would really love for you to read. Unfortunately, a few media organisations rejected it – they said it was too academic.

This week I had to move, they transferred us from one prison to another prison. It is exceptionally difficult for a prisoner to be forced to shift prisons.

New environment /

New architecture /

New people /

People who cannot tolerate seeing any newcomer in their prison /

It's like being smashed by hopelessness.

But at least I'm happy that my new room is close to the fences facing the jungle. And a few metres behind my room is a small garden with colourful flowers particular to the tropical environment – they balance the violence of the prison.

These few days I have put a white plastic chair in a remote corner between the garden and the wall of my room – I sit there and smoke and watch the lives of the birds over on the other side of the prison, birds that sit on the tall coconut trees or drift in flight.

I like this new environment, but it's really hard to write anything under these circumstances, to write something of high standard, to write in a way that readers will respect.

And at the same time there are two documentary filmmakers who are waiting on me to send a series of shots for them. In fact, during these days I don't get any opportunity to write. I'm like a vagabond who has just managed to rent a room in an unknown place within a foreign city.'

—

This essay draws out and presents aspects of the philosophical ideas, arguments and collaborative interpretations developed by the author and translator. It provides insight into the burgeoning theoretical framework and analytical methodology underlying the book. It builds on many of the themes and issues raised in the translator's note in order to assist with reading and interpreting the book and, consequently, Australia's border-industrial complex (in fact, the themes and issues are relevant to all nation-state border regimes). This is also only the beginning of a more in-depth and multifaceted project that we refer to as the *Manus Prison Theory*.

The outline of selected themes and concepts is important because it is inspired by Behrouz Boochani's research training, intellectual work and vision. I indicate how his writing and his position as a scholar speak to both academic discourse and activism, and how he challenges common perceptions of refugee-hood in general, and the phenomenon of imprisoned refugees in particular.

One major concern for Behrouz is reception, and the interpretative frameworks and criteria employed to evaluate and engage with the book. In this essay I will suggest possible ways to interpret the book that stem from Behrouz's own thinking, culture and lived experience.

Manus Prison Theory: an empowering knowledge ecology

One of the central concerns of our *Manus Prison Theory* is how the institution of Manus Prison, with its multipronged practices as part of a wider border-industrial complex, was organised to stifle pursuits for truth and understanding. In other words, Manus Prison as an ideology hinders or eliminates opportunities to *know*; to know in nuanced and multidimensional ways both about the violent atrocities and about the unique lived experiences of the prisoners. Behrouz is convinced that the general public have yet to grasp the horrors of systematic torture integral to the detention system. The primary aim of the book is to expose and communicate this very fact.

The refugees of Manus Prison were being held indefinitely without charge, but in many ways they have also been denied entry into communities of thinkers and planners and are only able to function in limited roles when working towards their liberation.

There exists a form of asymmetry in relation to collaborative strategies and initiatives. Interpretation and awareness suffer due to a significant intellectual and cultural gap. The authority possessed by detained refugees provides crucial insight and critical tools for analysing the logic of border politics and its wider social and cultural impact. However, the limited experiential and socio-political imagination of people with citizen privilege can at times distort meaningful and validating dialogue with the prisoners affected by border politics. Injustices occur and are cultivated within both government and non-government institutions as a result of this fundamental disconnect.

Behrouz: 'It's absolutely fascinating. It's something that needs to be considered in terms of epistemology . . . you know what I'm saying? This really is the case right here; you see, the refugees held in Manus Prison have modified their perception and understanding of life, transformed their interpretation of existence, matured their notion of freedom. They have changed so much – they have transfigured into different beings . . . This has occurred for everyone. The process has been unsettling and vexed, and some have become totally cynical and pessimistic of the world and life. But in any case, all of them are unique in their own special way; they have become distinctly creative humans, they have unprecedented creative capacities. And in my view, this is incredible, it is phenomenal to witness.'

—

Pro-refugee/anti-refugee disposition

Sensitivity to the individual and structural forms of discrimination described in this essay requires acknowledgement and rectification of what we term the 'pro-refugee/anti-refugee disposition'. This is a paradoxical posture involving a wide spectrum of roles and practices – a position that forms and evolves when inequitable collaboration, intersectional discrimination and intellectual undermining are not factored into the ethics of organisation and action related to refugee support. The same system that spawned Manus Prison created variable manifestations of this paradoxical positioning; therefore, in most instances it becomes possible and acceptable to be both pro-refugee and anti-refugee in different ways and the contradiction is rationalised away through institutional and social logics.

Different types of harm pervade. Refugees on Manus are undervalued or misread in terms of the testimonies they provide and other transactions they enter into; they are not involved in the construction and application of the concepts, critical debates and themes that affect how the phenomenon of Manus Prison is seen by the general public and, in some cases, affect their self-perception and self-understanding. Also, practices and institutions with various aims and objectives can reject, distort and undermine refugees in myriad ways due to socio-cultural and intellectual gaps and incapacities. Subsequently, complicity and shirked responsibility become factors when institutional practices, organisational networks and individual action are not challenged or changed after problems are identified.

The difficulty arises when particular communities of refugees – in this case the men in Manus Prison – are excluded from conversations that pertain to them. Another difficulty involves the overbearing and often unreasonable culture that demands multiple forms of justification so that a set of criteria incongruous with emancipation are satisfied (criteria that never serve to empower and liberate refugees, and instead perpetuate marginalisation and stigmatisation). The discourse is dominated by the limitations of 'traditional' or misplaced notions, theories, expectations and over-emphasis regarding legitimacy, authenticity and behaviour. Thus, norms rooted in conservative and colonial ways of thinking and acting are preserved and upheld. And these normalised attitudes function to orchestrate restrictive and essentialist performances of refugeehood.

The border-industrial complex is insidious and pervasive such that all citizens become complicit in different ways. Therefore, in order to be successful, activism must involve tactics and strategies that directly aim to dismantle the system. Action must avoid approaches that situate activism as an end in itself.

The following tropes are used to represent refugee identities, often diminish their experiences and capacities, and function to exclude them from discourse and justice movements. The tropes are rooted in a deficit/surplus dichotomy in which refugees are contrasted with citizens:

- Caged person – escape to the West
- Desperate supplicant
- Struggling overcomer – the battler
- Tragic and miserable victim
- Broken human being
- Mystic sage – quirky and mysterious, a trickster.

Used in variable ways, and sometimes in combination with each other, each trope has the potential to reduce refugees to essentialist, voyeuristic, patronising and disempowering narratives (the list is not exhaustive and is open to being expanded and modified).

Terms of empowerment

> **Behrouz:** 'After I watched Bahman Ghobadi's *A Time for Drunken Horses* (2000), I thought to myself that if I ever made a film it would turn out like that.'

Behrouz's book is a contribution to the Kurdish literary tradition and Kurdish resistance. Interpretations need to be situated within the styles and structures that have characterised Kurdish creativity for centuries, collective memories of historical injustice and Kurdish political history, and their relational concepts of being and becoming that are connected to the land. The book is also a significant work of both Australian and Persian literature, but the Indigenous Kurdish ways of being, knowing and doing are the most prominent elements. A schema needs to be deciphered from these elements, techniques and dynamics in order to encourage readings that invigorate the author's viewpoint, project and vision. Following is a list of guiding principles that can form this situated schema for reading:

- Indigenous Kurdish presence
- Evocation
- Self-determination
- Custodianship
- Decolonisation and liberation
- Intersectional and transnational rhetoric
- Horrific surrealism
- New knowledges.

In the translator's note I describe Behrouz's genre as 'horrific surrealism'. Reality is fused with dreams and creative ways of re-imagining the natural environment and horrific events and architecture. Reality is also presented as a form of free subconscious experience directed at multiple individuals, and including himself.

The role of the subconscious is central in Behrouz's writing, presenting a stream of consciousness – or, more appropriately, a fragmented or disrupted stream of consciousness. His writing is poetic and surreal, often presenting a theatre where both secular and sacred narratives and rituals are adapted and performed. This feature, in particular, revives Kurdish oral and literary history to meet modern accounts of resistance, political ambition and persecution – an established approach in Kurdish literature with roots in the work of the renowned poet Abdullah Goran. The terrifying, dark and pessimistic character of many parts of the book also entertains elements of empowerment and authority. In this respect, Behrouz's style and mode exhibits features of naturalism in ways that also manifest in the work of writer Sherzad Hassan.

The book is mythical and epic in many places; it also renders a critique of political ideology and coloniality/modernity[21] and evokes the history of Kurdish struggle against aggressors and occupiers. Behrouz weaves legend and myth together with tales from his own imagination and psychoanalytic examinations of people, as well as his personal response to the natural and built environments. The use of vision and dreams in his writing can be

---

21 Coloniality/modernity is a notion introduced by Peruvian scholar Aníbal Quijano and then further developed by other decolonial thinkers. The concept refers to how modernity is inseparably intertwined with western colonial expansion, exploitation and control.

partly attributed to the influence of poet and writer Sherko Bekas, although Behrouz also grew up listening to mythic fables, folklore and folksong recounted and sung by his mother. Bekas's more explicitly political works have also influenced Behrouz's thinking and creative work, and nuanced and multilayered elements of horror pervade the writing of both authors.

One may also make these kinds of connections and comparisons in Behrouz's book with the work of poet, painter and academic Choman Hardi. For literature that reflects dissident political critique and self-reflection, compare this book with poetry by Abdulla Pashew. For the prominent sense of surrealism and introspection in Behrouz's writing, compare with the poetry of Dlawar Qaradaghi and painters Jamal Hamed Ameen and Ari Baban.

For other Kurdish parallels of Behrouz's surrealist exploration and a longing for homeland and its natural elements one can also turn to similar works by Kajal Ahmad. Her poetry is deeply embedded in Kurdish traditions and landscape, and characterised by exile and its conflicting emotions. As with Goran, Hardi and Bekas, the political and horrific are present throughout the sensitive life of objects, animals and the natural environment. Behrouz and Ahmad are also journalists committed to Kurdish liberation and cultural preservation, as was Bekas when he was alive. Gender justice is an imperative in Behrouz's writing, an issue consistent with Kurdish literature particularly from Goran to Hardi, Ahmad, Bekas and many more.

The writing of Bachtyar Ali and Mariwan Wrya Kanie also deserve special mention in relation to the development of themes and ideas in Behrouz's book and the particularities of its Indigenous Kurdish presence. It is through a rich oral and literary history of Kurdish folklore that Behrouz constructs and develops his epic chronicle. He combines this heritage with genres such as journalism, autobiography, philosophy, political commentary, testimony and psychoanalytic inquiry to create a totally unique genre: horrific surrealism.

The concept of 'kyriarchy' plays a central role in the book and its philosophical foundation. Through his naming technique Behrouz brings into existence a new abstract entity, a scholarly term for a being that represents the multi-structural nature of Australia's border-industrial complex – a being that orchestrates the systematic torture inflicted in Manus Prison: The Kyriarchal System.

> **Behrouz:** 'The government have constructed this system and they create terms to establish and reinforce their power . . . 'Australian Border Force', 'off-shore processing centre', etc. I avoid using their language as much as I can when writing journalism, and through literature I can do whatever I like. I create my own discourse and do not succumb to the language of oppressive power. I create my own language for critically analysing the phenomenon of Manus Prison.'

For Behrouz, first and foremost, the Manus Island Regional Processing Centre was unequivocally a type of prison (he began using the term 'prison camp' after the PNG Supreme Court decision ruled the Australian-run detention facilities illegal in April 2016, thus allowing incarcerated refugees to exit the RPC and frequent Manusian society). The name Manus Prison is a literal translation from Farsi and is designed for a number of purposes, one of which is to draw attention to and scrutinise the carceral nature of Australia's processing of asylum claims on Manus Island. (In fact, it is also a statement and critique of border politics in general.)

As previously mentioned, in the translation we decided to use the term 'kyriarchy' to represent the structures ('The Kyriarchal System' is not a single superstructure) of power and domination that produced and governed Manus Prison. The term 'kyriarchy' is a neologism first introduced by radical feminist theologian Elisabeth Schüssler Fiorenza in 1992 to represent intersecting social systems of domination and oppression. The use of this technical term enabled a truer representation of Behrouz's thinking and experience because it purposely encompasses multiple, interlocking kinds of stigmatisation and oppression, including racism, heteronormativity, economic discrimination, class-based violence, faith-based discrimination, coloniality, Indigenous genocide, anti-Blackness, militarism and xenophobia. The term also captures the way that the intersecting systems are perpetually reinforced and replicated. This important aspect connects the prison with Australian colonial history and fundamental factors plaguing contemporary Australian society, culture and politics.

Closing remarks

As I write, Behrouz still spends his days on Manus Island, yet his work continues to reach new audiences and influence new discourses. In 2017 Stephanie Hemelryk Donald arranged for Behrouz's work to be presented at a conference at UNSW during which Behrouz also engaged with the participants through WhatsApp. As a result of her continued support Behrouz and my work will soon be presented and published in various scholarly forums. Soon after, Susan Banki arranged a talk for Behrouz at the University of Sydney and a joint submission to the United Nations (written with Susan and me). Mahnaz Alimardanian also deserves special mention for her intellectual and cultural exchanges with Behrouz on the last few chapters and for incorporating Behrouz's writing and resistance into her anthropology research; she has been active in raising the issue of Manus Prison in academia. And at the beginning of 2018 Behrouz was made non-resident Visiting Scholar at the Sydney Asia Pacific Migration Centre (SAPMiC) at the University of Sydney by the director, Nicola Piper. As the book was being prepared for release, Samia Mehrez from the Center for Translation Studies at the American University in Cairo invited Behrouz and me to speak at the Tahrir Square campus (again using communication technology for Behrouz) as part of the 'In Translation Lecture Series'. The presentation was about Behrouz's experience of writing from prison, our interaction and the translation process, and the philosophy behind the book. Also, Anne Surma from Murdoch University published a response to Behrouz's 'A Letter From Manus Island' in *Continuum: Journal of Media and Cultural Studies*, and the publication's Managing Editor Timothy Laurie commissioned the publication of Behrouz's reply and my essay about *No Friend but the Mountains* in the same volume. And Brigitta Olubas and Su Goldfish from UNSW arranged the first book launch in conjunction with Live Crossings magazine, UNSWriting and SAM (School of the Arts and Media). This event will involve Behrouz through communication technology and also feature a panel discussion involving Moones Mansoubi, Janet Galbraith and me, in addition to a presentation on art and exile by Matine Antle.

As the book was being prepared for publication, news came of the death of Michael Gordon. Behrouz wanted to acknowledge the work, dedication and friendship he received from his fellow journalist who communicated with him regularly and requested regular updates on the release of the book. Behrouz received this message after expressing his regret that his friend had retired from journalism:

371

Michael: 'Thanks Behrouz. You haven't lost me . . . I hope to write again about the situation on different platforms after a pause. Go well . . .'

In 2017, Critical Indigenous Studies scholar Victoria Grieves published one of Behrouz's articles in her role as editor of the *9th Annual Maroon Conference Magazine* (from the conference held in Charles Town, Jamaica organised by the Charles Town Maroon Council). The article is titled 'A Kyriarchal System: New Colonial Experiments/New Decolonial Resistance'. In her introduction to the volume she acknowledged his Indigenous Kurdish way of being and knowing, particularly in connection with his co-directed film *Chauka, Please Tell Us the Time* (2017, co-directed with Arash Kamali Sarvestani). In fact, Behrouz's most compelling conversations and collaborations regarding dispossession and oppression have yet to be initiated – I am referring to dialogue and sharing with Aboriginal and Torres Strait Islander peoples.

Behrouz's book would best be interpreted within the context represented by the multi-context schema I propose in this essay. Rather than categorise his writing as 'refugee narrative' or 'refugee memoir', the book is better situated in other traditions: clandestine philosophical literature, prison narratives, philosophical fiction, Australian dissident writing, Iranian political art, transnational literature, decolonial writing and the Kurdish literary tradition.

In contrast to the thriving 'refugee industry' that promotes stories to provide exposure and information and attempts to create empathy (if that is at all possible), Behrouz recounts stories in order to produce new knowledge and to construct a philosophy that unpacks and exposes systematic torture and the border-industrial complex. His intention has always been to hold a mirror up to the system, dismantle it, and produce a historical record to honour those who have been killed and everyone who is still suffering. Behrouz's book also functions as an edifying message to future generations.

Behrouz: 'Many advocates and journalists from different organisations and institutions have supported me throughout this time. In general, there is a lot of support from many people; for nearly five years I've had the opportunity to work with the largest media networks in the world. But sometimes I'm in situations where I do all the work requested by journalists so they can write their report without receiving the kind of respect I deserve. I don't feel there is recognition of my role as an individual. What I've learned is that journalists need to respect others; journalists need to respect the subjects they cover; they need to respect the people they write about.

I am convinced that if the refugees in Manus Prison were provided opportunities to form and present a different perception of our character, we would be able to challenge the system in much more profound ways. We could challenge the system with greater ease. But the reality is that Australia has done everything it can to ensure that we're not perceived as this kind of character, not recognised as professionals, as valuable and insightful contributors to the discourse. The government has tried to suppress us because they know that if we were seen in this light, things would be different. Consider the reputation we have acquired over the last two weeks (after the three-week siege starting 31 October 2017); our resistance is stronger, our fight is fiercer. The government knows exactly what we're capable of – this is why they have suppressed us. Respect is central. We need that to continue resisting, we need respect to become stronger and fiercer.

This will take time, but I'll continue challenging the system and I will win in the end. It's a long road, but I'll do it.'

Translator's Tale:
A Window to the Mountains

Omid: 'I read your recent article . . . I really admire your work.'
Behrouz: 'That's very kind . . . I just hope I wake up from this
nightmare soon.'

The experience of translating Behrouz's book is itself rich with
multiple narratives; some reaching back before our initial
communication, even before the construction of Manus Prison.
Over the last few years, especially after meeting Behrouz, I've
come to realise how integral narratives are to living life well, and
the translation process for this book has confirmed and expanded
my insights and experiences with storytelling. This translator's tale
provides some insight into the many experiences and conversations that have shaped the book and characterise our shared vision
of narrative and life.

——

I had only been on Manus Island for a few hours when I rushed
over to the central bus stop in Lorengau town. We met in person
there for the first time. Behrouz hadn't eaten a thing all day – he'd

consumed nothing but smokes for breakfast and lunch. He was still on his mobile phone when I got out of the vehicle to greet him. Earlier that day I learned that the body of refugee Hamed Shamshiripour had just been discovered within a cluster of trees near a school, beaten and with a noose around his neck; in fact, I had passed by the crowd of Manusian locals and police on my way in from the airport*. The circumstances were extremely suspicious and many refugees still claim he was killed. Behrouz is the first point of contact for many Australian and international journalists and at that point he had been engaged in interviews for the entire day. My first trip to Manus Island was supposed to be dedicated to working on the translation of the book – but on Manus only torture is allowed to proceed according to schedule.

At the time of publication seven people have lost their lives on Manus Island, four on Nauru and one on Christmas Island. Twelve deaths in total.

Mohammed Sarwar (Nauru, 2002)

Reza Barati (Manus, 2014)

Hamed Khazaei (Manus, 2014)

Fazal Chegani (Christmas Island, 2015)

Omid Masoumali (Nauru, 2016)

Rakib Khan (Nauru, 2016)

Kamil Hussain (Manus, 2016)

Faysal Ishak Ahmed (Manus, 2016)

Hamed Shamshiripour (Manus, 2017)

Rajeev Rajendran (Manus, 2017)

---

* See my translation of Behrouz's article in the *Huffington Post* 'The Tortuous Demise of Hamed Shamshiripour, Who Didn't Deserve to Die on Manus Island', published 14 August 2017.

Sayed Ibrahim (Nauru, 2017)
Salim Kyawning (Manus, 2018)

—

My familiarity with Behrouz's approach to writing began before I first came across his work – before I had even heard about this prolific writer incarcerated in Manus Prison. My father died suddenly in May 2015, approximately eight months before my first point of contact with Behrouz. He was also from a historically persecuted group in Iran and had lived most of his life in exile; after leaving Iran around the time of the revolution he never returned. His name was Manoutchehr, the name of a mythical shah from the *Shāhnāmeh*, a book of epic poetry which also features Behrouz's name. I practiced refiguring and incorporating myth, legend and poetry when writing eulogies for his funeral and subsequent memorial service, particularly the tale related to the last days of his namesake. In addition to Ferdowsi's *Shāhnāmeh*, my father's life was honoured with poetry from Omar Khayyām and Ṭāhirih Qurratu'l-'Ayn – poets and philosophers who were ostracised and oppressed in their own contexts. Commemorating the life of my father became something of a literary and cultural celebration for me and my immediate family, and it also involved performances and talks from close friends living in diaspora. So, when Behrouz and I finally had the opportunity to sit together on Manus Island and discuss the style and details of his book, including the translation method, we quickly realised that we both approach storytelling, philosophy, memory and performance in very similar ways. The realisation was uncanny. For me, translating Behrouz's book was a continuation of the festival previously inaugurated for Manoutchehr.

The opportunity to translate Behrouz's book was an unexpected blessing. He offered me the role after I'd spent six months translating a collection of his journalism. During this time, we'd started discussing other ways in which we could collaborate. He had mentioned very early on that he was working on a book, but we did not really discuss it since we were so focused on translating his journalism and brainstorming strategies for challenging the detention system. Once we shifted our focus to the book, the translation became a creative and intellectual fixture of our relationship with most of our interactions revolving around this project. It has also been a source of many inspirational and auspicious encounters and discoveries.

The whole project was carried out during my time in Sydney, Cairo and Manus Island. The method and perspective of translating developed and changed at different junctures. The themes of each chapter are contingent on specific events and dynamics in the prison and Australia's border politics. Therefore, shifts in technique, style and voice differ depending on the narrative settings and moments; in some instances, the events and occurrences were taking place at the exact moment of writing.

The story behind the translation functions as a framing narrative for the book itself; that is, the book contains the main story framed by a complex translation process as paratext. The relationship between frame and embedded narratives has roots in the distinctive narrative techniques common in the traditional and contemporary storytelling practices of Iranic peoples (including Kurds). By presenting some examples of this frame narrative, I will be able to briefly discuss key themes, concepts and issues. This approach will help to convey, first, how the translation involved literary experimentation, and second, how the collaborative efforts between author, translator, consultants and confidants matured into a shared philosophical activity.

Collaboration and consultation

Behrouz: 'With journalism I have no choice but to use simple language and basic concepts. I need to consider diverse audiences when writing news articles . . . they're for the general public so it isn't possible to delve as deeply as I would like. And this is the problem right here. I can't analyse and express the extent of the torture in this place. But I think it's inevitable that for years and years to come I'll end up opening critical spaces for engaging with the phenomenon of Manus Prison . . . this work will attract every humanities and social science discipline; it will create a new philosophical language. I'm prepared to provide you information about this place so we can begin the necessary research projects.

It's possible, for example, to examine Manus Prison using a Foucauldian framework and apply his philosophical critique of the prison, the mental asylum and psychology . . . or one could draw from Žižek or Gramsci's well-known reflections and the discourse around hegemony and resistance.'

Omid: 'Every time I meet with Moones and Sajad your book becomes the basis of a lot of critical discussion . . . the possibilities are huge.'

Behrouz: 'This place really needs a lot of intellectual work . . . It requires a team to produce research that is rigorous and academic . . . universities need to get involved.

At the moment I'm collaborating with friends in Iran on the subject of Manus Prison . . . Our aim is to publish our research in an academic article. Co-authored pieces are ideal.'

My initial conversations with Behrouz were conducted via Facebook, and over time our connection shifted to WhatsApp.

Because the connection on Manus Island is so poor we have only been able to text message each other or send voice messages. So there is no direct real-time conversation. Behrouz wrote his whole book (and all his journalism, and co-directed a film) through messaging. Sometimes he would send me his writing directly via WhatsApp text. But usually he sent long passages of text to Moones Mansoubi, a refugee advocate and another of Behrouz's translators, who arranged the text messages into PDFs. Once prepared, Moones would email me PDFs of full chapters. In some cases Behrouz would text me new passages later on to add to the chapters, usually for placement at the end. The full draft of each of Behrouz's chapters would appear as a long text message with no paragraph breaks. It was this feature that created a unique and intellectually stimulating space for literary experimentation and shared philosophical activity.

The translation process was a profound learning experience which helped us develop analyses pertaining to the incarceration of refugees on Manus Island, and many related issues. The translation began in December 2016 and the process since has been heavily influenced by the many disastrous events in the detention centre and the regressing Australian policies and socio-political discourse.

Behrouz's attempts to finish the manuscript and my translation work were hampered significantly by the three-week siege after the forced closure of the prison camp (31 October 2017), and the urgent need to report the unrelenting and targeted punishment of those who refused to be removed[†]. In ways reflective of the book,

---

† For excerpts of Behrouz's diary of the siege period see *The Guardian* article '"This is hell out here": how Behrouz Boochani's diaries expose Australia's refugee shame', published 4 December 2017. Translations by Moones Mansoubi and me.

Behrouz employed a mix of literary language and journalism to depict the strategic use of starvation, thirst, insomnia, disease and emotional and psychological pressure as tools of torture. And it is this same style and vision that helped structure and characterise his poetic manifesto 'A Letter from Manus Island' (translated by me and published in *The Saturday Paper* on 9 December 2017).

One of my aims in this translator's note is to share some of the stories that offer insight into how the translation process was shaped and directed. Behrouz's extraordinary individual struggle involves a plethora of creative and intellectually savvy strategies to overcome terrible oppression and unpredictable attacks. The collaborative efforts he engaged in make up another part of the backstory. In this respect, a number of individuals must be acknowledged; they are advocates who were integral to the translation process and provided ongoing support.

Janet Galbraith

Janet: 'This morning I woke remembering our earlier correspondences that were based around poetry – a kind of poetic correspondence that went on for years. It was really a profound creative relationship that I am very grateful for. I remembered that initially you, Behrouz, did not want to use your real name for publishing or for presenting your work. We talked a lot about names, pen names. We talked of birds as we often did, sometimes do . . . and decided to use the name Pacific Heron. Do you remember that? We used that name because the Pacific heron is a bird that flies between Manus and Australia. It was a bird we both saw. I was living in central Victoria as I do now but in a different small town. From time to time a sole Pacific heron would arrive

and sit for a few days above a small pond just outside the house
I used to live in.'

The book is dedicated to Janet Galbraith who coordinates and facilitates the writing group Writing Through Fences‡, an organisation that collaborates with incarcerated refugees (or previously detained refugees) and amplifies and supports their writing and art. Janet has been working tirelessly to support Behrouz since the initial phase of his writing career on Manus Island (in 2014 Janet was one of the very first people to communicate with Behrouz regarding his work and situation). She also worked with Moones to translate one chapter which was published in *Mascara Literary Review* (published as 'Becoming MEG45'), a text that was integral to securing the contract with Picador.

Arnold Zable

> **Arnold:** 'You say that four years after leaving Iran you feel yourself to be a stateless person, and you belong to no country. Where do you belong now? How do you sense the world around you? How does it feel to approach and move across unknown borders?'
> **Behrouz:** 'What is a border? . . . My whole life has been impacted by this concept of "border".'

Writer Arnold Zable has also been working with Behrouz from early in his writing and resistance. Arnold and Janet introduced Behrouz's work to PEN International, establishing his case as an urgent international concern. Since his commitment to Behrouz in 2015, Arnold has written a review of Behrouz's co-directed film

---

‡ For more information, please visit www.writingthroughfences.org.

Chauka, Please Tell Us the Time (co-directed with Arash Kamali Sarvestani), chaired panel discussions, and interviewed Behrouz for publication for a number of important media organisations. He is now working on a new literary project – a promising dialogue initiative. Like Janet, Arnold has provided valuable feedback and encouragement throughout the translation process.

Kirrily Jordan

Kirrily: 'Hi Behrouz . . . for one of my projects I'm trying to make a small artwork to try and bring more attention to what's happening on Manus Island and Nauru. I came across some of your poems online, and wondered if I can use some of your words in my project?'

Kirrily Jordan also played a vital role in Behrouz's writing process. An academic and artist at the Australian National University, Kirrily first met Behrouz through a collaborative art project in early 2016 that was inspired by Behrouz's poetry. Since then, she has regularly provided feedback on his work when he has written in English. Her correspondence regarding draft chapters of the book after translation from Farsi provided Behrouz with important context and sparked ideas and suggestions for consideration during subsequent drafts of the translation.

Picador

An early draft of Chapter 10, 'Chanting of Crickets, Ceremonies of Cruelty. A Mythic Topography of Manus Prison', was published in 2017 by *Island* magazine. The team at Picador immediately recognised the urgency of the project and the profound message it conveys, following Behrouz's plight and writing throughout the process. Many important aesthetic and structural decisions were a result of engaging with the editorial team, and correspondence with them led to original and creative outcomes. Picador, Behrouz and the translation team are also indebted to John Connolly, whose kind donation to defray translation costs helped make that work possible, and Sarah Dale, Principal Solicitor from the Refugee Advice & Casework Service (Aust.) Inc. Sarah's pro bono work was essential for reviewing the book from a legal perspective.

Najem Weysi, Farhad Boochani and Toomas Askari

Throughout his time in Manus Prison Behrouz has been communicating with three friends from Iran: Najem (Najmedeen) Weysi, Farhad Boochani and Toomas Askari. Najem and Behrouz have been close friends since they began university. Farhad and Behrouz are cousins (both on the paternal side) and have been close friends since childhood. Toomas and Behrouz are university friends. Najem, Farhad and Toomas are extremely important confidants for Behrouz and their influence has been critical to the book as Behrouz shared his work regularly with them through WhatsApp from the prison. Their exchanges and attempts to understand the phenomenon of Manus Prison open up a new discourse regarding collaboration in the context of creative and intellectual work. Their relationship, in combination with the translation process, also informs the notion of a shared philosophical activity.

Moones Mansoubi and Sajad Kabgani

Moones Mansoubi began translating Behrouz's journalism in 2015 and has been pivotal in supporting him in his ongoing description and analysis of the horrors of Manus Prison – she deserves special mention beyond her work on this particular project. Moones's role in the translation was integral; she assisted me from the beginning as a consultant. Her acute understanding of Iranian literary traditions (both classical and contemporary) was invaluable. Moones also employed her training in international relations and refugee support services to refine many of the social, cultural and political nuances of the book.

Sajad Kabgani also worked with me as a translation consultant. He is a researcher in educational philosophy and literature and, like Moones, his contribution greatly enhanced my reading of the original text. My consultation sessions with Sajad provided further multidimensional perspectives and resulted in a more profound translation.

Consultations spanned a number of weeks for each chapter. I would translate large sections at a time and identify words and passages for further examination when meeting with the translation consultants. During these sessions I would read in English while the consultants followed and reviewed in Farsi. I collaborated with either Moones or Sajad, one at a time, to complete each chapter. Meetings were generally once a week or fortnightly and lasted from a few hours to a major part of a day. From the very first meeting with each consultant our interactions took the form of dynamic philosophical seminars. We would spend long periods examining, interpreting and reflecting on passages; every so often we would contact Behrouz for clarification and feedback, or simply to share our thoughts and express our admiration. This translation is genuinely a multi-perspective, collaborative project. The conversations I engaged in with Moones and Sajad had a remarkable effect on the translation and it is crucial that fragments of our dialogues are documented and discussed here to contextualise the translation process, and to stand as testament to their indispensable contributions.

Meaning, structure and place

Moones: 'I realise now how inadequate many Farsi–English, English–Farsi dictionaries are . . . And Behrouz's use of words and phrases in this book is so complex and unique – the context in which he's using language is deep and challenging, and often bizarre in a remarkably creative way. The variety of situations and his imagination add new and profoundly original nuances to the terms and phrases.'

Omid: 'If there was time we could've created a glossary to explain key words and phrases.'

Moones: 'That would be an excellent follow-up project. However, working on this book makes me realise how urgent it is to initiate a comprehensive and multidisciplinary dictionary project. I think Behrouz's book expands the meaning of some words – he adds new layers of significance.'

Finding the appropriate English words and sentence structures depended on a number of factors. Literature written in Farsi mainly consists of long elaborate sentences with many different kinds of clauses in consecutive order. The subject is at the beginning with the verb usually at the very end after a series of varying clauses. Trying to translate while maintaining the integrity of the original sentence structure becomes cumbersome to read in English – the longer complex sentences and passages seem to function well in Farsi because of the language's poetic resonance and the rhythmic movements. In translation I decided to split the sentences in various ways and repeat key words and phrases accordingly. Sometimes I combined this technique with parallelism, alliteration and consecutive synonyms. In some instances I simply divided long sentences into a series of short sentences, or short sentences into single-word sentences. Other times I used punctuation in creative ways to communicate each idea or point easier and to create a kind of sustained cadence.

Paradox and juxtaposition are defining features of Behrouz's storytelling which created many opportunities for splitting sentences and restructuring passages. His style and use of literary devices allowed me to explore the use of antonyms and oxymoron in creative ways as I translated. The use of flashback (analepsis) and flashforward (prolepsis) direct and enhance the emotive power and messages, philosophical heuristics and the sense of wonder in the text. Behrouz incorporates these elements into his literary strategy in combination with Kurdish folklore and resistance, Persian literature, sacred narrative traditions, local histories and nature symbols, ritual and ceremony. The philosophical and cultural features are not exclusive to Kurdistan and Iran, they also include other examples, particularly from Manusian thought and culture. He also incorporates influences from Western literature (for instance, he was reading Kafka's *The Trial*, Camus' *The Stranger*, and Beckett's *Molloy*, *Malone Dies* and *The Unnamable*). Awareness of the techniques and influences, and refashioning them strategically in English using diverse literary tools, ensured that the poetic qualities and idiosyncratic literary style embodied in the original were not lost.

Behrouz's writing is rich with cultural, historical and political frames of reference and allusions. The social and cultural conditioning of the many intertwined narratives is grounded in

Kurdistan, Iran, Manus Island and Manus Prison . . . and also on the seas during the harrowing boat journeys. I felt the best way to capture those qualities was to present the sentences as fragmented or reconfigured, and to also style some sections as verse. In my view, some of the most captivating and intensely affecting passages of the book are when prose suddenly converts to verse, and back again. Remaining faithful to the poetic elements in the language and Behrouz's writing, translating prose as poetry turned out to be the best and most appropriate option.

Word choice was also determined by sensitivity towards place. Locations, situations and narrative settings operate in all the scenes to transport the reader. In order not to compromise too much of the sensory power that Behrouz meticulously constructs I tried to select words and phrases pertaining to the selected places and environments. Therefore, the English translation of nouns, verbs, adjectives and adverbs are in many cases metaphorical and particular to the geographical and physical aspects of the chapters and their different passages. In some instances, abstract and philosophical terminology is more prominent, while in other passages I depict the scenes with more direct realism. Translating with this place-based narrative approach in mind, the same word in Farsi could be translated differently depending on location, atmosphere, characters, objects, events, architecture and environment. The use of nature symbols, anthropomorphism and personification illuminates Behrouz's unique interpretations of trans-species understanding. In fact, Behrouz is adamant that had the refugees not established a relationship of respect with the environment and animals the oppressive force of the prison would have killed them a long time ago; nature works with the prisoners to combat the system.

Coloniality (colonialism as perpetual process and pervasive structure)

Moones: 'I'm reading *The Coup* by the Armenian-Iranian historian from England, Ervand Abrahamian. It reminded me of Behrouz's writing because Abrahamian recognises the importance of engaging in a nuanced and critical discussion regarding the role of colonialism.'

Omid: 'I don't think readers can truly appreciate the depth of Behrouz's thought and writing unless they recognise and understand the impact and consequences of colonialism on Kurdistan, Iran, Australia and Manus Island . . . and also the relationship between coloniality and forced migration.'

Moones: 'What's interesting in Abrahamian's book is that he examines how the term *estemār* (colonialism/imperialism) and *estesmār* (economic exploitation) are indispensably connected. In many situations the two could be used synonymously. Similar to this study, many of Behrouz's narratives illustrate the connection between the two; he emphasises how domination and control are related to aggressive extraction and manipulation of natural resources, the destruction of the ecosystem, and exploitation of human bodies.'

Behrouz's book is a decolonial text, representing a decolonial way of thinking and doing. In order to honour the nuances of his penetrating critique and his insight into the colonial foundations of the detention system, some technical terms needed to be incorporated into the literary work. In the supplementary essay that follows I discuss the issue of genre in more detail, but it is relevant to mention here that Behrouz intentionally fuses literature with political commentary and language from different scholarly discourses. This corresponds with the literary play involving forms and devices from different genres. These elements function together to expose the prison as a neo-colonial experiment and position his literature as a decolonial intervention.

The translation purposely uses academic language in places to convey the multidisciplinary vision behind the book. Behrouz's analysis of colonialism is the result of his education, scholarly investigation and lived experience – he understands colonialism historically, philosophically and viscerally.

Naming

> **Moones:** 'The name Behrouz means good/better (*beh*) day (*rouz*), prosperous or fortunate, and is also the name of a military commander from the *Shāhnāmeh*. It is somehow auspicious that his mother named him Behrouz; she gave him a traditional Farsi (Persian) name from classical literature, the name of a warrior. His name stands out from the names of most of his siblings and cousins, which have religious connotations. It is as though she imagined there was something different about this one.'

Naming has special aesthetic, interpretative and political functions in the book. For Behrouz, renaming things is a way to affirm his personhood and establish a sense of authority; naming is a way of reclaiming authority from the prison, disempowering the system and redirecting sovereignty back to the land. Naming is also part of the creative endeavour, and it works as an analytical tool for examination of the political and material circumstances.

Behrouz names many of the characters using a unique

technique. He uses humorous monikers and noun phrases when referring to particular individuals, either in order to protect their identity or as a way to help construct the character, or both. Farsi does not use capital letters, but we have the advantage in English of creating proper nouns out of phrases by capitalising every word (including the definite article). By doing this we make clear that in the context of the book the description or the moniker is the individual's name and also reflects their personality and characteristics (a physical feature, or their disposition or temperament).

An important abstract idea in the book is named 'The Kyriarchal System'. I explore the academic concept of 'kyriarchy' in the supplementary essay, a term that signifies intersecting social systems that reinforce and multiply with the aim of punishing, subjugating and suppressing. The Kyriarchal System is the name Behrouz gives to the ideological substrata that have a governing function in the prison; it is a title denoting the spirit that is sovereign over the detention centre and Australia's ubiquitous border-industrial complex. The Farsi term *system-e hākem* could also be translated as 'oppressive system', 'ruling system', 'system of governmentality' ('governmentality' is used in the book to describe particular applications of the system) or 'sovereign system'. However, the notion of kyriarchy amplifies the extent and omnipresence of the torture and control in the prison and highlights the subversive aspect of the name.

Behrouz also renames the Manus Island Regional Processing Centre. Throughout the book Behrouz refers to the detention centre as 'Manus Prison' – he names it, defines it and critically analyses it on his own terms. Each section of the centre is also renamed in similar terms. Conceptually, he owns the prison.

The combination of these two proper noun phrases – Manus Prison and The Kyriarchal System – bolsters Behrouz's reflections of the structural and systematic torture of the detention regime, and also reflects Behrouz's scholarly dexterity. In this sense, his significant use of academic terms in dialogue with literary language and style invites multifaceted responses and readings.

Another significant example of this multidisciplinary inspiration is the chapter titles. I shared ideas for titles with Behrouz at different times through the process and together we refined and expanded them. We decided that each chapter should have at least two titles that highlight a different aspect of the chapter. On first impressions the seemingly incongruous relationship between the multiple titles for each chapter helped create a sense of perplexity and absurdity; the non sequitur nature of the titles, and the illogical and unpredictable sense they evoke, is consistent with the techniques and themes Behrouz employs in the book. The title 'Our Golshifteh Is Truly Beautiful' occupies a special role for Behrouz because it represents for him the most significant passages in the chapter; the character of 'Our Golshifteh' is his greatest inspiration among the narratives.

Imagery and reality

Sajad: 'His use of metaphors related to wolves is exceptional and haunting . . . I once heard that in Iran when a sheepdog fights off a wolf to defend its flock it aims for the jugular. In most cases the wolves are too strong and ferocious for the dogs. But there are times when the sheepdog manages to lock its jaws around the wolf's throat and remains clamped onto it until the wolf can't withstand the pressure anymore; the dog persists until the wolf submits. The sheepdog emerges from the victory with an extraordinary self-realisation – the experience transforms the dog, the encounter empowers it. The sheepdog develops a new sense of self beyond self-confidence – it re-identifies as a wolf. The shepherds know the dangers of this phenomenon; they know that when a dog's identity morphs in this way it is no longer controllable. They put it down.'

For some time I interpreted Behrouz's use of mythical and epic visual imagery, dream visions and mix of fantasy and reality as a form of magical realism. However, there are also many self-reflexive passages in the book in which Behrouz analyses himself, his interpretation of the prison, his method of depicting the scenes and situations, and his own rhetorical modes and literary style. These components remove his work from the genre of magical realism, and place it in a field all its own. In fact, Behrouz's work resists many examples of genre even though there are significant features of numerous genres present through the text. But translating the work required at least some form of conceptual and theoretical framework, even if tentative and conjectural. For me, Behrouz's literary techniques and forms of expression have connections with horror realism and culturally- or ethnically-situated forms of surrealism. Identifying these factors facilitated the translation: it made expressing Behrouz's voice, choosing the words, developing the tone and style, and creating intertextual figures more compelling and consistent. I interpret his genre (or anti-genre) as 'horrific surrealism'.

Literature, politics and respecting what is left unsaid

Sajad: 'Does Behrouz offer an account of his persecution back in Iran or does he provide a critique of the Iranian government in any part of the book?'
Omid: 'No.'

Sajad: 'Good. There's no need to describe that or justify why he left. That's why it's such a beautiful and meaningful piece of literature. Everything you need to know about his life in Iran is encapsulated in the tale about the first boat journey. Everything you need to understand about oppression and discrimination back in Iran is right there in the ocean. All the political turmoil is narrated when he describes the waves. All the state suppression is explained when he depicts the vortex in the sea.'

I saw this translation opportunity as a chance to contribute to history by documenting and somehow supporting the persecution of forgotten people; translation for me, like writing for Behrouz, is a duty to history and a strategy for positioning the issue of indefinite detention of refugees deep within Australia's collective memory.

But as I read the chapters I asked myself if it is even possible to communicate in English Behrouz's experience in a way that does justice to his endurance and insights. His interpretations, critiques and expression are so raw, urgent, and relentless; the stories convey agony, contemplation, rage and revelation. There is also a strong and admirable sense of humour perfectly placed in some parts, which had to be communicated with care. Also, the imaginative richness of the text needed to reflect the unique viewpoint and voice of the author.

One aspect I was always conscious of was that Behrouz was writing in Farsi, not Kurdish. He was writing in the language of his oppressors, even though he is a fervent advocate of Kurdish culture, language and politics. And the book was being translated into the language of his jailers and torturers. In addition to the Australian citizen/non-citizen power differential, I had to remain aware that I was translating the work of an oppressed Kurdish man as someone who identifies with the ethnically dominant culture in Iran (my ethnic group is Fars [Persian], although I am not among the dominant socio-religious group that has defined the political establishment since 1979). Therefore, it was imperative that the translation be attuned to nuances relating to historical injustice, marginalisation and representation, and committed to consultation. I had to ask myself a series of questions:

How do I communicate the conditions under which this book is written?

How do I express the ideas, emotions and critique emerging through text and voice message?

How do I express the new forms and techniques Behrouz creates in Farsi?

How do I express the mix of the Kurdish experience with the prison experience, and so much else . . .?

In what ways can literature convey meaning through suggestion, by denoting, through pointing? What colonial tales are told by an incarcerated Kurdish-Iranian narrating his Manus Prison experience? What is special about the viewpoint of a Kurdish man with an inseparable connection to his homeland and dedication to liberation, about the perspective of someone indigenous to Kurdistan? What codes does he provide for interpreting meanings? What is the relationship between form and meaning? And are there layers of storytelling that prioritise other colonised peoples and places?

The responsibility was daunting; the possibilities were exhilarating.

Initially we had issues translating both the socio-political and poetic quality and character of the original Farsi. Behrouz's writing is part of various literary traditions and reflects conventions pertaining to poetic style. However, the difficulties of interpreting and translating the Farsi original opened up possibilities for new literary experimentation.

To evoke the atmosphere and features of the text in English we needed to experiment with different techniques. Therefore, the translation arranges and presents the stories in unorthodox ways and purposely fragments and disrupts sentence and passages, appropriating and blending genre and style.

Shared philosophical activity

Behrouz: 'In order to understand the combination of art and thought in this book you must become familiar with my relationship with Najem, Farhad and Toomas. As I was writing I interacted with them regularly, and these conversations influenced the text in terms of its dramatic features and the intellectual positions and themes. As a result the book is a playscript for a theatre performance that incorporates myth and folklore; religiosity and secularity; coloniality and militarism; torture and borders. Najem, Farhad and Toomas are intellectuals and creative thinkers. In Iran we would express our critical analyses in theatrical ways; for us, performance is a part of philosophy and advocacy. We act out our ruminations, we embody our thinking . . . argument is narrative . . . theory is drama. Najem, Farhad and Toomas are enlightened intellectuals in every sense of the word.'

The conditions under which the book was created and the relationship between writer, translator and consultants form a space for unique philosophical inquiries. Experimentation was necessary in order to convey this shared philosophical activity.

In 2015 when Moones began working with Behrouz, the

prisoners were under constant surveillance and always in danger of having their mobile phones confiscated. She tells me that there were regular raids during which officers would search for phones. These incursions were brutal and would occur around 4 or 5 am. Rumours always circulated regarding the prison system's plans to conduct a phone search, so refugees lived with constant fear and dread.

Behrouz's first phone was confiscated. For two to three months he would write his book by hand and use Aref Heidari's phone to send voice messages to Moones for transcribing. Aref is a close companion and supporter of Behrouz in so many respects, and he features in Behrouz's co-directed film *Chauka, Please Tell Us the Time* (2017) – he is the individual who sings the stirring and mournful Kurdish liberation song.

Behrouz eventually managed to smuggle in another phone. This time he created a secure hiding spot for the phone as he slept – he inserted the phone into a cavity he made deep within his mattress. The officers did not find his phone again, although his phone was stolen in 2017 and writing was delayed for a short period before acquiring another. There were also periods lasting weeks and even months when Behrouz's personal communication was suspended. During phases of extreme securitisation and surveillance he was forced to leave his phone hidden for long periods.

Behrouz's connections with Najem, Farhad and Toomas were vital. Their commentary and critical questions helped keep Behrouz connected with his Kurdish homeland and invigorated his native language and heritage (Najem and Farhad are Kurdish, Toomas is Fars). They also reinforced the attitude and savvy he acquired from the intellectual and cultural circles he engaged with back in Iran, and communication with his three friends diminished the many senses of distance. Similarly, his correspondence with Janet and Arnold added new dimensions and perspective to his writing. His interaction with two writers living in Australia gave Behrouz a sense of validation and contributed to the cross-cultural angles and nuances interwoven through the work. During the book's writing and translation process, Behrouz continued his other writing, research, art and advocacy projects: the book was produced simultaneously with journalism, investigative reports, a film, academic presentations, protest speeches and human rights advocacy.

I maintained the consultation process by regularly checking my philosophical reading with Behrouz. Our discussions also worked their way into Behrouz's writing of the text, and they influenced my later translations. One of the unique features of the book is that the planning, writing and translating were simultaneous (sometimes the stories were being written even as the events were taking place). The consultation and review process during my visit to Manus Island clarified many interpretations, corrected errors, and developed culturally and politically sensitive points. There are many ways to interpret Behrouz's narratives; however, his main objective is to draw attention to the realities of systematic torture in Manus Prison. The book functions to move readers to resist the colonial mindset that is driving Australia's detention regime and to inspire self-reflection, deep investigation and direct action.

The shared philosophical project is open-ended – it is an open call to action.

Omid Tofighian,
Sydney – Manus Island – Cairo,
2018